How to Negotiate a Raise

How to Negotiate a Raise

JOHN J. TARRANT

VNR **VAN NOSTRAND REINHOLD COMPANY**
NEW YORK   CINCINNATI   TORONTO   LONDON   MELBOURNE

Van Nostrand Reinhold Company Regional Offices:
New York Cincinnati Chicago Millbrae Dallas

Van Nostrand Reinhold Company International Offices:
London Toronto Melbourne

Library of Congress Catalog Card Number: 75-26732
ISBN: 0-442-28407-1

Manufactured in the United States of America

Published by Van Nostrand Reinhold Company
450 West 33rd Street, New York, N.Y. 10001

Published simultaneously in Canada by Van Nostrand Reinhold Ltd.

15 14 13 12 11 10 9 8 7 6 5 4 3 2 1

Library of Congress Cataloging in Publication Data

Tarrant, John J.
   How to negotiate a raise.

   Includes index.
   1. Wages. 2. Negotiation. I. Title.
HD4909.T27   650'.12   75-26732
ISBN 0-442-28407-1

preface

Getting a raise has never been easy. Recently it has become a lot more difficult. It will continue to be difficult.

Obtaining more money from an employer is a process of negotiation. The better you are at negotiation, the more chance you have of getting maximum pay for what you do.

That, in essence, is what this book is about. It is a step-by-step guide to raise negotiation. This does not mean merely the single interview with the boss during which you ask for more money. The raise negotiation is a much more extensive process than that. How you ask for the raise is important. But how you prepare for the request is usually even more important. The task of getting yourself into the most favorable position can take months.

The book covers the ways in which you can size up the people and situations affecting your chances; the selection of goals; the avoidance of pitfalls; the development of strategies; and the use of tactics that best carry out your strategy.

However, there is more to it than that. Even the most skilled negotiator is at a great disadvantage when there is little to negotiate with. One section of the book discusses methods for making the most of a weak case. But much of the content focuses on how you can make your case stronger by becoming a more valuable member of the organization in a variety of ways.

So — although we are talking frankly about tough-minded raise negotiation — we are also talking about effectiveness on the job. You want to be effective. You want to handle your job well, and to be recognized for your effectiveness, financially and in other ways. When you are able to get the most out of yourself you enjoy your work more — and you make more money.

This book is about how to become more effective, to like your job better, and to be paid more for it.

John J. Tarrant

contents

How to Negotiate a Raise

1

what you're up against

The Essence of Raise Negotiation

Little raises may come automatically. For the big raises you have to *negotiate.* So it's important to understand what a negotiation is all about. When we see the word negotiation in the newspapers or hear it on the television news, its context is all-encompassing. In recent years Henry Kissinger has come to be thought of as a prime negotiator. Dr. Kissinger's bargaining triumphs occurred on a massive scale, with the entire globe as the bargaining table. We hear constantly of other "big" negotiations: the UAW vs. General Motors; Richard Nixon vs. the United States of America; the Player's Association vs. the National Football League.

Many of us think of ourselves as being involved in negotiations only when we buy or sell a house. But the fact is that much of life is negotiation. Our careers are negotiations, marriage and family life are negotiations, sex is a negotiation. And getting a raise is truly a negotiation.

What does "negotiation" mean? Gerard I. Nierenberg, founder and president of the Negotiation Institute, says "Whenever people exchange ideas with the intention of changing relationships, whenever they confer for agreement, they are negotiating."

Well, when you try to get a raise out of your boss you are not trying to change your relationship with him in the commonly-understood sense. However, you will have to confer with your boss for agreement, so this part of the definition applies. But there is a lot more to a raise negotiation than the conference. What you do before the face-to-face confrontation can be more important than what happens when you are actually sitting across the table. Moreover, the definition just quoted does not seem, for our purposes, to stress heavily enough the adversary relationship that exists in a raise negotiation. Make no mistake about it. You and your boss may be the best of friends, get along well on the job, see each other frequently off the job. But when you are going after a bigger raise than he wants to give you, you are *adversaries*. Indeed, your cordial relationship with him may be a definite drawback in this situation. To get the employer to come through with the money you want takes planning, strategy, and tactics. In effect it is a game, but a "real-world" game in which you play for high stakes and sometimes take real risks.

So, as we look at it from that point of view, we may come up with a definition that more aptly fits our concern. Try this:

Negotiation is a process in which two parties maneuver, each with the purpose of gaining the greatest possible advantage.

Some negotiations are cloudy. It's often hard to see what the opponents are driving at. They deliberately conceal their main objectives. They feint; they try to make the adversary think they are after one thing when they are really after another.

The raise negotiation is, in this aspect, straightforward. You want money. The boss doesn't want to give it to you, or at least he doesn't want to give you as much as you want. If you don't know anything about negotiation you just walk in and ask him for it, hoping for the best but expecting the worst — and you'll probably wind up with the worst.

If, however, you bring the principles of negotiation to this important aspect of your life — after all, we do like to derive various satisfactions from our jobs, but we work for money — you will begin your thinking, and your campaign, well before that moment at which you actually go in and ask for the raise. If you handle the preconference steps properly, the meeting itself and the process of requesting the raise will be far less traumatic and far more successful than they are likely to be if the procedure is approached haphazardly and with an abundance of mystification and fear. Let's examine the basic steps in a typical raise negotiation.

Study your adversary's official position — Your opponent in the negotiation is the person who has the most influence over whether or not you get the raise. Ordinarily he's your immediate boss.

First you'll want to size up what we might call the "official position." This is the overall attitude of the company — and of your boss — toward the handling of raise requests. Your superior, whatever his own feelings about you and about the job you've been doing, must operate within the environment of his own job. He cannot be a free agent in deciding how much you should be paid.

Let's take the case of an employee who is going to request a sizable raise and follow it through. Ted Gross works for Dave Seymour. They both work for Superlative Widgets, Inc. Ted has been in his job for four years and has gotten three raises. While he has never talked with anyone else but Seymour about a raise, he knows that Seymour always reviews every money request with the president of the company, Evan Wynkoop.

Gross's three raises have all been fairly small ones. To the extent that he is able to find out, other people who work at similar jobs have gotten raises of about the same size. There is one exception. Superlative has three women who do work that approximates Ted Gross's job. Over the years these women have received less money than their male counterparts. For the past two years the women have gotten larger raises than the men. While there has been no official policy announced, it seems clear that Superlative is committed to enabling its female employees to catch up. Now, as far as Ted Gross can tell, the differential between men and women, if it exists at all, is not very great.

There is no official "range" controlling salaries in Ted Gross's job classification; in fact, the job descriptions themselves are pretty sketchy. Nevertheless, there is obviously a pattern that has been applied for some time, and Dave Seymour tends to stay within that pattern.

Superlative is budget conscious. As year-end approaches Seymour and other department heads involve their subordinates in the process of estimating needs for the coming year. It is reasonable to assume that Seymour, along with the other bosses, is given a stated figure for compensation, within which he may allocate more money to one individual and less to another, as long as he does not exceed the budget.

Current business circumstances have a significant effect on the official position. The economy is limping. Superlative is by no means having a banner year, but the company has shown a profit for the past few years and will probably manage to show one again this year. There has been general emphasis on cost-cutting — more so than previously — but at the same time Superlative is mounting plans for growth in the coming year. The plans are not wildly ambitious, but they are reasonably optimistic.

In gauging the "official" position of the boss and the organization, examine:

- The pattern of raises given to you and others in similar jobs.
- The extent to which compensation is part of a fixed budget process.
- The degree of freedom that your boss has in deciding on raises.
- The current condition of business within the company and the industry.
- The company's plans for the immediate future.

Study your adversary's personal position — The relationship between subordinate and boss is influenced by the official position, but may differ from it in meaningful respects. The raise seeker needs to know how his boss looks upon raises in general and how he is likely to feel about this particular raise request.

Ted Gross thinks about Dave Seymour as a person. Seymour is not a hard-driving boss. He is easygoing. When you show him that you have mastered your job he lets you alone. Seymour is friendly enough, easy to chat with at leisure moments. He does not consult with his subordinates about matters of policy to any great extent, but he does show some sympathy and will listen to people who have a legitimate gripe.

Gross concludes that Dave Seymour still has ambitions to move higher in the organization. Seymour has been in the same job for six years, but a couple of the people at the top policy-making level of Superlative are getting along in years, and it's reasonable to assume that Seymour is justified in thinking that he has a fighting chance. This ambition is reflected in the usual degree of seriousness with which Seymour talks about departmental goals for next year.

Ted Gross and Dave Seymour have always gotten along pretty well. The boss trusts Gross. He listens when Ted reports on a situation and usually assumes that he has heard the facts. Seymour seldom checks further. Ted Gross can assume with some confidence that Seymour is satisfied with his work.

During the past year Gross's job has gone pretty well. He has had some disappointments, but — while Gross does not go out of his way to seek alibis — it can be said that any shortcomings were not entirely his fault. And there was one project with which Seymour entrusted him that came off quite well. Dave Seymour has never been highly critical of failures. At the same time he has not emitted glowing praise of successes. By and large, Ted Gross concludes that the boss tends to take his steady good performance for granted. Seymour relies on Gross as a key member of the department, without thinking of him as being a uniquely stellar performer.

You will want to review:

- The boss's overall pattern of conduct with regard to you.
- The degree to which he praises or criticizes specific parts of your performance.
- His own position in the firm and ambitions for growth.
- The extent to which he takes you for granted.
- His knowledge of just what you do and how valuable it is.

Select a strategy – Having reviewed the boss's official and personal posture, Ted Gross is able to come to certain conclusions about the prospects for a raise and the best way to get one. His boss considers him a steady performer but not a star. The boss assumes a continuation of a good level of performance, and takes for granted that Gross will produce it. Personal relations are good between the two, but the boss is not keenly tuned in on just exactly what Ted Gross does and how tough it is for him to do it.

Seymour will not be expecting any unusual raise request from Gross. He will assume that this year, as in past years, he will budget a certain amount for raises and then divide that amount equably among the contenders.

Gross will have to do something to shake this frame of reference. Raise negotiations between him and Seymour have assumed a well-worn pattern. Somehow, if Gross is going to change the pattern and get more money, he will have to change the context in which the negotiation takes place.

One possible strategy would be that of *threat.* Knowing that Seymour is counting on him, Gross could advance a threat – implied or explicit – that he may leave. There are several reasons why Ted Gross does not want to do that. For one thing, he wants to stay at Superlative, and stay in the same generally pleasant working relationship he has now. The strategy of threat can be effective in the right circumstances, but there is no doubt that it can disrupt personal and working patterns. This strategy is therefore best for the employee who does not care that much about the maintenance of those patterns. Since the status quo is valuable to Ted Gross, he discards the idea of a threat (except to the extent that there is always *some* implication of threat in a raise request.)

For similar reasons Gross discards the PITA (Pain-In-The-Ass) strategy which would involve badgering the boss to the extent that the superior comes through with the raise just to remove the source of irritation. (This too is a legitimate strategy, as discussed elsewhere in this book; but it is not right for every situation.)

Ted Gross cannot point to an astounding string of triumphs in order to work the strategy of reward for exceptional service. There are others who do the same kind of work he does, and some of them produce results that are about as good as his. Reliance on this strategy is not likely to produce healthy fruit and might even have a negative effect.

But Ted Gross has several things going for him. He and the boss get along reasonably well. Seymour is conscientious, and he is also ambitious to continue to show good departmental performance. And Seymour, while he takes Gross's performance for granted, does not know that much about what this particular subordinate does every day.

So Ted Gross decides that his best bet is the *strategy of education.* This approach calls for the subordinate to gradually lead the boss into a greater understanding of his problems and a greater appreciation of his accomplishments. It is not as hard-nosed or as spectacular as some strategies, but it suits a situation in which the employee — although he wants more money — wants also to keep his good on-the-job relationship with the boss.

We go into greater detail about the strategy of education — as well as alternate strategies — in other sections. Here we are concerned with examining the basic framework of a raise negotiation.

Ted Gross begins to "educate" Dave Seymour. He does not do this by complaining about how tough his job is. Such a tactic is tiresome and counterproductive. Except when you choose deliberately to pose headaches for the boss, your approach should be as headache-free as possible. Instead, Gross chooses a relaxed moment and begins the process on a positive note: "You know, Dave, I'd like to make some suggestions about our training program. It seems to me that some of the trainees don't really get a full appreciation of all of the functions in this department. They just see the surface, and observe the results. They don't get that much of a feel for what goes into producing those results. For instance, the clearing process. . . ."

Gross goes on to give a fairly brief, but pointed rundown of one of the things he does, with emphasis on its intricacy. "You know how it works, Dave," concludes Gross, "but some of the new fellows don't. And while they don't have to do it, it might be a good idea if they had a better realization of how it all gets put together. Don't you agree?"

Dave Seymour did not know all that much about this particular function. Gross was aware of this. By using a "third party" approach and attributing the ignorance to the trainees he has been able to work a neat little rundown of the function into the conversation. Now Gross goes on: "Of course some of us have our own short cuts that we've developed to do the job better. I don't think it's wise to go into too much detail for guys who are just in training. Maybe it would be better to let them develop their own methods if they ever have to do the job. For example, on the clearance thing I've developed some little tricks that are a little different — and I think better — than the ordinary way of doing it."

This is an opening for Seymour to ask to hear more, and, as most bosses would do, he asks Ted to explain what he does that's different. Ted obliges, with a summary of innovations he has introduced into a routine function. "You don't have to get involved in all this, of course, Dave. You let me alone to do the job, and I appreciate that. I went into this now just to show the kind of different ways that a fellow can come up with if he's on his toes."

In the following weeks Ted Gross takes other opportunities to educate the boss about what he does and how well he does it. Gross is unobtrusive about this. He neither boasts nor complains. It's all done rather casually, "As you know, Dave, the trick here is to. . . ." or "Just as an aside, the reason we were able to get that job out so fast is not that the machines suddenly get more efficient — we should still consider replacing them — but that I was able to do a little rescheduling. . . ." or "I know you'll get a kick out of the way this was handled. . . ."

Ted Gross's preparation for the actual raise interview consists of letting Dave Seymour know just how difficult his job is and how well he does it. At the same time Gross is getting the message across that *he* has a pretty good idea of what he is worth. But Gross's process of education accomplishes something else. He is giving Seymour ammunition that the boss can use when he goes to his own superiors to justify obtaining more money for raises.

Ted Gross knows that he must get his formal raise request on the table early. Timing is always an important consideration, and earliest is not always best. But in this case Gross is aware of a number of factors. The boss needs time to consider a higher-than-usual request and to clear it with his own superiors. The money should be approved before the budget is set. And, since Gross is in competition with other people for what may be a limited total amount of raise dollars, it's important to stake out the claim before the others get into the act.

So Gross requests the interview as soon as he can. He reviews his accomplishments. He marshals his arguments. And he goes in ready to carry out the strategy he has chosen.

Executing the strategy in the raise interview — The interview itself is an extension of the tactics that the raise seeker should have put into motion some time before. Sometimes the strategy dictates that the size of the request should come as a complete surprise. In this case that is not a prime consideration. Seymour is likely to anticipate that something special is in the offing — and that's okay.

Ted Gross does not come out with the amount he wants immediately. First he talks about the job he has been doing, referring to the innovations he has made and the problem-free way he has been able to handle his tasks. He reminds Seymour of the one or two big things that he accomplished, saying: "I don't like to blow my own horn, Dave, but sometimes you have to. You just look for the results, and I like working that way — not having the boss looking over my shoulder — but at this point I think it's helpful if I go into some detail about how the results were gotten."

Gross spends some time talking about the things he plans to do in the year to come, and how he will be able to support Seymour's goals. Then he states how much he wants.

They discuss it. Seymour refers to the fact that it's a lot of money, and things have been somewhat tight, and that there are other deserving people as well. Gross sticks to his strategy, letting some of the boss's objections go and responding to others. (How to handle the boss's objections in the interview is covered in detail under the headings of various strategies.) At the end of the interview Seymour says he can't give Ted an answer right now, but that he will do what he can. Within a month Ted Gross gets his answer. He does not receive all that he asked for, but he receives a lot more than he has in the past.

After evaluating the boss's official and personal position, select a strategy. Begin applying the strategy in advance of the actual raise interview; effective raise-getting is not an overnight process. When you go into the interview, have your tactics thought out, and follow through on the plan.

This has been a capsulized review of the raise-getting process. Highlighting the principal elements are: evaluation of the boss's position;

selection of a strategy; early embarkation on a campaign to apply the tactics growing out of that strategy; and conduct of an interview as an extension of the right strategy.

The specific strategies and tactics covered in this book — except for some off-beat ones — fit into this pattern. Getting a raise is a matter of planning and execution, not of luck or of passionate entreaty. Approach it cold bloodedly, as you would any complex work problem that must be solved. This particular part of your work involves getting more money for yourself. Plan your work — and then work your boss.

Why You Hate To Ask For A Raise — And What To Do About It

One of the staples of comic-book continuity is the wife berating her husband because he lacks the guts to go in and ask his boss for a raise. Like many of the standard situations exploited by pop culture, this one is rooted in truth. It is not easy to ask for a raise; indeed, for many people it is one of the most difficult challenges in life. The most intrepid and outspoken employee may quail at the prospect of confronting his superior and requesting more money. So if you are distressed because you feel "chicken" about asking for an increase, rest assured that you are by no means unique. It is a feeling shared by millions from the top to the bottom of the employment spectrum.

Fear of requesting more money is understandable when the employee has reason to think that his action will imperil his job. But the problem is not confined to so narrow a scope. Even when you know that you have an excellent case to make, and when you are sure that your job-security is in absolutely no jeopardy, you are still apt to dread the confrontation.

The reason for this lies deeper than mere disquiet about keeping a job. Human beings have a deep-rooted abhorrence of rejection. We don't like to hear the word "no." Even when the negative answer refers to a specific area, even when logically a "no" reflects not the least discredit on the petitioner, it is still hard to take. Some people go to great lengths to avoid bad news, even when it is vitally important to discover the news, good or bad. The American Cancer Society has long been aware that one of its biggest problems is the fact that people who suspect they have cancer will put off going to the doctor because they are afraid that he will confirm the suspicion. And people will hold back from putting their fortunes to the test even when there is every reason to think that the news will be good. National marketing organizations acknowledge that one of the biggest difficulties in selling is that an experienced and skillful salesman who has made an effective presentation and has received many favorable signals from the prospect will still shy away from asking for the order. Sometimes the customer must almost literally seize the order blank and pen from the salesman's hands. The salesman's job is to get people to say "yes" and he usually has high confidence in his ability to do this; but he still hesitates at the climactic moment because rejection hurts so much.

Eminence is no guarantee against this hang-up. Longfellow's *Courtship of Miles Standish* has no basis in fact, but we never question the verisimilitude of the story that has the leader of the Pilgrims sending John Alden as his agent to ask for the hand of Priscilla Mullins because he fears to undertake the task himself. Getting a turndown can hurt far more than the logic of the situation or the specific aspects of the refusal would dictate.

This is particularly so in the case of asking for a raise. The job, and recognition by superiors of good performance on the job, mean more to us than we are often willing to admit. Many proclaim loudly that they work only to earn enough money to do what they want. Beyond that, they maintain, they could not care less what the boss or anybody else thinks of them. Nevertheless, even in the breast of the most outspoken "couldn't-care-less-er" there is a feeling that he handles his job well and that his ability on the job enhances his standing as a person. The job — even the distasteful job — becomes part of our lives.

In general we want other people to think well of us, but there are certain individuals about whose opinion we become particularly anxious. And one of these individuals is the boss. Even when the "boss" is a group or a faceless institution, there is an urge to win their approval. And approval of job performance — in spite of the many and various other means that have been devised to motivate workers through praise, challenge, opportunity for participation, etc. — is still measured primarily in salary dollars.

And so when the boss says, "I can't give you the raise you want," he is in effect saying that your results on the job do not warrant the increase. It doesn't matter if (as so often happens) he expresses his total satisfaction with your work but cites other factors as mitigating against the raise. It's still a turndown. And when our job performance is denigrated it is tough for us to say we don't care. For most of us the refusal seems directed at our whole selves. Whether we realize it or not, few of us work only for money. We want to think we are good at what we do, and we want others to think so, too. So failure to get a raise is a blow to the entire self-image. It's not just the money; if money were all, we would go in to the boss with no hesitation and risk failure to receive the desired raise without too much apprehension. It is what the rejection implies beyond the dollar area that we don't like.

So we hang back from asking the boss for a raise even when we have, ostensibly, nothing to lose. This reluctance to court rejection does not manifest itself until we have at least approached adulthood. The small child has no hesitation in making demands on authority. He trails around after his mother in the supermarket, tugging at her and asking her to buy candy, cookies, etc. She keeps on saying "no." The child protests, insists, maybe cries — but he is not deterred by rejection. He does not seem to feel that his mother is saying he is a bad child. A moment later he is back with another demand. It's when we are grown up that we begin to build up the implications of a refusal — like a turn-down of a raise request — into a rejection of ourselves as persons. Getting older does not always mean getting smarter or even getting more mature.

And so the gag in the comic strip is really not that much of a joke. We often have to be prodded, by ourselves or others, into asking for a raise. For example, Cindy Cullen has been working as secretary for Paul LeBlanc for eight months. Before that she was a member of the steno pool, moving around to fill in on various jobs.

Cindy's life is by no means confined to the office. She gets around quite a bit. She does not date any one man steadily, but she enjoys a full and sometimes swinging social life. Cindy has no low opinion of her skills. She thinks she is good at what she does and she wants to be paid at a level commensurate with her ability. During her tenure as a pool stenographer she was not at all backward about asking for raises when she felt they were justified.

But back then Cindy was not asking for raises from anyone with whom she really worked. Her boss was Marge Halpern, the assistant personnel manager assigned to the secretarial and clerical staff. Of course Marge got feedback from the managers for whom Cindy worked from time to time, and Cindy was certain that on the whole the feedback was favorable. So she was calm and resolute in asking for salary increases. She didn't always get what she asked, but this did not deter her from bringing the subject up again when she felt it was justified.

Now the situation is a little different. If Cindy is going to ask for a raise, she will have to talk to LeBlanc. This is the individual for whom she has been working, the man who knows best about her performance. In this company managers recommend raises for their secretaries within a fairly wide range based on performance and length in service.

Cindy Cullen has no reason to think that Paul LeBlanc does not appreciate her value. He has been generous in complimenting her. He listens to her suggestions. He is considerate. There is just one problem. It seems to Cindy that she has now earned her spurs as a secretary and that she should be getting paid closer to what the other secretaries get. But as yet LeBlanc has not brought the matter up.

Nor, strangely enough, has Cindy. She tells herself she is going to ask for a raise ("Tomorrow I'm going to walk in there and. . . .") She rehearses her arguments. But she doesn't ask for the raise. She keeps hoping she'll get it without asking. And Cindy does not know herself what is holding her back. She knows she's doing a good job, and she knows that her nice-guy boss will certainly not snap her head off. But still she holds back.

In part Cindy is deterred by the difficulty we have been talking about; the unwillingness to risk rejection. Cindy Cullen has achieved a comfortable one-on-one relationship with a superior who seems to have the highest appreciation for what she does. But, put to the test, will that appreciation stand up? Or will Paul LeBlanc bargain with her, point up faults in her performance, maintain that she should be satisfied with a lower figure? Realistically, Cindy should not be concerned about these possibilities. Realistically she should be eager to go in and ask for the raise anyway, even if there is a chance she won't receive all she's asking for. After all, what can she lose?

What she can lose is the illusion of perfect rapport between boss and subordinate. This fear is particularly acute when the boss is a warm, friendly person. The subordinate shrinks from bringing up the distasteful subject of money because it might damage the delicate texture of the relationship that has been achieved.

It can happen to people who have been around long enough to acquire considerable experience, job-security, and sophistication about the things you have to do to get more money. Walter Kamp has been with Borealis Inc. for more than twenty years. He has worked his way up from the lowest rungs of the ladder to department head. Kamp is a dependable manager. He establishes and maintains good relationships with the fifteen people who report to him. He is meticulous about training, even-tempered in adversity, fair in evaluation. In recommending salary increases for his subordinates he is always aware of the need to reward good and loyal performance; but he balances that awareness against his knowledge that he must keep the "big picture" in mind and keep his operation within the bounds of profitability.

Walter Kamp has listened to just about every argument there is for more money. When he doesn't think a raise is justified he holds the line, refusing to be moved by assaults or blandishments. Kamp is a veteran who is knowledgeable and adept in salary negotiation with subordinates.

But how is he in handling his own negotiations with his boss? Walter Kamp has been reporting to Jim Makoski for six years. Makoski is younger, has been with Borealis less than half the time that Kamp has put in. Kamp was somewhat disappointed when Makoski got the job; he had aspirations of his own for the post. However, Walter Kamp has never been consumed by ambition, and he took that disappointment as he takes most other things, in stride. As a boss Jim Makoski has been a pleasant surprise to Walter. The two men, separated in age and temperament, like each other. Makoski is ever anxious to call on Walter for advice and comment; he often expresses appreciation for Kamp's contributions to the division and the company.

It has been fifteen months now since Walter Kamp got a raise. He has no reason to think that he has reached his limit. The last time he and Makoski talked salary he did not get the raise he hoped for, but he did receive an increase that seemed reasonable. Makoski is by no means a pushover in money talks, but he is never anything but cordial and understanding.

But Walter Kamp has not asked for a raise. His wife, while not the virago of the comic strips, does bring up the subjects of increased living costs and the debt that Borealis owes to Walter. Kamp is agreeable — he is usually agreeable — but there always seems some reason to put the confrontation off. So he goes on from day to day, week to week, delaying his request for a raise.

Walter Kamp, although modest, is not unaware of the value of what he does for the boss and for the company. But he just does not like to ask for money, particularly when the person to be asked is such a nice guy with whom he works so well. (What if Kamp's boss were not such a nice guy — would he be more likely to initiate a salary discussion? Probably not.) So Walter Kamp waits for something to happen.

And what does Jim Makoski make of this? Kamp's boss is willing to work out a raise if and when the subject is broached. But right at the moment he is just as happy that Walter has not taken the initiative. There is some pressure from top management to keep costs down. Makoski knows he is in no danger of losing Walter Kamp, and he has seen no indication of unhappiness on the part of his loyal subordinate. And Kamp's work is as steady and dependable as ever. So, while Makoski assures himself that he will eventually do something about raising Kamp's salary without being asked, he is willing to let things go along the way they are for a while.

As a matter of fact, this seeming placidity about money has contributed to a general feeling in the company that Walter Kamp lacks the drive needed to handle a job with greater responsibility. This was part of the reason that Walter was not promoted at the time Makoski took over the division. Although Kamp does not know it, his failure to push hard for raises has tended to confirm the impression that he is deficient in drive. Not long ago top management was looking for somebody to run a newly-established operation; they passed over Walter Kamp as not being ambitious enough.

An easygoing approach to getting raises is always welcome to bosses; they want as few headaches as possible. And yet at the same time, it can help to label a worker as being overly satisfied with the status quo. This is what is happening to Walter Kamp. He is reinforcing his boss's appreciation of him as a nice fellow; he is also strengthening the impression that he is *too* nice a guy to handle a tougher assignment. It may not be just, but it is true; the employee who is not aggressive about raises handicaps himself in more than merely immediate financial considerations. He may be unwittingly helping to short-circuit his own career.

No matter how secure and deserving we feel, it often takes an added stimulus to push us into asking for more money. One such stimulus can be a flash of anger. Sometimes a spurt of annoyance — even when it is out of proportion to the cause — can get the adrenalin pumping and send us into the boss's presence prepared to make a case. This is what happened to Garry Loesser.

Loesser was relatively young for the responsibility that the company had given him. He had been jumped up from the ranks at a moment of crisis to take over a vital function and had handled the situation well. After a time the word "acting" had been deleted from Loesser's title and he had been confirmed in his new role. At the time of his promotion Gary Loesser had thought about money. He had asked for a raise, but his boss, Abel Chaseman, had convinced him that this was not the time. . ."Let's see how this works out, Gary. After all, you're a pretty young and inexperienced guy for this job. I don't have any doubts about you having what it takes, but after all, we don't really know, do we? But you don't have anything to worry about. If you're able to show that you've got the stuff, this organization will take care of you."

Loesser had shown that he had the stuff; and, in its own way, the organization had "taken care" of him. It had been three years since the crisis that put him on the spot. He had been confirmed as a section leader, and had received a raise every year since then. But these raises has been of the same order that he was used to getting when he had been just a toiler in the ranks. He had not received the one big jump that would bring him into the financial class of the older, more experienced people who were holding down jobs no more responsible than his.

Gary Loesser had made a couple of tries to obtain this big jump; but they had not been much more than half-hearted stabs. He was still somewhat awed by the turn of fate that had propelled him to his present job. He was pleased by the recognition that had come his way. He was intrigued by the promises of a great future that were constantly dangled before him. And, in Abel Chaseman, he was up against a skilled and highly-effective negotiator. Once, when Loesser had indicated mildly that he thought he ought to be getting a lot more money, Chaseman had laughed indulgently and then so maneuvered the conversation that Loesser emerged thankful for a small raise and equally thankful that the boss did not hold his outlandish demand against him.

This was the status on the day of the annual Christmas party. Traditionally, this was also the day when the company distributed small bonus checks to everyone on the payroll. These checks were never enormous — $100 was tops. Everyone from mailboy to executive vice president received the same amount. And this particular year Gary Loesser had no reason to think that it would be any different. He was counting on that fifty or one hundred dollars to help out with the last minute shopping.

The bonus checks were brought around in their bright Christmas envelopes. It was not until Loesser was almost finished distributing them to his staff that he realized there was no check for him in the batch. This did not bother him unduly; no doubt there had been some foulup. So Loesser headed for the party with a light heart. On the way he met a fellow section leader and, in the conversation, happened to mention the oversight. The other shook his head; "No, it's not a mistake.

Didn't you hear? New policy. Since we are members of management, we don't get the bonus anymore. It's just for rank-and-file."

At the party Gary Loesser exchanged the usual friendly greetings, but he continued to think about this bit of news. The amount was small, but for some reason he kept getting madder and madder. He couldn't forget about it. And so, as the festivities were at their height, he took an opportunity to draw Abel Chaseman aside, into an empty office near the company cafeteria in which the party was taking place.

Chaseman, with a look of amused inquiry, asked Loesser what was on his mind. Loesser replied, "I hereby withdraw my request for a $1500 raise." Assuming some kind of a joke, Chaseman smiled more broadly and waited for Loesser to go on. After all, the raise situation had all been taken care of in a series of meetings concluding just a few days earlier. Loesser's $1500 had been agreed upon. Loesser went on, "I take back that request and replace it with another one. I want a raise of $6000, effective immediately. It's not negotiable, I will not take any less. And I'll be expecting an answer from you by the end of the day on Monday."

Abel Chaseman was willing to laugh off the gag; but Loesser continued his insistence, and it began to dawn on the boss that his subordinate was not kidding. "Well, we'll talk it over next week, Gary," said Chaseman; but Gary replied firmly that he was unwilling to talk it over. This was his demand and he was standing on it. No longer smiling quite so broadly, Chaseman told Loesser that he would get back to him. Chaseman moved back to the party. Loesser went home.

Monday morning Chaseman called Gary Loesser in. "I thought we could talk over that matter you brought up at the festivities, Gary; that is, if you want to talk about it. I'm willing to forget it. Lots of stranger things get said at our parties. You know that."

Loesser shook his head. "I mean it now just the way I said it then. Six thousand. I won't go into the justification. You know as well as I do that it's merited. I'll be waiting for your answer."

At four-thirty Loesser was summoned to Chaseman's office. The boss sat frowning at a piece of paper. Gary Loesser waited for what seemed five minutes. He was determined — but that did not mean he was not anxious. And he had to confess to himself that he was more than a little scared. Chaseman finally looked up and, wordlessly, handed the piece of paper to Gary Loesser. It was a memorandum approving a $6000 raise. As Loesser read it Chaseman got up, grinned broadly, and slapped the younger man on the back. It was not until months later that Gary Loesser disclosed to Chaseman the trivial episode that had triggered his rebellion.

Do You Deserve A Raise?

It's quitting time. A man emerges from the front door of Sievers & Company. He is a man worth looking at. He wears a well-fitting sport jacket made of the finest material, with slacks to match. His shoes are obviously hand-tooled. The shirt and tie are glorious adjuncts to the rest of the ensemble. The man strolls to the parking lot, swings open the door of a low, lean sports car — a Maserati or something — enamelled bright red. The engine starts with a throaty purr, and the little car swoops arrogantly out of the lot into the stream of traffic.

Another man comes out of the building. He is wearing a suit, neatly pressed, but that is about all you would say about it. The suit carries the burden of years. It has narrow lapels, the ones they put on suits before narrow lapels started to come back into style. The tie is neat but a little stringy; the shirt has made many trips to the washing machine. This person walks to a 1967 Valiant with a somewhat crumpled fender and a fading paint job. After some grinding and clunking the vehicle gets under way and begins its laborious homeward journey.

There is a third man who happens to be watching all this from a second-story window. There is nothing unusual in the sight, he has seen it many times before, he hardly notices the details. But he is thinking.

The first man to come out, the sports-car buff, is Andy Villalon; the second is Roy Washington. The person gazing from the window happens to be their boss, Hank Stern. Both Villalon and Washington have applied for salary increases of some magnitude. Stern is considering these requests. At the moment, the question going through his mind is, "What would they do with the money?"

Now, we can all agree that this question is irrelevant. What an employee will do with the money has, logically, no bearing on his qualifications for a raise. In fact, it is none of the boss's business. However, fortunately or otherwise, the raise-giving and raise-getting process is not always a logical one. Emotional factors creep in, and subterranean currents sometimes influence what happens on the surface of the boss's mind.

This is what is happening to Hank Stern. He is familiar with the life-styles espoused by each of his subordinates. Andy Villalon lives as flashily as he dresses and drives. He knows the best places to eat, is always the first to report on the new shows, seems perfectly at ease in the poshest drinking places. Headwaiters call him by name. He does things in style, spends big. Stern has seen Villalon's house, and it seems every bit as costly as his own. He has met Villalon's wife, a coruscating blonde who is emphatically not a favorite with Stern's wife or the spouses of other men in the office, but who certainly catches the eye. Maggie Villalon is a dish, and she looks like an expensive dish.

Nor is this all. Stern has heard the talk around the office that Andy Villalon has usually got one or more amorous intrigues going on the side. While never exactly admitting anything, Villalon does not go to any lengths to disabuse anyone of the notion. He is smilingly evasive when, over a drink, he is kidded about it. Furthermore, Stern has once or twice seen Villalon in the company of a spectacular redhead who in no way appears to fit the description "business contact"; at least not the kind of business carried on by Sievers & Company. Hank Stern is not a bluenose, and yet this does not sit well with him. Perhaps "envy" would be more accurate than "disapproval." Whatever the term, Stern is not enthusiastic over the way Andy Villalon lives his life.

Hank Stern has, whether or not he admits it to himself, scrutinized Villalon's work for a sign of adverse effect caused by these high-rolling activities. He has not found any. Villalon is cocky, sometimes abrasive, but the boss has to admit that he is bright and that he gets the job done. Moreover Villalon is an idea man. Some of his notions are half-baked, but a pretty good percentage of them are worthwhile. Villalon is not a superman, but he is good. Therefore, Hank Stern should be considering his raise application strictly on the basis of merit and ability to pay.

But he's not. On the one hand Stern has always asked himself, "How the hell can he afford it?" But he has an ingrained antipathy to giving Villalon more money so that his swinging subordinate can afford to enjoy even more of the good life.

What a contrast between Andy Villalon and Roy Washington! Washington never seems to spend an extra penny. He usually brings his lunch in a neat little sack. He always, as they say, "makes a good appearance," but no high-fashion clothing store is getting rich on Roy Washington. His home is modest; his wife is a pleasant, uncomplaining, self-effacing person who keeps the place, and the kids, spic-and-span. The Washingtons do not live it up. They take budget vacations, and give every evidence of thoroughly enjoying them. They may be just getting by, but they appear to be quite content about it.

And Roy Washington is a valuable worker. He is not a bundle of energy, throwing off sparks like those that streak from Villalon's vicinity. But he plugs along, getting the job done. Washington is a quietly determined, effective performer. He is never going to achieve any cosmic breakthroughs. But he gets the job done, and Hank Stern is well aware of his worth. Roy doesn't make a fuss over money, but he does ask for what he thinks he deserves. Now he has indicated that he wants a pretty big raise.

Well, Hank Stern should be willing and ready to satisfy Roy Washington's request, shouldn't he? Given the contrast between Washington and Villalon, he is highly likely to come through for the quiet man, right?

Wrong. Again, logic has nothing to do with it. Hank Stern, after all, wants to keep payroll costs down. He will pay what he has to for continuing good performance, but no more. This, in itself, is an understandable and legitimate concern of the manager. But Stern, under even the normal pressure to hold the line on salary, finds himself looking at Roy Washington and asking, "What does he need it for?"

Of course this is no more of his business than is his reluctance to provide more fuel for Andy Villalon's swinging lifestyle. What Washington is going to do with more money is for Washington to decide. It is not a matter of "need" at all. People are not paid on the basis of need. They are paid for what they contribute and what they may contribute in the future. Consciously Stern admits all this. And yet he feels, without any rational basis, that it is unjust for his life to be made more difficult by people who want more money when they are doing perfectly well on the money they make now. Furthermore, Stern has developed a feeling toward Washington that he is conscious of only at rare moments. He envies this unobtrusive subordinate for his ability to live what seems to be a contented life on what he earns. Stern, struggling to keep up the payments on his much bigger house and endeavoring to put enough aside to send his kids to the best schools, contemplates Washington's apparent accommodation with his financial station in life and sort of wishes he could manage things the same way, or at least that his wife was as efficient at stretching a dollar as Mrs. Washington. And Stern is faintly resentful.

So, for widely varying but equally illogical reasons, each of these subordinates is going to have a tough time getting the raise he wants. It will probably never be mentioned, but the boss will drag his heels because he is thinking about what the subordinate will do with the increased stipend.

There is no way to keep the boss from speculating on what you will do with the money, do you really need it, etc. But there are things you can do, and things you can avoid doing, that will minimize the problem.

It has been pointed out that *need* is not a logical basis for consideration of a raise. However, as we have seen, it does enter into the equation. So, if you can enhance your chances of getting a raise by showing that you need the money, you should do just that.

However, it's best that need be kept to one side as a "silent" factor in the negotiation. When boss and subordinate get down to cases, the bargaining should be on the basis of qualifications — at least on the surface. If the boss is sympathetic toward his employee's need for money, his feeling should be capitalized on — but indirectly.

Here's one way to do it. Andrea Murchison is looking ahead to a salary negotiation with her boss, Martha Tippett. The confrontation is a month or so away. Right now Murchison has the opportunity to report some good news to Tippett. She is able to go in and demonstrate that a project has been completed successfully, a little ahead of time.

Tippett listens to the details and then smiles. "Nice going, Andrea. I know it couldn't have been easy to pull off." (Actually it was not as hard as it looks to Tippett; Murchison has been using some good tactics in maximizing her triumphs.) Murchison nods, somber-faced. She says, "You'll note there that we project a continued upswing of 5 percent for the rest of the quarter. We'll be trying hard to do better than that." Martha Tippett goes on to make some more pleasant comments about the job. Andrea Murchison continues to be serious and somewhat subdued. Finally the boss says, "I thought you'd be walking on air. You seem a little gloomy. Is there some problem here that I haven't spotted?" No, Murchison tells her, the project went off just fine. Her state of mind has nothing to do with work.

Under the circumstances most bosses will pursue this opening. Tippett presses her subordinate to find out what's wrong. Finally Murchison says, "It's really nothing that you should be concerned with, Ms. Tippett. It's just, well you know, everything is so high these days, and now it looks as if I'm going to foot some big medical bills for my mother. . . ." Tippett expresses her sympathy. Murchison thanks her, but seems anxious to get off the subject and back to work-related topics. No more is said about Andrea Murchison's financial bind. But the seed has been planted.

When the time comes for Murchison to present her case for a maximum raise, she makes no direct reference to her need for the money.

However, at one point she becomes quite vehement in declaring that she deserves the raise. Then she stops, sits back, and says: "I'm sorry. I guess I got a little carried away there. Forgive me if I seem to be stressing some of these things kind of heavily, but this raise does mean a great deal to me. Naturally I know that's got nothing to do with whether or not you feel I've earned it." Murchison proceeds to make a strong but factual pitch for the raise.

And she gets it. Martha Tippett has been convinced of the merit of the request; but at the same time she has been influenced — at least a little and perhaps more than a little — by the need factor.

Plant the seed of need in the boss's mind before the raise negotiation. If possible work it so that you mention your strapped condition in answer to a question by the boss — a question that may be brought on by your unusually sober demeanor, or perhaps just a casual query in an off-hand moment ("God, with prices the way they are these days I don't know how any of us manages. How are you making out?").

Give the impression that you don't want to intrude your personal problems into the work situation. After making it clear that your head is barely above the surface, get off the subject and back to job-oriented matters.

And, if you have any control at all over the occasion when this comes up, see that it takes place in a context that is favorable to you. The best kind of situation exists when, like Andrea Murchison, you have acquitted yourself with at least some distinction. Certainly you should not do your sowing when you have been the bearer of bad news or the cause of problems. Your seed would then be apt to fall on stony soil ("Too bad about him. I've got my own troubles."). Then, in the actual salary negotiation, you can make some glancing reference to your need for the money — but never present it as an argument for getting the money. Need should be used, not as a selling point, but rather as a factor that makes the boss more receptive to your factual arguments.

Since it is true that bosses think about what their subordinates will do with more money, you can and should explain the need element as indicated above. However, you will have real trouble if the boss resents the way you are going to spend the increase.

If you enjoy a lavish lifestyle, swell. But if your boss is not the type who appreciates that kind of living, do everything possible to keep him from being aware of the way you get rid of your money. You don't have to poor mouth it around the shop — that just makes you look ridiculous — but you don't have to dress to the nines and give everybody a blow-by-blow description of your most recent big-ticket purchases or "sky's-the-limit" nights on the town.

Even if the boss is a big spender himself, it is wise to be careful. He is likely to look with more tolerance on a subordinate who likes to live it up — but he does not want competition. Don't drive as expensive a car as this kind of boss. Don't wear clothes that have obviously come from a better store. Don't let your conspicuous consumption match his. It may not be a bad idea to show your admiration for his swinging style by emulating it, but always — at least as far as he can see — on a somewhat smaller scale. If the boss is an Olympic-size check grabber let him bask in that reputation unthreatened by you. Otherwise you may bring about a situation in which he tries to stifle competition by curtailing your income.

At the same time it is not advantageous to seem to be always content with your lot, always able to manage handsomely on the money you make. For one thing this may irk the boss who feels that somehow you are showing him up by being able to conduct your affairs better than he does, even though he makes more than you do. And then of course he is apt to ask himself, "Why does this guy need a raise? He's doing fine right now." From this question it is just a short step to a determination to put the oil on the squeaky wheels. The boss may let himself be persuaded into giving bigger raises to people who have less of a case, because they are apt to complain more about it, and may drop off in performance. If you convey the impression that you are "doing fine" and can continue to do fine even if you don't obtain a deserved raise, you increase the danger of missing out. The boss will not deliberately want to be unjust — but he may figure, "Well, he will make out all right anyway. I'm sorry about shorting him right now, but I'll take care of him the next time around.

Even if you do manage well on your present salary, don't make a federal case of it. When the others are talking about how hard it is to make ends meet, don't smile your secret smile and rejoice in your own superior fortune. Join in the conversation. Detail some of your own hard-times stories, even if you have to embellish them a little.

No matter what lifestyle you espouse, it's a good idea to always look a little hungry. Bosses like people who will appreciate raises, appreciate the giver of those raises, and who will work hard in response to the raise. So, unless the circumstances are extraordinary, you will do well to appear as neither St. Francis of Assisi or Diamond Jim Brady.

Come on as if you need money, work hard for what you get now, and will be grateful and work even harder for what you request in the way of a raise. Let the boss think that you are not a spendthrift or a competitor, but a guy who needs the raise without making your need a basis for asking for it.

No matter how you play it though, you may run up against the situation in which the boss is obviously inclined against giving you the money just because he does not approve of your having it or does not feel that you need it. (This falls short of the situation in which there is a real rivalry or antipathy between you and the boss; that we cover elsewhere in this book.) How can you overcome this problem in the salary negotiation?

Let's go back to Andy Villalon, the possessor of the flashy sports car and even flashier women and bar tabs, and see how he might handle it. As we have said, Andy should not have gotten himself into this box. But as long as he has, he should do the best he can to climb out of it.

Here the direct approach to the problem can be the most useful. Andy has indicated his raise requirements. He goes on to say: "Hank, I hope you agree that I rate it. I think I can show you that I do. But let's get one thing out on the table right now. I know some people look at me and wonder how the hell I can afford the wheels and the threads and all the rest of it. I admit it — I like to live. Get it and spend it, is my motto. You're dead a long time. But I think you'll have to go along with me on one thing. When I walk in that door in the morning, I'm all business, and I stay that way until I walk out at night, and sometimes that's pretty damn late. I give the job everything I've got, Hank. Do you have any reason to be able to say that I don't?"

Hank Stern can't point to any contrary evidence, and Villalon knows this. But Andy's strategem goes beyond merely pinning down the boss's agreement that he does not permit outside pleasures to affect his work in the office. Villalon is challenging the boss. Without coming out and saying so he is implying very strongly: "I know that you don't like some of the things I do with my money. If I get the raise I will do more of those things, and I would be a liar if I told you I wouldn't. But if you are a fair and objective boss you will not permit this to influence your decision."

By getting it out in the open this way Villalon prods the boss's conscience. It is one thing for a manager to permit himself the luxury of inclining against giving a raise because he disapproves of how the subordinate spends his money. But it is quite another thing to deliberately say to oneself, "I will not give it to him because I am prejudiced against him." The first can happen with the boss being only a tiny bit aware of it. He can feel in no way blameworthy for his reluctance. But the second situation is a lot tougher. When the possibility of bias is deliberately — if indirectly — called to a boss's attention, he would have to be a calloused creature indeed to say to himself, "I don't give a damn what he says. I'll fight him to the death on this simply because I don't want him to have it."

When you let the boss know — not by direct imputation but by oblique reference to what "some people" might do — that you are aware of the possibility that he might be inclined against you because of a reason like this one, you make it a lot tougher on him to follow through. Some bosses may even lean over backwards to be objective about it.

Another way to circumvent the road block that exists when a boss doesn't want to give you the money because of how you may spend it or because he doesn't think you need it, is to emphasize the symbolic meaning of the raise rather than what it will buy. Let's look at how Roy Washington, the quiet, capable fellow who never seems to be strapped, might approach it.

Washington says to Hank Stern: "This raise will mean a lot to me, Hank. It's not just a matter of buying things or of having greater security against emergencies, although God knows we all need that, and I'm sure I'll be a more relaxed and better operator when I have it. But what's even more important to me is what the company thinks of the job I do for it and the loyal service I give it. Some people might think this sounds like flag waving, and maybe it does, but my association with Sievers for all these years means a lot to me. I'd like to think that I've given as good as I've gotten. I think I have. And I think this is a time for the organization to show me what it thinks of my worth by giving me this increase."

Roy Washington is asking, not for greater spending power, but for evidence that the firm appreciates his service. The fact is that we all think of a raise as a measure of our worth, at least insofar as it is measured by our employers. But we don't always use this factor to any advantage in bargaining for more money. When it is put on this basis, Hank Stern is not going to forget entirely about his feeling that Washington probably doesn't need the boost all that much, but this factor will inevitably dwindle in his considerations. Washington has put it on an entirely different basis. And both men know that, in Sievers as in most companies, pats on the back and accolades in the house organ are pretty cheap and not too meaningful. It is the recognition in the pay envelope that counts.

A certain amount of prejudice is always a possibility in the raise-seeking situation. The wise person conducts himself so as to keep it to a minimum. He does not flaunt a style of living that will enhance the boss's inclination to withhold money from him. He does not go out of his way to give the impression that he is free of financial concerns. To the extent that his need will be a favorable influence in the negotiation, he lets the boss know about it, but he refrains from asking for money *because* he needs it. And if money as buying power becomes a problem, he tries to shift the ground by challenging the boss's conscience and by emphasizing the symbolic aspects of the raise.

No matter what, the boss is not going to be falling all over himself to give you a raise. The big thing is to keep down the number of reasons for him to feel that way. If his motivations for reluctance are narrowed down to one or two points — points that he is willing to talk about — you stand a much better chance. It's those reasons that the boss won't express — or isn't even fully aware of — that are the most difficult to cope with.

Can You Be Motivated By Money?

Some managers are great followers of the prominent business philosophers. They read *Harvard Business Review* and other journals that convey the latest theories of the profession. Other managers pay little if any attention to the "art of management." They run things by the seat of their pants.

But, whichever category your boss falls into, when raise time approaches he is likely to adopt the coloration of a disciple of Dr. Frederick Herzberg. The boss may do this wittingly or unwittingly. Either way, you are up against one of the major theoretical obstacles in your path toward a healthy raise.

Dr. Herzberg is the leading industrial psychologist who propounded the "hygiene" theory. This theory seeks to articulate the things that motivate people to work. Probably the most distinctive feature of Herzberg's proposition — and the one that has garnered for him the widest recognition — is his assertion that, above a certain level, the granting of a salary increase does not motivate workers to work harder or become more efficient.

The Herzberg theory names two sets of factors that can affect a person's approach to his work. One set is called motivators; the other is called the hygiene factors. Hygiene factors cannot satisfy. They can merely keep a person from being dissatisfied. If each of the hygiene factors in a man's job comes up to a certain minimum level, then improvement under these headings does nothing toward making that man a more effective performer. So the manager is encouraged to regard the hygiene area as one in which he should fulfill a subordinate's basic needs, and then forget it. Anything more than those basic needs is rather a waste in buying better work.

The five principal hygiene factors designated by Herzberg are: company policy and administration; supervision; interpersonal relations on the job; working conditions; and *salary*.

The company can revise its procedures, improve the dispositions of its managers, induce greater congeniality on the job, provide carpets on the floors, and so forth. Doesn't mean a thing. If these goodies are taken away, the worker will, to be sure, be less well motivated and his performance will suffer. But giving him more of them will not make him work any better. This is what Herzberg is saying.

More to the point, he is saying that, after the employee is getting enough money to satisfy certain needs, you cannot motivate him to a greater extent by giving him more money. "It would seem," says Dr. Herzberg, "that as an affector of job attitudes salary has more potency as a job dissatisfier than as a job satisfier." (*The Motivation to Work*, Herzberg, Mausner, Synderman, John Wiley & Sons, 1959.)

It is this last point that is the kicker. By relegating money to the status of a nonmotivator, Herzberg gives the boss solid and respectable theoretical underpinning for what he wants to do anyway; namely, not give you a raise. And of course Herzberg's theory has achieved wide acclaim and acceptance among businessmen. Indeed, a cynic might speculate that it is the anti-money content that helps to make this proposition so attractive to employers today.

Well, what — according to Herzberg — are the things that *do* motivate a worker toward better performance? He names five principal areas: the work itself; achievement; recognition of achievement; a feeling of responsibility; and the desire for advancement. According to the theory, the boss should concentrate on providing his subordinates with more under these headings, and this will result in greater satisfaction and enhanced effectiveness.

You will have noticed — as have thousands of bosses — that Herzberg's five motivators include no mention of the vulgar subject of money. This in itself is a source of great satisfaction to the boss, but it is a headache for you. In asking for a raise you are not only up against your superior and the company; you must grapple with a widespread theory as well.

True, there are quite a few behavioral scientists who take issue with Dr. Herzberg about some facet or other of his theory. For a time one could hardly pick up the *Journal of Applied Psychology* without coming upon an earnest refutation of the formulation. But the refutations, no matter how much research and insight they may reflect, have never come within light years of catching up with the popular theory. Dr. Herzberg and his followers have spread the word assiduously, in speeches and writings, and now in many places the idea of motivators vs. hygiene factors has become an article of faith, and the notion that you can't motivate a man by paying him more money has been inscribed in letters of fire.

Let's construct a salary interview in which we can see the theory in full flower.

Earl Glick has gone up against his boss, Chet Hallinan, for a raise. Glick has gone through the routine of displaying his triumphs, emphasizing his value, and underscoring his worthiness to receive the money. He has talked about the soundness of the investment from the company's point of view. Now it's the boss's turn.

"You know, Earl, it's a pleasure to see a guy like you work. I was saying to the old man just the other day how much you seem to enjoy the job. You really tear into it. I know how many problems you've been able to solve out there, and you can be sure we appreciate it. But we never run out of problems, do we? There are always others coming up. We think you're the guy who can tackle some of the trickier dilemmas we're facing. I'll be talking with you about that. It means more responsibility, but we're sure you can do the job. In order to give you the kind of clout you need, I think it would be a good idea if you assumed the title of Supervisor of Special Internal Transactions. It's a step that reflects the greater challenges you'll be facing, and recognizes your success in accomplishments in the past. As you move up the ladder like this, I am sure that you're acquiring more of the management viewpoint. You see things from the perspective of a man who is arriving at a position of distinct importance in the organization. So I'm sure you see that, at the moment, it is unfortunately not possible to give you any more than a minimum raise at this time. However. . . ."

And so on. In this telescoped example we have shown our fictitious boss ringing all the chimes on the hygiene-motivator theory. The big thing is to give the worker greater responsibility; let him come up against challenges; pat him on the back when he surmounts these obstacles; move him along so that he has even more to handle; and try to see that he retains a certain gusto in doing his job.

But, more money? Give him as little as you can get away with. It's not a motivator.

The boss in this example may or may not have heard of Frederick Herzberg, or his theory. It doesn't matter. His little speech is a capsulized version of the approach of conscious and unconscious "Herzbergers" to getting more work out of people without paying them more.

How do you offset this? It's not enough to bluster continually that you are interested only in the buck. Knowing managers nod wisely and murmer, "He *says* that; but deep down inside he doesn't mean it. He is really motivated by responsibility, accomplishment, etc."

You can threaten to quit if you don't get the raise you want, but you had better have another job lined up. Even if it does some good, such an extreme and abrasive tactic can lose points for you in the company. It's not pleasant, and not really effective.

It's much better to implant the idea that, for you, money really *is* a motivator. This is best done by talking of money as the true recognition factor. In fact, at one point Dr. Herzberg offers support for this technique. Describing the reactions to money among workers he studied in one of the research projects leading to his theory, Herzberg says, "salary was mentioned. . .as something that went along with a person's achievement on the job. It was a form of recognition; it meant more than money; it meant that the individual was progressing in his work."

As a general rule Herzberg claims that money is a potential dissatisfier rather than a motivator, but he does recognize that it may represent recognition of achievement. The above quote is a good one to remember, particularly if your boss is an aficionado of Herzberg.

There are a number of things you can do to get the idea across that money means more to you than buying power. (Of course people who toil in certain industries don't have to do this. Advertising copywriters, for example, are well-known for their tooth-and-nail dedication to the pursuit of the buck from their earliest association with the industry. In the creative end of advertising, for reasons that are not germane here, money is recognized as *the* badge of accomplishment.)

Here's one way. As soon as you have received your first raise — no matter how small — tell the boss what it means to you. If appropriate, put it in writing: "This increase means more than just more money.

It is an indication to me that you and the company appreciate my efforts and feel that I have a future here. I will try my best to be worthy of that confidence, and will do everything I can to earn more money by increasing my ability and broadening my range of responsibility." Stuff like that. Talk about your salary as if it were a decoration bestowed on you by a grateful government for heroism. Don't say, "Oh, boy, now I can buy that matched set of Sam Snead irons." Rather say, "Emily was really touched when I told her. I've often said what a great place this is to work, but this raise proves it."

In negotiating for the raise, establish an order of priority. The boss will want to talk about challenge, recognition and all that other stuff first, with money last if at all. You give money its proper weight. Say "I believe we should talk about the raise first. All of these other things, although I value them highly, fall into place when the salary situation is taken care of."

By all means permit the boss to "motivate" you with all the non-monetary goodies. Let him give you more to do, greater responsibility, work you can get your teeth into. Welcome his words of encouragement and praise. But, when the crunch comes, consider these things as chips which can be cashed at the teller's window. For example, you bring up the fact that you were able to save a particular account for the firm. The boss replies: "By God, you sure did, and we all realized what a job you did on that one. I put out a companywide memo about it, didn't I? That kind of recognition doesn't come often around here. R. J. himself was very impressed, I can tell you." You nod in acknowledgment and say "I'm happy to hear it. Surely that will clear the way for approval of this raise."

At some point the boss, confronted with this constant relating of his motivating ploys to money, may assume a pained expression and say something to the effect that he is disappointed; you seem to think of nothing but money. He thought you were different, etc. Don't protest that you don't just think of money. Don't deny his assertion at all. Instead, look as if you are pleased that he has grasped the key to the situation and say, "Well, there is a time for everything. I try to give all of my concentration to the subject at hand, and I like to think it helps me get things done. The subject now is money. I'm not ashamed to say that I believe fully in the profit system. And I know that you believe in it too, and that you recognize the value of a man enjoying the fruits of his labors. This raise will mean a great deal to me in terms of recognition of achievement and evidence that the company believes in me, but if I talk about it in those terms it will just confuse the issue. So let's talk about it in terms of salary."

Don't permit yourself to be sidetracked by the boss's appeals to your "better nature," no matter how touchingly they may be put. The great George Bernard Shaw was a literary artist who well knew how to be recompensed for his efforts. Once, when a particularly tight-fisted producer tried to whittle down Shaw's price by referring to the glorious contribution the forthcoming play would make to the everlasting theater, Shaw sent back a wire: "That is the difference between us. All you care about is Art, and all I care about is money."

Your stance is not quite that. Your position is that you care very much about Art — recognition, opportunity, advancement, the job, the company, and all the rest of it. You expect and hope that the company will reciprocate with a similarly pure interest in you. How do people demonstrate their loyalty, affection, confidence, friendship, etc. in each other? By doing for one another the most that they can do. You, for your part, have given and will continue to give the company your best efforts and your intense involvement with the job. The company, in return, can give you resounding job titles, greater responsibility, and occasional accolades. But if that's all the company gives — well, you are sorry and terribly disappointed, because the organization is not giving you everything it can. The firm can manifest its true feeling for you by bestowing on you a little more of what, after all, constitutes its life's blood. And that is money.

So, when the boss attempts to keep you satisfied with "motivators," accept them with a certain reserve. You will not be constantly asking for raises, or talking about money every time they pat you on the back. But you can occasionally remind your manager of how you see it. He tells you you did a great job on something or other. You reply with thanks and the assurance that you were happy to be able to come through for the company. And then you add that, while this is not the time to talk about it, you are frankly happy also because this accomplishment, you are sure, will be remembered when it is time to talk about your value to the organization. That's enough.

None of this is really intended to constitute debate or judgment on Dr. Herzberg's thinking. Whether the theory is sound or not is not the point. We are talking here about getting more money, motivator or no. If a theory stands in the way, you must cope with it as you cope with any other obstacle.

2

the art of positioning

Campaign For Your First Raise When They Hire You

The strategy for getting your first raise, and all subsequent raises, begins before you get hired.

Most employment interviews are charades with respect to money. Both participants tend to skirt the topic. The job seeker does this for obvious (if dubious) reasons. He wants to come on as a high-minded person to whom the biggest thing by far is the opportunity to work for such a fine company and meet such stimulating challenges as will be offered him. Most employers stay away from detailed discussions of money for two reasons. The first is that the standard interviewing techniques concentrate on determination of the applicant's qualifications and his fitness in terms of personality, motivation, and character. The books on interviewing tell you to do it this way. For example, Benjamin Belinsky and Ruth Burger, in *The Executive Interview,* offer a definitive treatise on how to handle interviews of various types (including the selection interview) but they don't talk about money.

The second reason is that most people do not like to discuss compensation with job candidates; or, for that matter, with subordinates. They feel uncomfortable with the subject. The reasons for this discomfort vary with the type of individual conducting the interview and with the circumstances under which it is conducted.

Some employers shy away from talking about money because they are afraid of the topic. They do not have the power of the purse. They are limited in what they can offer. A superior, orally or through a policy directive, has put a limit on how much they can offer. Few people like to acknowledge — overtly or even tacitly — that they lack full authority. So they resolutely stick to the safer paths of outlining the job requirements, getting the candidate to talk about himself, etc.

There is another kind of job interviewer. He has ample scope for establishing a starting salary; nevertheless he keeps off the subject. He wishes to keep the transaction on a high plane. He hopes that the job seeker is a dedicated individual whose principal motivation is the self-less solution of corporate problems. Of course the businessman who possesses such an outlook is often disappointed, but he tries to stave off disillusionment as long as possible. Thus he avoids the crass topic of how much the job pays.

And then there is the employer who "sells." He is always trying to use his powers of persuasion to work the applicant into the position of slavering at the mouth to get the job. Some executives do this automatically; they sell everybody. Some do it in selected cases; they have fixed on a particular candidate as being the right man or woman and they build up the nonmonetary values of the job. They forestall discussion of salary for as long as possible, fearing that it might turn the candidate off.

Another type of employer plays it differently. He brings up compensation early and bluntly — "Let's get this settled first." His aim is to get the difficult subject out of the way first and then settle down to a statesman-like conversation about the "big picture." This business-man may not enjoy talking about money any more than his counter-parts, but he knows that it comes up sooner or later and he figures it might as well be sooner.

As for the job applicant, his readiness to plunge into the subject of money can be rated along a continuum according to his hunger for the position. The individual who has been unemployed for fifteen months and whose savings have run out will agree to just about any amount, whenever it is brought up. The fellow who is happily and successfully ensconced in a good spot — but who has been persuaded to at least consider making a change — will have few inhibitions about getting tough.

So money is not out in front as a topic for frank and extended discussion in most job interviews. It lurks around the fringes, peering out at the two principals. But it has a considerable influence. The potential employer is asking questions designed to draw out the candidate:

"What kinds of things do you like to do best?"

"Why would you like to work for this company?"

"What do you feel you accomplished on your last job?"

"Do you work best on your own or as part of a group?"

"Where do you want to be in five years?"

Now, a lot of candidates, if they were really honest, might answer such questions along these lines:

"I like making money best."

"Because I thing this company will pay me more than the last one."

"What did I accomplish? I made more than anybody else had ever made in that job category."

"On my own or part of a group, as long as the dough is there."

"In five years I'd like to be making three times what I'm making now."

Of course he doesn't answer this way. That wouldn't be playing the game. He would be dismissed instantly from consideration. So he goes along, talking about his interest in the prospective job, his admiration for the prospective employer, his love of a challenge, his lust to solve problems, his burning desire to lead men, and his unique ability to combine innovativeness with cooperation. He tries to spot and handle the trick questions; those pet queries that many job interviewers rely on to cause the applicant to unfold his soul. He struggles to project the image of a ball of fire who will at the same time be absolutely loyal and no threat whatever to the boss. Eventually, of course, money comes up. But most applicants do little or nothing to establish a good bargaining position for the present or the future.

You can begin to build a foundation for your more-money program before the subject comes up in the interview. You can do it, for example, when you are describing your present or previous job.

Here's how one job candidate answers the question about what he did in his last job:

I supervised twelve people. My department was responsible for all final processing. I was responsible for hiring, training, and managing the staff. I reported directly to the Director of Manufacturing. . . .

Wrong. He's describing the details of what he did. He's not talking about what he accomplished. This would be a better way to cover it:

When I took over the department, average processing time was thirty minutes per unit. We did not have a unit cost for this operation so I figured it out; a hundred and ten dollars. With my boss, the Director of Manufacturing, I worked out some goals. Cut the processing time to twenty-three minutes and the unit cost to ninety dollars. We established a deadline. These objectives were to be accomplished within nine months. Part of the understanding was that the staff size would remain at twelve. We were able to get the time down to twenty minutes and the unit cost down to eighty-seven dollars, and this was done before the deadline — within seven months. The annual lowering of costs came to. . . .

This candidate is talking about accomplishments, not details. But he's doing something more. He has introduced the concept of *standards of performance.* He indicates that he expects standards to be established on his job; and that he expects to participate in the establishment of those standards. And by strong implication he is working to establish the idea that, if he accomplishes more than anticipated by the standards, then his accomplishments are worth more to the company.

It is important right from the start — from before hiring, even — to concentrate on the setting-up of standards of performance: not vague standards, under which the boss forms a general impression about whether you are performing well or not, and not unilateral standards which are established by the boss without discussion. Elsewhere in this book we go into the details of a program that will enable you to work against specific criteria that will measure how well you are doing. And we spell out the ways in which you can influence the establishment of standards so that your strongest qualities are rewarded most highly.

You can — and should — draw out the employer on his present approach to performance evaluation. You may or may not want to ask him about the day-to-day duties that the job involves. But it is important to ask him questions like this:

"Looking at the job overall, Mr. Langer, what do you consider its most important aspects?"

"What are the biggest problems that the new person in the job will have to cope with?"

"What do you consider to be satisfactory performance in the job?"
You will find out certain things. You will learn whether or not the employer has meaningful standards at present. Whether or not he has them, you will pick up an idea of the aspects of the job that he considered important. If they are areas in which you are sure of looking good, fine. Go on to assume that they are the primary requirements of the job: "Yes, I can see how important it is to be able to maintain absolutely smooth relationships with the other departments."

If the standards he is talking about are not particularly shaped to your strengths, you may want to introduce, gently, the notes that will constitute a prelude to a little re-shaping: "Yes, I can see how important it is to maintain smooth relationships. But I wonder if I might ask about a situation in which you were convinced that a certain plan was right and would significantly improve the department — even though you ran the risk of some temporary friction. . . ."

You're not going to get into a full-scale discussion of job standards now, of course. That comes after you have the job. But you can plant the seeds. And while you are planting the seeds you are probably strengthening your chances of getting the job because you are talking about performance and accomplishment in a way that probably makes you look better than the competition.

Keep talking about standards and accomplishments. Don't be in any hurry to get to the financial question. In fact as a rule it is best to *delay talk about money for as long as possible.* As you go through the interviewing process — and of course it may involve multiple interviews — you may be gaining in favor. If this is the case, then time is working for you. The more the employer is leaning toward you, the stronger you will be when money is mentioned.

And if your chances are not particularly improving as time goes on, you still do not lose anything by holding off on a discussion of money. Precipitation of the salary issue at a time when you are not too solid may merely serve to shut off further consideration.

Most bosses will go along with a tacit agreement to postpone the financial discussion. After all, the employer has a general idea of what he thinks he is willing to pay, you have some feeling for the possibilities, and your track record gives some indication of what you have been making.

Of course you may run into the interviewer who does raise the question directly before things are very far along. Here's a snatch of dialog from an interview:

Interviewer: You know what the job pays?

Candidate: Well, I understand that the range is from twenty-two to twenty-five thousand.

Interviewer: Yes, that's the general range we indicated, but of course the upper part of that range envisions someone with extensive experience in exactly our line of business. We wouldn't be talking about anything near twenty-five.

If the job seeker goes along with this — and he is in a poor position to struggle with it at this point — then he has just cut himself off from even a crack at $25,000. Furthermore, he has given the first inkling that he might be pretty soft-boiled when it comes to asking for subsequent raises. He would be better off if he had stalled on the discussion:

Interviewer: You know what the job pays?

Candidate: No, not really, but I don't have any worries about being able to agree on a figure if you decide you want me. I know your firm is well-known for recognizing ability. But right now I thought we might go into. . . .

Much better. The candidate has given a gentle indication that he knows what he is worth. Few interviewers are going to battle to pin him down to a figure at this point. It would seem premature almost to the extent of being ridiculous. And the employer who is told that he has a good reputation for "recognizing ability" is unlikely to reject that accolade.

Wait until they want you for the job. And then make your discussion of salary firm and business-like. For the average job hunter it is difficult to be firm about salary. It seems like "getting off on the wrong foot." The candidate fears that he is compromising his chances of getting the job.

Not so. While blind unreasoning stubbornness about salary will eliminate a candidate, logical and persuasive insistence on a figure that is "in the ball park" is highly unlikely to have this effect. When an employer finds himself leaning favorably toward a candidate, he may wish to land him at the lowest possible figure, but he will respect him for insisting on a higher one. And remember this, a couple of months or even a few weeks after you are hired, any conceivable hard feeling about your tough line on salary will be forgotten if you are doing a good job.

So when the question of pay comes up, *assume* that all other questions have been answered and that this is the last detail to be taken care of before you sign on board. By this time you should have formed an impression of the leeway your employer possesses in fixing your compensation. There are three categories:

- The boss who can pay you anything you ask within reason.
- The boss who can give you more or less within a fixed range.
- The boss who does not really have the final say over salary.

Watch him when he is talking about money. Observe his "body language." Does he talk about a higher figure with confidence, or does he become uneasy? Few interviewers will confess flat out that they don't have the authority to fix on an amount (although some will, and a few will pretend that this is their situation.)

If you conclude that he is going to have to talk to someone else to get an okay on the amount you ask, give him arguments that will support his request. Recap your accomplishments, to the extent possible, in terms of measurable accomplishments; money saved, volume sold, what it all meant on the bottom line. Emphasize the contributions you will make to this company and to this particular boss in terms of making him look good and spotlighting his hiring of you as a wise decision.

If the individual you are talking to does have the power to decide, you will still want to make your case in terms of the accomplishments that can be expected in the light of what you have to offer. Here's a fragment of how it might go:

Employer: Fine. Well, I think we've been over everything, and I must tell you that you're under very active consideration, although of course we are still looking at some other excellent candidates. (They usually say something like this.) Now; about compensation. If we were to decide on you, we are thinking about $17,000. Would that be satisfactory?

Candidate: (This is the time to be firm.) I'm afraid not. In the light of what we've discussed and what I think I can accomplish for you, I would expect $20,000.

Don't set a "bargaining figure" that is highly-inflated with the idea that you will split the difference. It's embarrassing and unrealistic. You are not haggling with an Armenian carpet merchant. State a figure that is believable, but from which you can back down a little, if only to let the employer save face. (Saving face is quite important in salary negotiation; we go into it at some length elsewhere.)

Make him give you a reason for his lower figure. Ask, "Why do you say $17,000? Is there a limit imposed on the position? From our discussion I assumed that you attached more importance to what could be accomplished on the job."

Stay calm and loose. The employer may try to justify the lower figure by commenting on your lack of experience in this particular line of business.

If you have focused the discussion on standards and accomplishments you are in a position to say: "I don't pretend that there are not people with a lot more experience in this particular business. No doubt there are many right in your organization. But I know from the way you've talked with me about the challenge that you place great emphasis on the importance of overcoming problems and the value of high accomplishment. I'm ready to undertake that challenge. I don't think either of us wants to have the start clouded over by a problem about salary. Tell me, if I am able to accomplish a significant proportion of what we talked about, won't that be worth what I'm asking?"

He may talk about the existing compensation range, and how too much money for you would throw it off. You can reply: "If, as I hope, I join you, I'm going to be giving the job everything I've got to make the organization go. I hope to make a contribution as part of the team, but also as an individual. I wouldn't think of myself as just a cog in a big, impersonal machine, and I know that's not your approach to the job." And so on.

Don't be a pushover. Work for the salary you want — or something close to it. If he says he'll have to think it over, wait for a few days. If they want you, they won't knock you out of contention out of hand. They'll call you in again. And you may get the figure you want; or the one you'll accept. Or, you may not. If you conclude that you have to settle for something less, you have at least established yourself as an individual who will not be a patsy when raise time rolls around.

You can underscore this message: "I want to work for this company. I think I can do things here. And so I accept your offer. However, there is one question. Can I be reasonably sure that a good record of accomplishment will qualify me for appropriate salary consideration later on?"

The boss says yes. You haven't gotten the starting salary you were aiming at; but you have made the initial move in your campaign for a substantial first raise.

Establishing Your Money Position With the New Boss

You have a new boss. You want to establish yourself with him for various reasons — continued cordial relations on the job, security, advancement. And *money*. You will want to begin working on the new boss for your next raise early in his tenure.

When a manager comes in fresh — without much previous experience with the people he'll be managing — he is under a certain amount of strain. He wants to get off on the right foot. To do this he must establish good working relationships with his most important subordinates. Some of these important subordinates he can, of course, readily identify by rank and title. But most managers with any experience know that there is an invisible echelon of "influentials" within an operation, and the people who constitute this group are not, at first, so easy to spot. If the new boss makes enemies out of certain functionaries his life in the job may be hard — and relatively brief.

So the newly-arrived manager is seeking those who will mean most to his success, and trying to set up good working relationships with them. He can't concentrate on everybody, willy-nilly he will write off some people as useful but not very important. (Making the right guesses about these relationships is one of the most important things a manager can do when he takes over a new responsibility.)

However minor your role has been in the past, when the new boss arrives make a systematic effort to convince him that you are someone whose involvement and good will are well worth fostering. Establish the impression that you are an "influential."

To do this you'll have to talk with the boss. You'll have met him, and been at one or more meetings with him. He is also probably conducting one-on-one sessions with workers in the department, making his way down through the ranks according to the rough ideas of preference and relative importance that he has formed.

If you wait for this process to run its natural course it may be a long time before the boss gets to you. By the time you have your shot he may already have hardened in his feelings about who is vital and who is not. So don't wait for nature to take its course. Make an opportunity to have a chat with the new boss.

Mary Duryea has shaken hands with her new manager, Bernie Gruen, but that's about all. Gruen has been in the job a week. So far he has spent most of his time with three or four key subordinates. Mary Duryea decides that it's time for her to get to know Gruen better. She comes in briskly with an impressive sheaf of papers in her hands. After a few pleasantries, she comes to the point: "Bernie, I'm sure you know that one of the real potential bottlenecks in this operation is the difficulty of making sure that all outstanding charges are accounted for before a file is closed. When you close one and then other stuff trickles in, it can be embarrassing. But you can't keep the files open forever — that's not so good either. Now, we're coming up to the point of the month where we try to close out as many as possible. I've worked out a method of getting the input we need, and it seems to be working pretty well if I really go all out on it, but since it involves some touchy areas of interdepartmental contact, I thought it important to check it out with you."

Now the fact is that Mary Duryea is embroidering a little bit. The process she is describing is not all that critical, and while there have been problems, they are not earth shaking. But she is saying some of the right words: "potential bottleneck". . ."embarrassing". . ."touchy areas. . . ." Bernie Gruen certainly does not want to trip over some hidden stumbling block right at the outset, so he listens. Mary goes over her procedure. The procedure consists in essence of going to people in other departments and asking questions. Mary Duryea does not put it quite that simply. "I have established regular contact points in the activity centers. I try to be alerted in advance on any difficulty, and I activate a plan to fill out the input requirements by the deadline." She goes on to give a detailed and not altogether comprehensible description of this supremely intricate function.

Bernie Gruen doesn't follow it all, but he gets the idea that — although Mary Duryea is not a highly-visible member of his team — her continued efficacy is important in making sure that he does not stub his toe. So he decides that it is worthwhile to cultivate this particular subordinate. He tells Mary that he wants her to proceed in the way that she has been going, and then he settles down to ask her more about herself and her job.

Mary Duryea has accomplished step one. She has impressed the boss that there is something about her work — whether or not it looms large in the job description — that is important to him. Now she is ready to solidify her position.

Any new boss wants information. But there are two kinds of information — official and unofficial. The official information is couched in the files, the correspondence, the job-evaluation forms, and the utterances of the top brass who have hired him. The unofficial information is more nebulous. Some of it may be largely gossip. But it can be more important than the official variety, because it may contain keys to the true "feel" of the place and the unorthodox channels through which work really gets done. The new boss is going to receive these insights from somebody. It might as well be you.

Mary Duryea brushes over the more obvious details of her job and then moves on to the "inside" stuff. "As you may have already found out, the toughest department we have to deal with is Account Service. It's not that they have anything against us — I've been able to stay on pretty good terms with the right people over there — but some of their procedures are not helpful to us in doing what we have to do. So in a way I have to become a kind of consultant to their department. I've gotten so I know what stage something is at with them, or I know the people who can tell me. Why, only last month we were struggling with some real hangups on a very important deal. . . ." Mary relates how, through her contacts, she was able to straighten out a tough problem.

Give the new boss the distinct impression that you are thoroughly familiar with not only your own job but also with the ins and outs of the operation and the company. You know how to get things done.

Along with this you will want to let the boss know that you are willing and eager to put all of this know-how at his disposal, not only to get the work done, but to make him look good. Mary Duryea says, "I don't know what procedure you want to follow in making the monthly reports. They are read very carefully by the executive committee. (As a matter of fact they are glanced at by one member of the executive committee.) When I was working with Duane Phillips (Gruen's predecessor) we decided that certain highlights were good to include. They tend to flesh out the bare figures and give top management a better picture of the job we do. If you would like to continue on that basis I am willing to do anything I can to help out."

Bernie Gruen welcomes this evidence of loyalty and tender of help. He is beginning to feel that Mary Duryea is one of those unsung people who don't hit the headlines, but whose support and assistance are crucial in the success of any manager. He is quite willing to accept the idea of a close working relationship.

Mary Duryea is extremely forthcoming in her offers of information and help. In her comments about how she feels about the company and the job she is somewhat more reserved. "Oh, I like working here," she tells Gruen. "There are a great many things about the place that suit me very well. I don't expect a lot of recognition for what I do. In fact, since I work behind the scenes, so to speak, for me or anybody else to make a fuss about some of these things would hinder my ability to accomplish what needs to be accomplished. But everyone likes in some way to be recognized, and I'm no different. However, I'm very hopeful about the new arrangement, and for my part I will do what I can to make it even more productive than before."

When Mary leaves Bernie's office she is in a far better position to build a campaign for a good raise than she was before.

You can appeal to the new manager's anxiety about not making a mistake by alluding to some of the hidden pitfalls that may lie in his path. You are his guide through this part of the jungle — or at least you are willing to be. He will be keenly alert to possibilities of making mistakes. (Much more alert than he would ordinarily be to the opportunity of making sweeping changes in the minor details of the way things run. New bosses like to look as if they are making changes — but these changes will be cosmetic ones, affecting the big-picture "look" of the operation. They are chary of fooling with existing routines about which they know little.)

Give the new boss information, particularly "inside" information. It is not a bad thing for him to look upon you as a reliable and respectable source of gossip about the organization. At first keep your tidbits innocuous; as the relationship progresses you can move into the more titillating areas of speculation. ("Not that I ever thought there was anything to it, but for a while there people were wondering about Mr. Kenby and Ella Lorimer, who used to work in purchasing.")

Impress him with the thought that your loyalty is important, and that it is at his disposal. However, your loyalty and cooperation are not just there for the taking. You want to cooperate in keeping things running and in making him look good, and you are willing to assume that he will continue to merit your cooperation. The implication is that he will extend loyalty down the line, notably when it comes to a raise.

Show at all times that you are absolutely in control of what you do. *Don't ask the new boss questions that require tough answers.* Have a workable answer for the problem, and merely ask the boss if he wants you to apply it. He may want to hear more, and you can tell him more, in language that emphasizes the complexity and the delicacy of some of the things you do.

Demonstrate involvement with your job as a matter of professional pride — but at the same time give the impression of a certain amount of remoteness and self-sufficiency. The boss should never get the idea that you would never think about leaving. You expect certain things as your due, and you are confident that he will come through for you.

Reassure the boss. He has a lot on his mind. Provide him with the feeling that in this one area, at least (and he should feel it's an important area) he doesn't have to worry. You will take care of it all. You will see that there is no horrendous calamity to mar his introduction to the job. And, as time goes on, your efforts will contribute to positive results that will enhance his reputation.

First impressions can last a long time. The coming of a new boss gives you the chance to make an impression that will stand you in good stead. When you become, in his eyes, one of the "influentials," you have established the underpinning for a successful raise campaign. Of course you will continue to do the best job that you can. The important thing is to get the new manager to understand that your function is critical to his well-being. If he sees it that way the picture may linger for quite a while — well into raise time.

How To Set Job Objectives You Can Meet

What's your job description?

You have one, whether you know it or not. Job descriptions don't have to be formal, written documents. Whether there is anything down on paper or not, the operative job description is the one that exists in the minds of your boss and others in the organization who influence the decision on your next raise request.

If your job is described in writing, become familiar with the document if you are not already acquainted with it. There may be a job description in your boss's files, or in the personnel department. If such a piece of paper exists it may not be very important. Nevertheless it can't do you any harm to find out what's in it, and it may do you some good.

Job descriptions come into being in various ways. Business consultants are often called upon to make them up. Whoever handles the personnel function may decide that job descriptions are needed. Sometimes a line manager writes, or requires somebody else to write, a set of specifications for the positions reporting to him.

But somehow the concept of the written job description has never caught on as securely as many of its proponents thought it would. The problem can be summed up in this question: After you have the job description, what do you do with it? The fact is that a written depiction of the work that a certain job entails is not that useful a tool. For one thing requirements change, so that a job description can become outdated quite rapidly. For another thing, the formal document may be a drawback rather than an advantage; by rigidly defining what a worker does it may tend to inhibit creative incursions into other areas.

Written job descriptions can be of some help in a number of areas. They can serve as guidelines in hiring people. They can be of use in the building of a training program. And, in larger organizations, they are sometimes associated with the setting of pay scales. It is the last function that we are concerned with.

If you work for a company that has established salary ranges for types of jobs, then as long as you occupy that type job you have little chance of getting more money than the scale indicates. And pay scales that spread over a large number of jobs are slow to change and tough to crack. The employee may feel that he is doing exceptional work, but the boss can spread his hands helplessly and point to the existence of the pay scale as a reason for not giving him more money.

But the rigid job description is not as pervasive a hindrance to the raise seeker as it might be. Most bosses don't pay much attention to formal descriptions, and this is usually fortunate. The boss may have inherited the document, which now resides in a file drawer someplace, because its value is limited. For the classic job description outlines functions without assigning standards. A job description will say, "Balance all transactions by the end of each calendar month," or "Provide liaison between field representatives and merchandising department," or "Supervise the scheduling of departmental work," or something like that. Ordinarily it does not indicate what constitutes good or acceptable performance in the functions it covers. It does not even say they should be done well.

There's another job description with which you should be more actively concerned. This is the one that exists in your boss's mind, perhaps supplemented by notes in writing. Your boss has certain expectations of you. He expects that you will do certain things, but also that you will handle them in a way that satisfies him. The functions on which he lays the greatest emphasis may not be the most important aspects of the job, and his expectations may be too low in some areas and unrealistically high in others. Furthermore, this mental job description may fluctuate with changing circumstances.

To get the raise you want, you should appear to be exceeding the boss's expectations in the areas that he considers most important. So you will want to get as accurate a line as possible on the job description that he carries around in his head; not just his idea of the functions you perform, but his feeling about the standards against which you perform them.

Do you really know what the boss expects of you? A lot of people assume that they do, but assume wrongly. One widespread problem is that job standards are seldom spelled out in any detail. An employee is indoctrinated into a task. He goes along, doing his best to pick up enough knowledge to handle the job. He gets advice and tips from the boss, and an occasional word of warning or approval. But rarely does the boss sit down and talk about what constitutes good performance.

Of course the boss will set up goals — but these, more often than not, are specific short-run objectives relating to a current job. "This has to be finished by four o'clock. . . .We need all the figures by Friday. . . . You'll have to turn out five thousand acceptable units." These are sub-goals, short-range targets to shoot at. They are helpful; but they don't fill the need for more broadly-based standards of performance.

You want standards for at least a couple of reasons. Everybody needs guidelines. No matter how much an individual may insist on a "free hand" in his job, that same individual would feel lost if he were working in a totally unstructured situation. We all ask ourselves, "How am I doing?" — and without standards we have a hard time giving ourselves an answer. When standards are cloudy or nonexistent, it is easier for us to kid ourselves that we are doing fine. Then, when raise time comes around, we find that we have not been satisfying the boss at all. It's much better to know what is expected.

But just knowing what the boss expects of you is not enough. He must know that you know. Standards should be agreed upon between boss and subordinate. Only then can you use the meeting or exceeding of standards as the basis for requesting more money.

How can you arrange for giving your job a set of standards that are congenial to you and that you're able to meet? The best way is the simplest: talk with the boss.

Here's Pete Ervin sticking his head into his boss's office, "Got a minute, Chuck?" Chuck waves Pete in. Pete starts out by saying that he hasn't come in with a problem to drop on Chuck's desk, everything's going fine. Then Pete goes on: "I just thought that, if you have the time, I'd like to talk about the job, where I think I've got it under control and where maybe you can help me. But first, I wonder if you'd tell me how you see the job. Not how I'm doing, but the job itself. What do you think are the most important parts of it?"

Pete has done several things right. He has precipitated an informal chat, and has assured informality by taking any possible edge off the occasion. He has, right at the start, reassured his boss on several counts. Pete is not there to raise a problem. He does not want an evaluation of himself. And he doesn't begin by monopolizing the conversation. He has deferred to the boss's wisdom, suggesting that Chuck comment on the more important elements in Pete's job.

Thus reassured, the boss is relaxed. Bosses feel it necessary to hear about problems — they will rebuke subordinates for not telling them bad news ("Why wasn't I informed of that?") — but few people really enjoy being presented with problems. And since many managerial and supervisory situations seem like just one damn problem after another, a lot of bosses will welcome an easy going, feet-on-the-desk exchange, particularly when they get a chance to expound their own ideas.

The ultimate ideal in the establishment of job standards is for *you to set the standards yourself.* This is not normally possible to do in its entirety, but you can have a significant role in shaping the criteria by which you will be judged, if you work it right. The first step is to initiate the right kind of one-to-one conversation with the boss. The next is to find out what the boss thinks is important.

As your leader begins to make his observations on your job, listen carefully. There may be some surprises. An element of the task that you assumed was of only the most trifling importance may loom amazingly large to him; and something that you figured to be of great moment may not rank very high with him. For example, Pete Ervin is barely able to conceal his startled reaction when he hears Chuck say: "One thing I've noticed, Pete. You always answer your phone on the first ring. That's good. Some of the people that call this department are funny. They want us to be alert, right on the ball. Answering fast gives that snappy feeling. Otherwise they wonder what you're doing." Well, of course this is not the only standard that Chuck mentions; but since he seems to lay such stress on it, Pete is interested.

As you get your boss talking about standards, keep in mind the things you do well and not so well. When he refers to an area that you handle effectively, encourage him to dwell on it. As Pete Ervin's boss begins to discuss job requirements of a bit more consequence than how quickly the phone is answered, he touches on such an area: "Well, it's important to get those reports in on time, every time; and they should really be detailed. People are depending on us to give them the dope they need to make decisions. So this is one of your bread-and-butter things."

Now, Pete Ervin knows that he does well with the preparation of reports. He is painstaking and well-organized. So a discussion of report writing as an essential of the job is a good thing and should be pushed along. Pete pursues it: "Yes, I feel pretty strongly about the responsibility we have there, so I always try to do a super job on the weekly report. But there's always room for improvement, I know that, too. Do you think I've been handling that part of it okay so far?"

Chuck says that Pete's reports look all right to him. But Pete wisely does not leave it at that. When you are engaged in a standard-setting conference, the idea is to milk the things you do well. Solidify and magnify them as vital parts of your assignment. But do more than that. Work it so that you and the boss agree on goals for improvement — goals that you are sure you can meet.

Pete does this now: "I have some ideas about that weekly report, how I think it could be made even more useful and more of a credit to our department. One idea is that I think we ought to break down the shipment figures within each region, in other words for each territory. This would make it possible...." Pete spells out a number of notions for improving the project. Chuck advises that he hold off on some of them ("We've got a good thing going and we don't want to change it too much.") but on others he accepts Pete's ideas for improvement with enthusiasm.

Now Pete completes the job of establishing a favorable standard in this area. "Okay, Chuck. It won't be easy, but I know we'll have a lot better report when we do these things. It will take some research and some dry runs — we want to be sure of what we're doing — but I think we can have every one of these changes installed and working smoothly by September 1. At least I'll do my damndest to get them in by then."

Pete is quite sure that he can accomplish the task comfortably in this time, and in fact he is reasonably sure that he can do it by August 1. So Pete has accomplished something useful. He has gotten a standard applied to his job in a way that he is bound to look good; because he was able to control the institution of the standard.

In establishing a standard, make sure that there is more than just a description of what is to be done. See that there is at least one criterion that will measure how well the job is done, whether it is a criterion of time, volume, money, or whatever. And, to the extent that you are able to influence it, see that the standard is set high enough to be impressive to the boss, and yet well within your capacity. This is often not too difficult to do. Many bosses have a tendency to minimize the capabilities of subordinates. So they are pleasantly surprised when an employee undertakes to accomplish more than the bare minimum.

The job standard that works in your favor at raise time need not be one that involves the most important elements of the job. Sometimes it can be a minor facet of the position, but one that reflects credit on the boss. A snappy report that is seen by the higher-ups and which conveys the impression that the department is on the ball may be more welcome to the boss than an improved technique that is appreciated only by those thoroughly familiar with the work.

When you have managed to win the application of a standard to your job that will enable you to look good, pin it down so that the boss will not forget it when the time comes to discuss an increase in salary. If possible, get him to put it in writing ("You expressed that so well, Chuck, I'd appreciate it if you could dictate a memo to me just the way you said it, so I'd have something to refer to."). At the very least, *you* put it in writing ("Great, Chuck. I'll do my damndest to accomplish it.

And the first thing I'll do is spell it out in a memo."). If you can send information copies of that memo to any other influentials in the company without awkwardness, by all means do so; but don't be too obvious about it.

How do you handle the other situation — the one in which the boss articulates a standard that will be tough for you to meet. Here's Pete Ervin's boss, Chuck, "Another thing that's important, of course, is that we have to do something about getting these people in on time and cutting absenteeism. It's running too high."

Pete is aware of the problem. He has reasonably good relations with the people he is supervising, but he knows that cracking the whip and effecting a startling change in their habits is not his long suit. So here's how he proceeds: "Yes, that's a real headache, and I realize it's not a new one. I've been looking around to see if anybody in the organization has any really good answers to that one, and so far I've come up empty. Tell me, Chuck, what would you recommend?"

Well, Pete has introduced a note that is not too comfortable for his boss, but that's all right; it's necessary and they will not dwell on it for long. Chuck doesn't have any specific answers; his bag is to tell Pete to do something about the problem. So his remarks, while earnest, are likely to be somewhat light on specifics. Pete keeps emphasizing the difficulty of the dilemma. He mentions extreme solutions: "Some days I'm tempted to really crack down and lower the boom on them, but considering the overall needs of our operation I guess that would not be a good idea." The boss agrees; they can't just fire people or pressure them so much that they quit, because there is no reservoir of replacements that will work out any better.

So Pete says, "The first thing, as I see it, is to keep the thing from getting any worse. And then I'd like to put together some recommendations for improving the situation, which will serve as a basis for discussion. I think we ought to have personnel sit in on the discussion, and maybe traffic. You, of course, Chuck, should chair it, if you're willing."

What Pete is doing is working toward the establishment of standards that don't require any improvement. He is pretty sure that things are not going to get much worse, so he is safe in saying that his first objective is to hold the line. Then he goes on to say that he will prepare a piece of paper and that there will be a meeting to discuss the problem. This is frequently a most effective approach in an area where no real accomplishment is possible. Certainly Pete will do the report, and the meeting will be held. When raise time comes Pete may even be able to cite his report as an achievement worthy of monetary recognition.

These are the elements of establishing job standards for yourself. Arrange for a face-to-face discussion with the boss, in a relaxed atmosphere. Get him to talk about what he considers important in the job. When he gives you a lead in an area that you handle well, follow it. Underscore the idea that, yes, this is a truly vital function, and you will do your best to accomplish more than has ever been accomplished before. Agree with your boss on a standard of performance that you are able to meet. It's helpful to describe the standard in terms that will redound to the credit of the boss, or that will help him to PR your accomplishment to his bosses ("Ervin was able to take an essential report that was already good and improve it in ways that make it even more responsive to the needs of the firm.").

In areas where you are not so strong, invite the boss's recommendations. If he doesn't have any red-hot ones, this gives you another reason to comment on the awesome difficulty of accomplishment. Then work towards the establishment of a standard that involves motions without necessarily involving accomplishment: paperwork, meetings, etc.

And when the boss and you have come to terms on a standard or set of standards that you like, get them into writing. They will serve as your documentation for a "job-well-done" when you ask for a raise.

How Much of a Boss's Pet Do You Have To Be?

Apple-polishers don't automatically get fatter raises than those who are not afraid to disagree with the boss; but chronic boss-baiters run into a lot of trouble when they ask for more money. You want to get as much salary as possible, but you don't want to abdicate your self-respect and make yourself a doormat in the process. Somewhere in the middle is the course that will permit you to speak up when you feel it is justified, and yet avoid the erection of vindictive barriers to financial advancement. How do you take issue with the boss without jeopardizing your next raise?

Obviously a lot depends on the boss. If he is a maniac or an ogre, any hint of disagreement is apt to foment resentment that carries over to your next increase review. You're in trouble with this kind of boss, but your trouble is not merely a matter of money. It's a matter of self-respect and sanity. If your superior is unreasonable about honest disagreement, and rewards only supine conformity, your choices are limited. You can get out; and if it looks like you are stuck with this boss you should make every effort to do so. If you can't get out, you can stifle your logical reservations and act like a yes-man. This is debilitating over any extended period of time. Furthermore, it may not work. The paranoid boss who demands total agreement is always looking for hidden disagreement. If you are not a consummate actor, he may see through your deception and you will be a loser in all ways. He will still resent you, you will have compromised your principles, and you will have just as big a battle on your hands at raise time as you would have if you had acted according to your better instincts.

There is one other course that you may take with an unreasonable boss. You can voice your disagreements, document your case, and then hope that the boss doesn't last too long; or, if he does, that you may be able to go over his head. This extreme strategem is discussed elsewhere.

But let's proceed on the optimistic premise that your boss is not paranoid. If he is like most people he will declare that he welcomes honest disagreement, and he will try to live up to that declaration. He will make a real effort not to hold your divergence of opinion against you. But at the same time he will expect "loyalty" from his subordinates. And, no matter how much he may try to be totally objective, he will be hurt at what he considers disloyalty. The trouble is that disagreement and disloyalty may get mixed up in his mind.

Watergate, with all its ramifications, placed the spotlight on the problems of loyalty and the limits to which it should extend. The country has been confronted with the dispiriting spectacle of confessed or convicted perjurers, spies, and aborters of justice saying that they realize they did wrong, but they did these things out of loyalty. The problem, in politics as in business, is of course not a new one. Few men in positions of power have been as blunt about it as William Lamb, Viscount Melbourne, British Prime Minister of the early 19th century. Shortly after Melbourne had been elected, a colleague approached him and said, "You may be sure that I will always support you — when you are in the right." Melbourne replied, "Why, that is no use to me at all. What I need are men who will support me when I am in the wrong."

The question of loyalty must be considered in a larger context than the paycheck. While this book is concerned with hard, realistic procedures for getting more money, none of its recommendations are based on the assumption that you must altogether abandon every principle in order to extract a few bucks more from the powers-that-be. True, you will find in these pages certain tactics that involve pressure, tough bargaining, even threats. But these things are all legitimate within the arena of salary negotiation. Every game has its strategems. In a game we try to overpower or mislead the opponent. Money negotiation is a "reality game," and as such has its own rules. But those rules do not encompass wholesale abandonment of conscience or ethics.

Once we have said this, there remains the problem of squaring the requirements of loyalty with those of intelligence and self-respect. In your resolution of the proposition you will not think only of money; but you will not forget about it either.

One point to consider is that, in a job, loyalty is multiple. An employee should feel some obligations of loyalty when he takes a position. But his responsibility is to the interests of the company as much as it is to the particular individual to whom he reports. Even if the boss is the person who runs the firm, person and company are not indivisible. The organization must prosper and grow. Its employees, its customers, its suppliers, and the community at large have a stake in honest and effective company practice. You are paid to do your best. Implicit in your unwritten job contract is the understanding that you will contribute any ideas that will help the firm to grow and prosper. So you should have a chance to make your voice heard on moves and policies that fall within your scope.

After you have expressed your thoughts the decision may go against you. Then it is incumbent on you to carry out the decision, whatever it may be, with full vigor. At the same time, the boss gears down a responsibility for loyalty. He should listen to your ideas if he is to do his management job properly; and he is not entitled to hold your disagreement against you if you accept a negative decision gracefully and go on to address yourself to the task at hand.

You need not be an apple-polisher. You have every right to say what's on your mind about things that concern your job. But there are ways and ways of doing this. If you do it the wrong way, you imperil your chances of obtaining a maximum raise. In fact, sometimes *agreeing* with the boss the wrong way can work against you. So now, having had our little homily about loyalty, let's consider the tactics of agreement and disagreement as they bear upon the negotiation for more money.

Let's suppose that you just naturally agree with your boss about most things. Maybe you feel that this is an unadulterated plus in your quest for more money. It isn't; at least not in every way. You may find yourself getting shortchanged on raises at the same time as more disputatious colleagues come away with large increases.

There are several reasons why this may happen. If your agreement is always quick and full, you may give the boss the idea that you are buttering him up. Oh, he may not complain; he is not going to go out of his way to make trouble for himself. But he may nevertheless put you down as a yes-man. Nobody thinks much of a yes-man, even if he sometimes welcomes the flattering agreement that a yes-man bestows on him.

Or maybe the boss knows that you are always entirely sincere in your agreeableness. This situation also can militate against your ability to get the money you want. It is a human tendency to undervalue that which comes too easily. The boss who is used to your "going along," no matter what, will not give you high marks for initiative. This may be paradoxical and unfair; after all, when you concur with his ideas and his wishes you are following his leadership, and this should hardly be held against you. Nevertheless, that's the way it frequently works.

Arthur Borzage has three assistants. One, Tim Diamond, is as amiable as they come. The last time Borzage called them together and enunciated a plan, Tim was the first to respond. "I'm persuaded that this is the right way to go about it," he said. "We've been needing a stronger policy in that area for some time, and this is it. I'm one hundred percent with you on this, Art." Borzage nods at Diamond in acknowledgment, but at the same time he notices the looks that pass between the other two assistants. They seem to be thinking, "There goes old Tim, brown-nosing again." This bothers Art Borzage. He can't believe it's justified — he's not the kind of man who requires subordinates to kow-tow to him — but it bothers him anyway.

The next to speak up is Herman Grillo. Grillo is blunt: "I can't see it. We'll be putting too much emphasis on a part of the overall program that does not justify it. I don't go along." Before responding to this, Borzage asks, "How do you feel about it, Mike?"

The third assistant, Mike Hemingway, says, "Well, right now I'd have to say I see Herman's point. Maybe I don't have all the facts, or I'm misinterpreting some of them, but I can't say I agree. I wonder if you could spell out the part about the revision of the schedules?"

Borzage goes into more detail. Hemingway asks some tough questions, as does Grillo. Hemingway brings up one or two more points, and Borzage tries to handle them. Then Hemingway says, "This makes it a little clearer. I would be kidding you, Art, if I said that I have no reservations whatever. But when you lay it out this way I can see a lot better why you feel this approach will work. I'll go along with it."

Grillo shakes his head and grins. "It looks as if I'm outvoted. I'm not going to waste any more time on questions — I may have some more as we get into the procedure — but let's just say we'll do it this way."

The plan is put into operation. Each of the three assistants does his best, as Borzage was sure they would. The project doesn't quite achieve all that it was meant to achieve. When it concludes the four men get together for a critique. All Tim Diamond has to say is: "Well, we gave it all we had, and I think things panned out reasonably well." Grillo has a couple of points to make: "You remember I raised the question of emphasis. As we look at the results I think we can see that one of the problems was that we concentrated too intensely on this one thing and let things slide in other areas. I'll have to take my lumps for that along with everybody else."

Mike Hemingway says, "By and large I think it went pretty well. In one or two places we fell short, and the reasons are fairly obvious. As far as my own performance is concerned, I think I learned some lessons from this." And Hemingway goes on to spell out the elements of his performance that he feels could have stood improvement. The meeting ends. Nobody is mad at anybody else. But that's not to say that the meeting is forgotten. When raise time comes, Art Borzage is more receptive to the claims of Mike Hemingway than to those of Diamond or Grillo. Certainly this is not just because of the recently-concluded project or the meetings that preceded and followed it. But to the extent that those meetings had an influence on Borzage's reactions — an influence of which he is not fully aware — they are worth some contemplation.

Borzage likes Tim Diamond, but thinks of him as something of a lightweight. Tim contributes to the impression by being so quick to agree with what the boss says. Also, Borzage is anxious to be fair. He has a tendency to lean over backwards in order to assure evenhandedness. So he will curb his instinct to be generous with Diamond because he is afraid that in some way Diamond's willingness to say "yes" has influenced his decision. In a way this is not fair to Tim Diamond, who just happens to think the same way as his boss. But it happens; and similar things happen in many other companies.

Herman Grillo's outspoken disagreement does not turn Borzage against him. He knows that Grillo is a good man, and he respects this assistant's willingness to speak out. But at times Grillo comes pretty close to being contemptuous of the boss's suggestions. Herman Grillo does not mean to be contemptuous; it just comes out that way. And Borzage knows this. Nevertheless he wishes that Grillo would not be quite so spectacular in opposition. This is not something that he can bring up comfortably in talking with Grillo, so he suffers in silence, but he does fight the abrasive assistant pretty hard about money.

Hemingway has the easiest time getting the full raise he wants from Borzage. Of course Hemingway is a good man; but there's a little more to it than that. Note how he handled himself in the first of the two meetings. At first he disagreed with the boss, or at least expressed strong reservations. But as the boss argued in support of his position, Hemingway came around to agreeing. This makes a good impression on Borzage, and that good impression is of some significance when Hemingway's raise comes up for consideration.

There is a good reason for this. Behavioral scientists always seem to be proving things that we sort of knew already, but hadn't thought about in just that way, but this is one of the big values of the discipline. Psychologists and sociologists have conducted experiments that show we have higher regard for those who at first disagree with us, and are then won over to agreement, then we do for those who agree with us right off the bat. When the boss has to work a little to convince you, there is no question of yes-manship. You have expressed your independence — and he has prevailed through logic and persuasiveness. Often the good feeling he derives from this will color his whole attitude toward you, and this is emphatically not a handicap when you are bargaining for more money.

During the critique meeting that followed the conclusion of the project, Hemingway confined his critical observations to his own performance. Grillo, however, referred back to Borzage's initial arguments for the plan and to his own points of disagreement. Herman Grillo may not deliberately be trying to say, "I told you so," but Borzage can certainly read a suggestion of this into his assistant's observations. And it rankles.

It's not whether you agree or disagree with the boss; it's how you do it. There are certain precautions to follow in agreeing and in disagreeing if you want to build up your line of credit to a point at which you hav a comfortable bulge to call upon when you go to the mat for more mone

Don't get into the habit of agreeing too readily with what the b says, even if you go along completely or feel that your points of d agreement are too inconsequential to insist upon. Let yourself be persuaded at times. It does no harm, it forces the boss to support his ideas, and in the process he can do some useful rethinking of them. And it helps to mark you as someone who is willing to speak his mind, but as a person who can understand and bow to superior argument.

When you disagree, you must be careful not to make it too visible or too personal. It's one thing to express disagreement with something the boss proposes. It's another thing to put such disagreement in a way that seems to cast doubt on the boss's intelligence or his reasoning power. And, even when your disagreement turns out to have been somewhat justified — or even completely justified — a little forgetfulness can be a useful thing. Don't bring it up. Most bosses will be far more appreciative of the employee who foregoes a chance to remind them of their mistakes than of the guy who seems to keep a mental dossier of everything that went wrong.

The time to capitalize on your reasonableness and your forbearance is the negotiation for more money. Here you will use a certain degree of subtlety and indirection to turn your astute behavior into concrete advantages. But those advantages must be there to be called upon.

So it's well to equip yourself with a kind of double vision in your dealings with the boss on disputable points. On the one hand you will want to get your points across, whether you are in complete or partial opposition, or in total disagreement. On the other hand you should be looking forward to your next request for an increase. This reality should not be allowed to control what you do or say, but it should have a certain modifying influence on how you do or say it.

Your loyalty to the boss calls for support, but also for expression of constructive ideas. Your loyalty to the company makes it incumbent on you to operate in the best interests of the organization. Your loyalty to yourself and your family dictates that you should be intelligently aware of the impression that you make on the boss in terms of how it is likely to influence his reaction to your raise request.

The individual who appears, overall, to speak up but who is also willing to listen to reason, who may disagree but then forgets his disagreement and pitches in to get the job done, is positioning himself advantageously for the forthcoming money negotiation.

Making Yourself into a Mini-Profit Center

Kate Crandall is a research assistant at Melmoth Inc. Her job involves the selection and use of various research methods to test market reaction to Melmoth products, merchandising devices, and advertising campaigns. But the job involves more than knowledge of research techniques. It requires her to interpret results with sophisticated insight so that she can communicate hard, useful information to the line departments. These interpretations must be brief, clear, accurate, and above all, relevant to the important problems the company faces in its marketing of consumer goods.

Kate Crandall is good at her job. Moreover she is a highly attractive person. She is intelligent and well-educated. In appearance she is crisp and businesslike when she wants to be, stunning when the occasion calls for it. And she is pleasant in personality, but very quick and perceptive in interpersonal exchange.

Since her arrival on the scene, Kate has been an object of keen scrutiny by the office Lotharios. Male optimists go out of their way to drop by Kate's office to "check something out" or just to chat. Talking with Kate Crandall is always rewarding; she is funny and insightful, and she knows a lot about the business. Just going over a problem with her — whether or not it lies directly in her area of activity — usually gives the other party a better grasp of the situation. But these are about the only rewards. In the vernacular, "You can't get to first base with Kate." Invitations for lunch, dinner, drinks are accepted most infrequently, and then only when there is a clear and immediate business connotation. More imaginative propositions reach a dead end. There can be no doubt that somebody as "all-together" as Kate Crandall can enjoy an active and brilliant social life if she wishes, but — as one discouraged operator put it — "As far as the guys around the shop are concerned, she might as well be a nun in a convent."

With the women in the office Kate Crandall is not quite as popular. Nevertheless, she gets along well with members of her own sex. She is highly regarded professionally, is always pleasant and helpful, and she works hard and cooperates fully on joint projects. Everybody agrees that Kate has a lot on the ball.

So there is considerable surprise when people see Kate Crandall going out to lunch with an insignificant male employee of the company. Most have seen him around but can't remember his name. He turns out to be Herbert Brenner, who does something or other down in accounting. Herbert Brenner is not very big in the company; nobody ever comments on his creativity or predicts for him a bright future. He is an obscure functionary in a department that is virtually ignored by those who work closer to where the action is.

But Kate Crandall can be seen now and then with Brenner, at lunch or having an after-hours cocktail. Many wonder: "What the hell is it that he has got?" (Frequently with the unvoiced addition, ". . .that I haven't got?") Men are puzzled; some women are indulgently amused. Herbert Brenner would never turn any of *them* on. There must be something a little odd about Kate.

They would be even more surprised if they were to overhear the conversation that passes between the seemingly ill-matched duo. For example: as they wait for the waiter to bring the beef bourguignon, Kate asks, "Is a percentage figure based on sales a good way to measure profits?" Herb launches into a somewhat lengthy dissertation, illustrating with precise little numbers written swiftly on the back of an envelope. Kate listens closely, putting an occasional question. A little later she introduces another topic: "How do you make up a break-even chart?" Again Brenner obliges with description and illustrations.

The question-and-answer exchange flows in the other direction as well. Brenner wants to know, "How closely do they read the monthly close-out statement up in client service? Do they really understand it? Would it help if some written explanation went along with it?" Kate Crandall considers this, and then tells her companion that most executives pretend to look at and understand this material, but that they are in the dark about most of its implications.

And so on. Kate Crandall and Herbert Brenner have formed a symbiotic relationship. Unlike as they seem to be, they provide each other with benefits. Kate is receiving a practical education in the financial side of the business. Herb is obtaining tips on how to give more relevance and impact to the work he does. (Those who know Kate would be even more amazed if they learned that she augments these informal sessions with a one-night-a-week course in basic accounting.) Years ago, Katharine Hepburn made a pithy comment about such mutually-rewarding associations when she said of the team of Fred Astaire and Ginger Rogers, "He gives her class; she gives him sex."

The joint teaching effort being conducted by Crandall and Brenner is devoted to one important purpose; making more money. Obviously their relationship can help to make each better at the job; but they are focusing on the more specific goal of getting their bosses to give them super-sized raises.

When the time comes to talk about salary for next year, Herbert Brenner is ready. He reviews his work with the manager of his department. That work is reliable but unspectacular. But then Brenner begins to range afield. To his somewhat astonished superior he demonstrates a considerable breadth of knowledge, not only about how various financial documents should be prepared, but also about what happens to them after they leave the financial department — and what should happen to them. He produces examples of revised reporting techniques that are calculated to make the numbers more understandable to "the people upstairs." Brenner's boss, who has long felt (as many financial executives feel) that the "glamour boys" neither grasp nor appreciate the importance of his area of responsibility, is interested. Some of Herbert Brenner's ideas seem a little far-out, a little bizarre, particularly as they emanate from this quiet functionary. Would it really be wise or dignified to change traditional ways of doing things to this extent? But there is no denying that Herbert Brenner's suggestions have a certain racy audacity that might just help to give the financial department a better image. Whether or not they would actually make the operation more effective is neither here nor there. The boss is tired of the line departments with the "action image" getting all of the kudos. (And Brenner, with the potent assistance of Crandall, has spotted this feeling and is playing to it.) If nothing else, Herbert Brenner has shown a refreshingly innovative approach to things. The boss chokes a little when Brenner names the figure he wants as a raise; but the subordinate is armed with proposals about how, in addition to his regular work, he will undertake to make the department's product better known. The boss is interested; he considers carefully; and in the end, without agreeing with Brenner's more breathtaking flights of fancy, he okays most of the raise.

Kate Crandall goes to her boss, Joe Young, to talk about an increase in salary. Young is on his guard. He knows how effective and persuasive Kate can be. But he has other things to consider. Kate Crandall is not the only person in the department. She's good, but Young is determined not to give her a raise that will louse up his salary arrangements with the others. He expects Crandall to present a dramatic case that features some of the more interesting reports she has turned out and some of the more imaginative uses of techniques that she has pioneered. Young expects this, and he is ready for it.

But this is not the approach that Kate Crandall takes. She goes into Young's office loaded with charts and figures. Donning a pair of spectacles, she begins to talk about things like contribution to net profit, maintenance of adequate margin, the traceability of research efforts to fluctuations in the cash flow, and so forth. Some of Kate

Crandall's statements and implications may be dubious — but Young is not enough of a financial man to be sure of this. Furthermore he bears the scars of policy-level sessions at which his operation has been attacked for being nonprofit-oriented, careless about costs, indifferent to the "bottom line." Now here is one of his assistants, transformed into a veritable human computer, appearing to present a strong case for the profit-connection that resides in the research operation in general and her own contributions in particular.

Calmly Kate Crandall works to her point. She has laid the groundwork for an arithmetical computation of her value, tracing her research work through the line divisions and down to that magical "bottom line." She comes to her conclusion: "I think this proves what we are worth and what I am worth. I can spell out anything that you want to go over again, Joe. But today we're talking about raises. I am fully justified in asking for eight thousand dollars more. But I know there are other considerations that have nothing to do with the logic of the situation. So I'm going to settle for six thousand."

Joe Young argues mightily against the six thousand. But Kate Crandall has an answer for everything, and her answers are supported by an impressive array of figures. Finally Young agrees to the raise, and at the same time enlists Kate's support in enabling him to make a case to top management for more money in the budget for research. Young is by no means euphoric about his chances; but Kate's presentation has given him hope that at last he can accomplish what he has wanted to accomplish for a long time.

Most people who do not actually work in the financial area of a company are woefully weak on numbers. They cannot really understand P & L statements or any of the other effusions from accountant or computer. They regard the financial people as glum and sinister enigmas who are always saying that there isn't enough money for this or that — and then proving it with serried rows of figures incomprehensible to an ordinary mortal. Henry K. Astwood was for many years head of the Sales Manpower Foundation, a New York based organization devoted to helping marketing people find jobs. Astwood remarked on his amazement at the innocent ignorance of marketing men when it came to profitability. "A lot of them don't even know that percentages are supposed to add up to 100," he observes. Thus the sales personnel were frequently at the mercy of the comptroller and his merry men.

You can give yourself an important boost toward making more money by learning the arithmetic of your business and how it affects you. Find out what profits and losses really are, how they're computed, what happens to the money, where costs have been tending, what relation those costs bear to income, and so on. Find out how to understand financial statements and talk about them. You will accomplish much. To begin with you will know more about an important side of the business than practically any of your associates. You will become identifiable as a profit-minded person. And you will be able to back up a healthy raise request with weighty figures, which the boss will find hard to refute.

The foregoing applies, of course, to those who are not in the financial end. The figure people have a reverse problem. They know the numbers, but often that is all they know. They work in isolation, knowing little about the connection that their numbers have with the rest of the business — and caring less. If you are a financial person, find out what happens with the numbers after they leave your bailiwick. Who looks at them, how fully are they understood, how can they be improved? By demonstrating that you are tuned in to the larger picture you give yourself another dimension that can be most compelling when you ask for a raise.

Some of what you need you can pick up through some form or other of adult education. For the nonfigure-minded there are courses in accounting; for those who are saturated in numbers or in some particularly confining area of technology, there is a plethora of books and formal instruction.

But a quicker and better way to give yourself this added dimension is by teaming up with somebody else from a totally different part of the business. In this way you get information that is keyed directly to your interests. And you get it for nothing, by repayment in kind. You provide the other person with what he needs to enhance his chances of getting a raise.

Image is important. You don't have to become the world's premier expert in the function that you're investigating. It's sufficient that you learn enough to talk about it knowledgeably and with assurance, and that you know more about it than your boss does. Often this latter requirement is surprisingly easy to fill.

Knowing more about the whole business will make you a more valuable worker. Some managers don't agree; they like to keep people compartmentalized, possibly because it helps to control requests for salary hikes. But they are wrong; this kind of knowledge will enhance your value. However, whether it does or not, it will help a lot in enabling you to build a raise-getting strategy that throws the boss off balance and impresses him with another side he never knew you had.

Keep quiet about your symbiotic seminars. It's best not to let them grow into group exercises — one-on-one is not only unobtrusive, it is the best way to pick up what you need. If you would like to learn about more than one area of the business, work with a person from each, but keep the contacts separate.

When you can talk with confidence about figures and about what makes the business go, you can come on strong for more money.

Getting Out of The Box

Here's a pitiable situation. Alex Alexander wants a raise — a big one. He has knocked himself out on the job. He has put in long hours and performed some prodigious feats. And he hasn't made any notable mistakes. His campaign for an increase cannot be faulted.

Alex Alexander's boss is Rob Robinson. He knows about the work Alex is doing, and appreciates it. He values Alex's contribution on the job, is impressed with the resourcefulness and determination with which Alex has gone after the raise, and would like to keep this useful subordinate functioning and happy. Robinson would like to grant Alexander the raise.

But he can't.

What's the trouble? The trouble lies in the boxes — the boxes on the organization chart. With each of those boxes goes a job description. And each box joins other boxes within a salary range. The range may not be officially spelled out in any formal document; nevertheless it exists. The raise that Alexander wants — and that his boss wants to give him — would exceed the range for Alexander's box. Rob Robinson must operate within limits. No matter how he feels, or how hard he sells his own bosses, he cannot give Alex a raise that goes beyond the range.

Of course one answer would be to move Alex to a box that sits higher on the chart. There are a couple of reasons why this should not be done. One is that the higher box carries a different description, calling for greater and sometimes different capabilities from those assigned to the lower box. Alex Alexander is valuable in his present job. Promoted to the next box up, he is an unknown quantity. He may become a liability. Alex's boss suspects that this might be the case. He doesn't think Alex is ready to jump boxes.

Even so, the temptation to move Alex up a box is strong. This happens frequently when a boss wants to give a subordinate a raise, but cannot find a rationale as long as that subordinate stays in his present job. Since a promotion is the only way to justify additional money for the deserving worker, the boss promotes him. All too often the worker can't handle the bigger job. He is in trouble. The boss spends an undue amount of time trying to bail him out. It can't be done. In the end, hope is abandoned and the subordinate is fired. Meanwhile, the box that he vacated is filled by someone who is not nearly as good as the previous occupant. This is the basis for much of the validity that lies in the famous "Peter Principle," which states that people are promoted to their level of incompetence. Under pressure to find rationales for paying more money, bosses promote workers who should not be promoted.

In spite of this, Rob Robinson might still take a chance and promote Alexander — except that there is another obvious problem. There is no box to promote him to. They are all filled. Sometimes companies play the game of creating higher-level boxes for deserving employees who continue to do exactly the same work, but this is a form of organizational inflation that is not widely practiced. When carried to even a moderate extent it results in a plethora of chiefs with a concomitant paucity of Indians.

If there is any chance that you may be trapped in your box, it is urgent that you take steps to find a way out of the trap. Otherwise, when you apply for a raise, you will find yourself scrabbling at the walls of your organizational cubicle. If the boss is ambivalent about giving you a raise he can use the box as a convenient excuse. Worse, even if he is sympathetic enough or impressed enough or pressured enough — or all three — to want to give you a raise, your position in the box will keep him from doing so.

You can try to get promoted. This puts you in a box that is higher on the chart, but it's still a box. You will encounter the same problems when you try for a raise that exceeds the range. Promotions are fine things. They bring greater prestige and power as well as more money. They also have their dangers. But within the confines of this book we are not talking about promotions. Our subject is how you can get the maximum possible raise while you remain in your present job.

Briefly, what you should try to do is to build yourself a somewhat larger box in your present location on the chart — or to append one or more little boxes which you occupy at the same time as you perform the main duties attached to your position.

In examining how you can do this, let's take another look at the phenomenon of the boxes. They are not just a problem for the worker who wants a raise. They are a problem for business in general. Managers tend to acquire the "box mentality." When a job is to be done, the project is invariably assigned to the person who occupies the box whose description comes closest to conforming with the task. This happens irrespective of the talent or personality of the occupant of the box. For example, the marketing department faces some difficulties in customer relations. Some long-time profitable accounts are becoming increasingly unhappy and are showing signs of restlessness. Loss of these accounts would be very bad. The marketing head may call his team together for discussions, but when someone must be assigned to improve customer relations, there is only one choice. It is the sales manager. Why? Because the job description that goes with his box includes customer relations. The sales manager may be ill-fitted to handle this problem at this time. There may be better ideas and abilities in the persons of, say, the merchandising manager or the advertising manager — but it is impossible to give the assignment to these worthies. This would do violence to the organization chart, and who knows what might emerge from the Pandora's box that would be opened by such a heretical move? The problem remains the sales manager's to grapple with. If his inability to cope becomes insupportable he is fired and another sales manager is brought in. The newcomer's first responsibility is to settle the customer relations issue. He will probably have been chosen for his skill in this area. However, once the problem has been reduced to manageability, it may turn out that this new sales manager possesses no qualifications besides the ability to placate customers. Since customer relations can only be practiced when you sell customers, the new man is soon in trouble, and so is the company.

In an effort to shake off the tyranny of the boxes, a lot of managers are resorting to the "task-force" approach. This is a way of tackling major problems by bringing to bear on them a combination of the best talent available, and at the same time preserving the fabric of the organization chart. A problem is identified. One or more individuals — regardless of position — are named to the task force that will seek to solve the problem. They are expected to handle their present jobs at the same time. The person who would — by "box" logic — be the one assigned to the problem may be the nominal chairman of the task force, but he may not exert overwhelming power.

That's the way the task-force approach works in its more formal embodiment. The same thinking can be seen in a less formal, simpler manner when an individual is asked to volunteer to help out with something.

And here is where you come in. You may have heard, in the service or out of it, the old maxim "Never volunteer." That doesn't apply. Volunteering is a good way to reshape the confines of your box so that you can qualify for a raise.

You can do it with a less-than-earthshaking problem. Let's say there are some unsatisfactory aspects to the way your office is laid out. Nobody likes it, but nobody is doing anything about it. You suggest to your boss that you have some ideas. You ask if it's okay with him if you — without interfering with your current job — pursue some of your ideas. The boss says yes.

You make yourself visible as somebody who is staying around after hours, studying charts, poking into corners. You give your boss a couple of progress reports, and you send copies to some others who would be interested. You talk to the heads of other departments. The boss seems pleased. You get into conversation with some colleagues who seem amenable to working with you on the project. (Their reasons may be similar to yours.) Now you have a task force. The force pursues its objectives, issues reports, and — we hope — accomplishes something. At the very least it can clarify objectives, articulate problems, lay out plans; all the things that we do in this workaday world when we can't quite come up with the definitive answer.

That's one way it can happen. Another way is when the boss asks you to look into something. You happily accept and go to it with energy. He may have put his request rather informally, but you proceed to formalize it by your comportment and the reports you issue. Take the assignment very seriously. Don't kid about it. It's not a throwaway, it may be your ticket to more money in the pay envelope.

For when raise time comes, you have the makings of an addition on your box. You will make your pitch for a raise on the basis of your excellences in the regular job. Having exhausted those, you can then turn to your additional volunteer or task-force duties. When you can cite such extras, you are doing two things. You are presenting additional reasons for getting a raise; and you are giving the boss a way to circumvent the range that may have been set by the configuration of the boxes. Your raise can be justified by your extra duty.

Doing a little extra — if packaged right — can help you climb out of a salary box.

3

preparing your attack

Sizing Up Your Competition

You're always competing with others for more money. Generally it's best to make your case on the basis of your own qualifications, without reference to the competition. However, this does not mean that you shouldn't consider the others who will be striving for more money at the same time you are.

The amount of money that management will be able to pay out in raises is probably somewhat flexible — but it is finite. A compelling demand from one of your colleagues can make it a lot tougher for you to get what you want. So, as you prepare your strategy, scrutinize the competition. Begin with the individual within your classification who would seem to be the most formidable rival in a head-to-head battle for more money. Ask yourself some clarifying questions:

- How long has he been here?
- How good is he?
- What is management's perception of how good he is? (The answer to this one often varies widely from the answer as to the rival's objective merits.)
- What are his strong points? His weakest points?
- How do I compare to him, point by point?
- What is management's perception of my strengths? My weaknesses?
- How much does he figure to be making?

- What kind of a raise is he likely to ask for?
- Does he seem to be successful in getting good raises?

There are other questions that will occur to you. You should make an assessment of your principal competitors, not so that you can attack them in the raise negotiation (ordinarily you will not mention them) but in order that you have a better understanding of the circumstances that will bear on your chances for the increase.

As you look around and evaluate the information and impressions available to you, you'll see that the people whom you rate as being the best performers are not always those who get the largest raises or who are most highly regarded by the boss. Some individuals — who boast only modest skills — seem to be able to extract salaries that exceed their qualifications. Others appear to toil along without being paid what you think to be enough. None of this is your problem, but it all has an influence on your problem.

Curiously, your biggest difficulty may lie in the person who never asks for a big raise. The toughest "competitor" is the "old reliable"; the individual who has been around longer than you, who does, on the whole, a better job than you do, and whose quiet worth is recognized by the boss. If this other party is content to settle for minimal raises, then you are in trouble. When you come in with your request the boss is mentally comparing you with your less-demanding counterpart. He may not mention it, but he is asking himself, "Why should I pay this guy all this money when old Willingham over there doesn't bug me for that kind of bread?"

And there are people like that. They are good at what they do. Management would pay them more if they forced the issue. But they don't force the issue. It may be diffidence — some folks just cannot stand haggling over money. It may be excessive company loyalty. It may be illogical fear of losing the job. It may be that they are somehow content to get along on what they make, and see no need to ask for more.

Whatever the reason, this character presents a problem. It is paragons (from the company's point of view) like this who drag the rest of us ordinary mortals down. You may decide that your own chances of getting a raise will be markedly improved if your acquiescent colleague can somehow be gotten to ask for a larger share of the pie.

Here's an example of how it might be done. Jean McCormick has been with the Simkin Company for three years. She would like to boost her income considerably. But she feels blocked. It has dawned on her that management measures raise requirements against the standard set by one of her colleagues, Sid Booth. Booth has been with Simkin for ten years, the last six of them in the same job. He does about the same kind of work that Jean McCormick does, and he does it smoothly, effortlessly, and efficiently. And Sid doesn't seem to press for more money. Jean is not privy to the figures, but she has observed enough to know that Sid Booth takes what the boss offers him.

Sid's lack of combativeness and enterprise is obviously going to be a problem. Jean McCormick determines to make an attempt at shoring up her colleague's resolve. Finding Sid munching a sandwich in the cafeteria, Jean asks, "Mind if I join you, Sid?" and slips into the seat next to him. Soon they are exchanging shop-talk, which is about all Sid Booth is interested in.

First Jean has to get a little better line on the source of Sid's lack of financial ambition. She already knows something about him. Sid has a small comfortable home and a wife and one child. He does not spend money needlessly. Although inflation has affected him as it has everyone else, Sid seems to be able to handle his needs adequately. At any rate, he does not feel enough financial pressure to be stirred into rebellion.

Is it fear? Jean McCormick doesn't think so. While Sid is a quiet person, he knows he does a good job. Indeed he is heavily involved in his work, and gets a great kick out of overcoming problems. He realizes his value to the company and takes pride in it.

Jean McCormick turns to the subject of the company in general. Sid says, as he has in the past, "Simkin is a good outfit. They've always been good to me. They let you do your work without bothering you. I like to be left alone. They know I can do the job." Jean doesn't want to ask Sid directly why he doesn't demand more money, so she uses the third-party approach. "You know, Sid, you remind me of a guy I worked with on my last job. He was a real tower of strength in the same way you are. We all looked up to him. And the company sure thought a lot of him. But the company didn't play it on the level with him. They used him for a patsy. They were paying him a salary that was, well, unbelievably low for what he did. And this man went along for years, just getting little raises. But one day it came to him how he was being used. He walked into the boss's office and demanded top dollar, a raise that would make up for all the years they had been screwing him. A lot of us thought he'd be fired, or that they'd get back at him in some way. But no. They gave him the raise, and you know something? They respected him more from that day on."

Sid considers this. "Well, I don't believe in that kind of stuff. Money isn't everything. If you can't trust the people you work for, you shouldn't work for them. Mr. Simkin always gives me a fair shake. I talk to him direct, and he gives me what he can give me. Why make trouble?"

Sometimes it is possible to reach this kind of person by implying that the company is making a sucker out of him. It's usually worth a try. But Jean McCormick has made her try, and it doesn't appear to have much of a chance. So she moves on to another angle.

"You're a real professional, Sid," she says after some preliminaries. "Everybody recognizes that. Do you really feel you're treated like a professional? I'm not talking about how nice the people at the company are. Let's face it, I'm talking about money. After all, money is the way that professionalism is rewarded. Do you feel that you get paid what somebody with your ability should be paid?"

After a pause, Sid answers, "I never thought about it that way. I suppose I could maybe get more some other place, but I don't want to go some other place. And I don't think it's just a matter of what they pay you. I know what Mr. Simkin and the others think about my work."

The appeal to professional pride is another useful lever for stirring the acquiescent ace. In this particular case Jean pursues what she sees as a slight opening, but concludes that she still has not reached Sid Booth. So she tries yet another tack.

"You were a lot of help to me when I came to you about that Des Moines thing. I think all of us have been able to get help from you when we need it. I don't know if you realize how much we rely on you. But, do you know, in a very real way you're a problem for us, Sid?" Sid naturally wants to know why. "I'll be frank," says Jean. "Unfortunately there are a lot of us who just can't seem to get by on what we get paid. We like the company, and we take pride in our work. We're not as good as you, but we keep trying to improve, and that's the main thing. But we can't seem to break out of the salary box they have us in — and I'm afraid, although it's not your fault, it's not really anyone's fault, that you have a lot to do with that."

Taken aback, Sid Booth asks how on earth he is causing problems for his colleagues. "I hope I'm not talking out of turn, and I hope you understand why I feel I have to say this, Sid, but frankly it's because Mr. Simkin scales down the pay ranges for all of us from what he pays you. You must realize that." And she goes on to lay out the picture, indicating that Sid's modest salary requirements have a heavy influence on the money that is paid to others.

This kind of person is usually highly conscientious. Sid Booth has now been brought face-to-face with the thought that he bears an obligation to his fellow workers. He is uncomfortable with the thought, but he can't disavow it. "I don't mean you should try to get the rest of us more," says Jean, "But if you were to insist on more realistic pay, all of us in this kind of work would benefit. And it wouldn't be just in terms of money. It's a matter of pride. You're secure enough not to worry about those things, but there are others who really need this kind of reassurance." Jean McCormick goes on. Sid Booth listens earnestly. She has given him something to think about. In subsequent conversations Jean McCormick refers to her theme again. And, in the end, Sid Booth is motivated to ask for a bigger raise than ever before, giving Jean McCormick more leeway to pursue her own raise.

There are a number of ways to appeal to the good performer whose unwillingness to ask for raises sets a low standard for all. You can try to overcome his fear, if that's the hang-up. You can implant the notion that the company is taking advantage of him. You can appeal to his professional pride, emphasizing that his efforts should be recognized in the form of higher compensation. Or, as in this case, you can get through to him by indicating his position as bellwether, whose actions have a bearing on the well-being of his friends and colleagues.

There are other competitive problems. A familiar one is the raise-getting expert. This colleague is not necessarily any better than you are, nor does he necessarily possess greater length of service. But he is at his best at raise time. He has an instinctive mastery of the techniques put forth in this book. One way to offset him, of course is to use the stratagems presented here. But you can even do a little better than that.

Here is Lanny Enquist, just preparing to make his pitch to the boss. "This isn't easy for me," says Lanny. "In fact it's the toughest job I can think of. I don't consider that the ability to bargain for a raise makes a person a better performer. I'd prefer to just do my job. But it doesn't work that way. It isn't fair to you to expect you to figure out on your own how I feel and why I think I'm entitled to what I'm asking. That comes naturally to some people, not to me. But I do want this raise, and I feel I've earned it, so here goes."

Lanny does not have to name the individual to whom it comes naturally to make a spectacular pitch for more money. The boss knows who he's talking about. And the boss is put on notice that Lanny is aware of that person's capabilities. The message to the boss is that he should reward real merit, not allow himself to be snowed. Most bosses will want to avoid any hint that they are patsies. Lanny can now give it all he's got — and the boss may be a little more sympathetic.

You don't bring the names of others into the raise negotiation. You work against your competition indirectly. Having sized up your rivals by asking a series of questions about each, you can then choose to deploy your strong points in the fashion that is most effective.

Let's say, for example, that you have figured out that a competitor is going to ask for a big raise and is likely to get it. This competitor is able to show a record of solid accomplishment during the past year, and you know he is going to milk that record hard. In displaying your own qualifications it may be well for you to take a little ride on the competitor's coattails. Show that you accomplished similar things. Indicate how, if possible, you contributed to the other party's triumphs. Associate yourself in positive ways with the other guy so that you may enjoy some of the benefits of the clout that he will be exerting.

If, however, the boss is apt to be comparing you to people who have not accomplished much, differentiate yourself from them to the greatest extent possible. Let's say the boss is still rankling because somebody in your department let a situation get out of hand by failing to follow up on correspondence. You don't have to say, "I know Eddie screwed up that project, but I'm different." You can say, ". . . .For instance, when we're working on something big against a tight deadline, I've learned that you can't depend on the mail. I always follow up by telephone, and it pays off." When you know the boss is picturing a colleague who sits next to you, build up the contrast in your own picture without directly defacing the other one.

The boss may refer to others who work for him. Most often he will make a collective reference, rather than naming one individual. He will say something like, "Well, there are five people in that area, all doing the same kind of work. It really doesn't seem to me that we should differentiate one from the others."

There are several ways to respond to this. One is the direct method. Since the boss has raised the question of competition, you can act as if you feel entitled to have him spell it out. "Do you mean they get paid less than I do? Or that they're not asking for as much?" The boss will not want to specify. You can then go on to say, "I'm sure that, although we all do the same kind of work, you think of us as individuals.

I've always assumed that, and it's one of the things that makes this a nice place to work. We don't feel as if we're cogs in a machine. I'm hoping that you'll be able to talk with me as an individual." Bosses don't like to tabbed as thinking of their subordinates as faceless automatons.

You can press the boss to enunciate the principles on which he gives raises. When he refers to the others, ask: "Do you mean that you give the same raises to everybody?" That, he doesn't mean. "So," you go on, "there are differences. I'm concerned with my own qualifications, and of course I can't ask what other people are asking or getting. But it would be helpful to know this. What are the standards you use in deciding? Do the people who have been around the longest make the most money? Or are you able to spot differences in individual contribution and respond to them?"

Few bosses will say that they give raises "by the numbers" without reference to individual accomplishment. Most will say that tenure has something to do with it, but not everything. Try to get the boss to talk about principles. Is he most impressed with volume of work? Quality? Innovation? Reliability? Practicality? When he says something about his standards, make your pitch on that basis.

Of course an occasional manager may try to con you by rigging the standards. He might, for example, emphasize something like the number of units cleared per week, when this is obviously your weakest point. If the boss seems to be going too far in posing such ad hoc criteria to blunt the thrust of your appeal, you may want to throw him a curve. One way to do it would be to affect surprise at his choice of standards. "I didn't know you set such store by that particular aspect of the job. I've been trying to concentrate on cutting costs and building profits. But if this is the way you feel we ought to go, then I guess a number of us should think about doing some things differently." The boss does not want his phony standards to be applied to the work; he offered them only as a ploy to cut down your raise request. So he is likely to back off. You can make your response even more pointed by saying, "Well, I have to admit that this area is one where I might need some improvement and some help. I didn't think it was as important as completing some of our major projects. But this will be good news for Tom Helfer. Tom happens to really shine at this sort of stuff, so I imagine he will make out fine. I'm glad for him." Again, the boss is not anxious that the picayune standard he has articulated be used against him by another subordinate, and he does not want to be in the ridiculous and dangerous position of outlining different criteria to each worker who asks for a raise. So, when the manager goes overboard in building up your competition to your own detriment, you can probably persuade him to modify his views.

Every once in a while a hard-pressed boss will actually name another subordinate, in his battle to keep your raise down. "You don't accomplish any more than Jeff Burger," he might say, "And Jeff isn't asking for half the raise you are."

One reaction to this is to slide over it with a combination of knowingness and deprecation. "Everyone knows his own value best. I'm surprised to hear that, but I don't see that it enters into our discussion."

Here's another response. You can look startled and assume the worst. "I thought Jeff was doing a pretty good job. Didn't look to me as if he had stubbed his toe anyplace. I guess maybe it was that project back in August, huh? He must have blown it." Jeff probably didn't blow anything, at least not to that extent. The boss, not wishing to appear to be running down another subordinate, will try to set you straight. You can nod in acceptance, indicate that it's all right with you if the boss doesn't want to give you the facts — they're none of your business — and then go on to continue your pitch.

You can ask for more information. "It hadn't occurred to me that this would be a factor. I planned to base my case on what I have done and expect to do. But, let's see. I'd like to know more about this. For instance, I don't know how much Jeff makes now. . . ." Here again the manager will veer away from a chummy disclosure of confidential information.

Or, you can meet the argument directly and plunge into a point-by-point comparison between yourself and the other party. If you have sized up the competition you are prepared to do this. You might even take a piece of paper and launch into a comparative evaluation; "I hadn't thought of it that way, but it may be useful for me to see how I stack up against Jeff. One area I'm sure would be customer relations. How do you evaluate the two of us there?" The boss probably won't play. If he does, you can work to maximize your strengths. At the same time, you can ask him to tell you just what it is that makes the competitor so outstanding in his areas of greatest strength; and then you can turn the interview — temporarily — into an evaluation session as described elsewhere in this book.

Before beginning your negotiation, size up your competition. You are not likely to be called on to match yourself against them in so many words, but they are a potent, unseen presence in the bargaining session. Where it is advantageous, emphasize what makes you different. Make sure that you underscore at least one area in which you are either unique or indubitably stronger than anyone else. This provides the boss with a rationale for giving you more money.

Associate yourself with the others in areas where their strength may be greater than yours. As you are doing this you also enjoy the opportunity to build up your colleagues instead of knocking them. You don't want to be perceived as a knocker.

When the boss seems to be making comparisons that are not to your advantage, ask him to spell out standards. He should be prepared to talk about the yardstick he applies. As he gets into the subject of standards you will spot ways in which you can reemphasize your plus points. Do this totally in relation to yourself, not by comparison with others.

Ask for facts. When the boss refers to the rest of the group, or to some individual, respond as if he has given the signal for a confidential discussion of how much they make, how good they are, and what they are asking for. The boss probably won't go along with this. You can work the conversation back to your own qualifications. If he does get into it you can find opportunities to make comparisons that will be helpful to you.

Aim for a posture that enables you to look outstanding in comparison with the general run and makes you look very much like the real star. Don't introduce the subject of your colleagues on your own; but if the boss introduces it, respond squarely and confidently. Remember, when a manager uses other subordinates as a reason for opposing a raise he has probably not got good arguments to muster against your individual qualifications.

Be Your Own Public-Relations Expert

As children we learn to be scornful of the individual who "blows his own horn." Kids look askance at the braggart; they make fun of him. This inclination stays with most of us as we reach adulthood. We feel that pushing ourselves forward is unseemly. And with that feeling we often enjoy the comfortable assurance that the boaster is always found out in the end, that the pushy person comes to grief, that "pride goeth before a fall," and so on. Shakespeare refers to those who seek "the bubble reputation," and we are inclined to agree. Good people earn good reputations by working hard and accomplishing good things, not by inflating themselves artificially.

This is a nice straightforward view of the way things should be; but unfortunately it clashes with reality. Little as we may like it, blowing your own horn does have its uses. Public relations has become a good-sized industry. People are able to obtain the "bubble reputation" by paying for it — or by acting as their own PR men. There are many in positions of prominence, power, and affluence who have gotten there and who stay there partly through ability, but in good measure through adroit self-promotion.

The art of self-PR can be important in getting raises. If there were complete justice and objectivity in this world every increase would be based strictly on merit. But the human condition does not permit this. You will often see a colleague, who has no more on the ball than you have and who has not accomplished any more, go on to obtain much bigger chunks of the pie than you enjoy. You ask yourself, "How can he get away with it? Don't they see through him?" He can, and they don't.

You don't have to be a one-man brass band in order to avail yourself of the help of some of the principles of public relations. You can do it subtly. And your promotion of yourself may be important, particularly when you are trapped by the "box syndrome." Many people would be able to qualify for more money if they were working on their own within the organization — but they are held back by the presence of others who may not be as accomplished but who do work at about the same level. The boss may acknowledge your good points, but he can't give you that large raise because you fall into the same classification — formal or informal — as a number of others, some of whom have been around longer. You have to find some way to break out of this box. And one way to do this is to mount a self-PR campaign that helps the boss to perceive you, not just as one of a crowd, but as someone who offers something extra.

Here's an example. Every summer, the Maricol Corporation holds a three-day work/play outing for its staff at some countryside watering place. There are talks and discussions, but the schedule is light and people have a chance to do a lot of playing and socializing. Every year the job of organizing this affair is given to one of the junior managerial personnel, and the assignment is, to put it mildly, a pain in the neck. It's a lot of extra work. Headaches abound. Things always get fouled up at the last minute. There are inevitable changes, requests, complaints, bottlenecks, and headaches, both large and small. As the time approaches, those who might receive the assignment cringe in fearful anticipation. The poor soul who is tapped for the "honor" grits his teeth and tries to get through it as best he can, copying what has been done before and struggling to avoid problems.

At least that's the way it went until last year. Last year the unwelcome assignment was given to Don Forbush. Forbush, a young graduate of the Maricol executive training program, is in charge of a minor department. He is bright, but he knows that he is in competition with several others who act, look, and talk about the same as he does.

Don Forbush's friends chortled gleefully when he received the memo asking him to act as chairman of the outing (this memo being traditionally known as The Black Spot.) But Forbush went ahead quietly and laid his plans.

The first hint that anything unusual was afoot came in a generally-distributed memo from Forbush. The missive bore the subject heading "Project Interaction." This was the title that Don Forbush had conferred on the three-day picnic. The opening memo was philosophical. It talked about the need for greater rapport and communication among Maricol people, the great opportunity afforded by the summer get-together, and how this year there would be certain innovations that would assure that, while everybody had a good time, the participants and the company would benefit from the festivities as never before. Of course all of Don's contemporaries scoffed at this, jeered at Forbush's imposition of such portentous language on what was, after all, only an excuse to have a big blow-out.

They continued to laugh in the succeeding weeks as memoranda streamed out from Forbush's office. There would be sensitivity sessions at the conclave. There would be buzz groups, and role-playing, and drill on crisis intervention, and something that Forbush called Fun-for-Profit Interludes. Other young managers held their sides in mirth as they read the torrents of jargon with which Don Forbush coated even the simplest procedural directive — "Accommodational assignments will be allocated with an eye toward the professional and social ecology effectuated by the interpersonal dynamics of the organization" — which translated meant that deadly enemies or total strangers would not have to room with each other.

Oblivious of the kidding that came his way, Forbush went about his task. The summer get-together finally came off. In reality it was not much different from those of previous years. There were speeches and meetings. The same people got the same grievances off their chests as they had in the past. The same people made spectacles of themselves. There were the same difficulties and hang-ups that had enlivened all other company parties. The one thing that was a little different was that Don Forbush was always to be seen with a clipboard in hand, frequently handing out imposing-looking pieces of paper that nobody read. At the end of the thing each employee present received a detailed questionnaire covering a great many aspects of the occasion, both business and social.

But this was not the end. Two weeks later many people discovered, in their in-boxes, a multi-page document circulated by Don Forbush. This was a "preliminary analysis" of "Project Interaction" – "Complete data and analysis will be furnished at a later date, but some of the immediate findings may be of interest. . . ." There followed a somewhat bewildering conglomeration of prose, charts, percentages, all devoted to drawing a set of conclusions from "the important interactive experience" that had just taken place. In another three weeks those who cared to had an opportunity to peruse the complete report, a thick blue-bound production that offered exhaustive analysis of every phase of the project (adroitly milking the questionnaires that had been handed back and skirting the issue of how many people had actually responded.)

And then there was a set of conclusions and recommendations, featuring the discoveries that the top management of Maricol was in the forefront of psychological thinking in its recognition of the importance of this kind of interaction; that Maricol people on the whole responded maturely and resourcefully to the plentitude of developmental experiences through which they had passed, that certain refinements might be introduced to make next year's project even more rewarding in terms of growth and self-fulfillment, and much more.

Don Forbush's colleagues were convulsed. They were particularly amused to note that the poor boob didn't even see what he was doing to himself. He was sure to be given the chairmanship of the party permanently.

But they were not laughing as loudly when word leaked out that Don Forbush had received a bigger raise than anybody else at the end of the year. Could it be, they asked themselves, that all Don's b.s. about the party might have had something to do with it?

It could be, and it was the case. When Don Forbush went in for his salary review, he made a great point of his efforts on "Project Interaction." Now, Don Forbush's boss was not so naive as to think that his subordinate had achieved a cosmically important breakthrough with the project; in fact, Don's boss had not really read Don's stuff with any care. But he suspected that the higher-ups in the organization might just have read the stuff and been deeply impressed with it. And, whether they had or not, Don Forbush's name was better known now than it had been. Some members of top management rather liked the formalization of the annual party. It seemed to give a rationale to something which cost money and with which they were stuck. Without looking too closely into their reactions they were able to feel that the company was doing more than just getting people together for a good time. Forbush's earnest and heavy-handed efforts had given the annual bash a patina of modern behavioral theory.

Forbush had done well at his regular job. However, his rank on the organization chart placed him in a general salary range with five other fellows. All things being equal it would have been difficult to justify an unusual increase for Don. But all things were not equal. Don Forbush had done something extra, something that took him out of the ranks. And he had PR'd it to the hilt. True, the accomplishment itself was not of enormous importance. But the way Forbush had worked it, it was easy for the people who counted to invest the episode with more significance than it truly merited.

You may be in a situation in which your regular work assignment does not give you a chance to lift yourself clearly above your associates. When this condition prevails, you can be held back from the realization of your salary ambitions by the boss's compulsion to be even-handed, not to give one person too big a raise because he might then have to do it for the others.

Look around for the possibility of "extra" performance. Every company has problems and recurring chores that require volunteer effort. The "task force" approach to solution of perennial difficulties is becoming more popular in business. It gives management a chance to turn people loose on assignments without worrying about channels and reporting relationships. Of course this is extra work. Some people shun it. Others bemoan the fact that they are stuck with it. But when you use the extra assignment as an opportunity to mount a PR campaign that will give you that valuable slight edge in the salary negotiation, you make it all worth while.

Sometimes the opportunity is forced on you; sometimes you have to seek it. Sometimes the assignment is of real substance; sometimes it is a "nothing" chore like running the company party. It doesn't matter;

the idea is to take the job on and give it some innovative twists that enhance your dimensions — even slightly — in the boss's eyes.

We are talking here about the boss's perception of you, and this is not always the same as his objective evaluation of your work. If you take yourself seriously, and present some basis for it, the boss will sometimes be willing to go along with your self-evaluation. He may not fully understand the importance of the achievement that you are advancing as a reason for more money, but it is enough if he concedes that it may have some importance.

The individual who undertakes a campaign of personal PR in order to win more money must be ready to withstand a certain amount of scorn, good-natured or otherwise. This is a hangover from the childhood propensity to ridicule pomposity. However, in the adult world, a certain amount of well-distributed pomposity can command dividends, so if this strategy seems to have promise for you, thicken your skin and proceed.

One more word about Don Forbush and "Project Interaction." It is true, as his friends gloatingly predicted, that he would wind up with the assignment again. Don has been named chairman of the party once more; but he has been assigned a team of assistants to do the work. All he has to do is sit back and write his memos.

The Timing of The Raise Request

Ann Pearson has been talking with her boss, Ginny Berg, for half an hour. They have been going over routine departmental business. Now all the topics have been covered, and Pearson gathers her files together as she prepares to leave. As an afterthought Berg says, "Oh, by the way, Ann; I guess it's time for us to review your salary, right? Well, as you know things are tight, but I'm going to do the best I can for you. I'll get the machinery working and put something through. You should know, oh, in about two weeks. Okay?"

Right here is where Ann Pearson could blow it. If she accepts this casual handling of her raise she permits the situation to be taken out of her hands. Sure, if what Ginny Berg finally offers is not enough, Pearson can protest; but she will be in a stern-chase. Her position will be weak and practically irreparable.

Ann's response should be something like this: "Ginny, I want to talk with you about that, and I think we can have a constructive discussion, but now is not the time to do it. You're busy and I want to get going on some of these things we have agreed on. How about tomorrow morning at ten? Will you have some time for me then?"

The question of your raise should not be handled in an offhand manner. Don't let it happen that way. Make a date with the boss to talk about money. If he puts it off, persist. If all else fails, arrange a meeting with him on some work-related pretext and go prepared to negotiate salary. Try to assure that there will be enough time to give the topic ample attention. But by all means see to it that your raise is the subject of a full-fledged head-to-head meeting with your boss.

The next question — and it's an important one — is whether or not you should disclose the size of the raise you are asking in advance of the negotiating session.

Let's assume you're requesting a big increase. Notification in advance prepares the boss for the figure; if he's the nervous type he will not fall senseless to the floor when you broach it in the meeting. But at the same time it alerts the boss who may be intent on fighting your request; the more you ask for the more strongly he will marshal his arguments. Examine the factors involved: your boss's make-up, the surrounding circumstances, the relative strength of your case. Then decide whether or not to tip your hand in advance.

Let's say it's about a month before you plan to go to the mat with your superior on the money question. What's going to happen within that month? The answer to that question will be one leading indicator as to the advisability of an advance warning.

Bruce O'Connor has decided to ask for a raise that is almost three times as big as any he's gotten in the past. He has been doing a good job, and he has every reason to believe that management is satisfied with his work. There is one good-sized project that still pends. One of O'Connor's assignments has been to cut the average time of materials-handling in his area of control. He has whittled away at the problem and there have been slight gains. But now Bruce is sure that he is on the edge of a breakthrough. Within the next two weeks a new plan, which he has instituted recently, will have taken hold. Bruce O'Connor expects the handling time to drop dramatically — and he will see to it that the word gets to his boss.

Basing his decision on this assurance, O'Connor concludes that his best course is to let the boss know how much he wants. He does it with a bare statement, this is how much I will be requesting, and I am looking forward to being able to support my request when we talk during the last week of the month. Bruce's boss will be thinking over the amount, and then he will receive the encouraging figures on handling time. O'Connor may not have to work hard at all for the raise when he actually moves into the negotiation.

If you have reason to believe that developments just before negotiation time will strengthen your case, then it might be a good idea to let the boss know in advance how much you want. If, however, there will be nothing in particular that will make you look any better — or if there are apt to be developments that shed an unfavorable light on your eligibility for a handsome increase — the better course may be to wait until you actually face the boss.

But it's important to consider the kind of person your boss is. Is he a chronic haggler? Does he inevitably bargain hard, trying to wear you down as far as possible from your original request? If he has acted this way in the past, or if you suspect that he is likely to act this way, don't disclose your asking price beforehand. This will only give him more time to figure out ways to counter your arguments. You are apt to run into some interim sniping; he stops you for a moment in the hall and says, "I got your note about money. Of course the figure you name is totally unrealistic, but I'm sure you'll give me a more realistic number before we actually discuss it." This puts the ball back into your court with a lot of spin on it, and that's not what you want.

But maybe your boss is a reasonable and amicable type, but one who needs time to get used to any unusual situation. Whenever anybody suggests a new idea to him, he takes time to think it over. This doesn't mean that he turns it down; he just wants to "sleep on it'" Often he asks for more discussion and for supporting evidence in order to make the most judicious decision. This kind of boss should probably be given the word in advance about the size of the raise you want. He will not reject it out of hand. He may be surprised, even shocked, but his initial reaction will be modified by time. And when you get together with him he will ask you to back up your demand. The raise negotiation interview can then be put to a productive use.

If your boss is a more mercurial type — the kind of person who prides himself on being a "quick study" who moves fast and decisively — then it's probably better to hold off the disclosure of your asking price as long as possible. You want him to make the decision under the circumstances that are most favorable to you, and this means that you want to make your supporting case at the same time you make the request. If he learns how much you want before you have an opportunity to negotiate with him, he will make the decision unilaterally. Your meeting may be a frustrating effort to reverse a *fait accompli*, a decision that has already gone against you.

There is another important factor to consider in deciding whether to name your figure in advance. How much leeway does your boss have in giving raises? If he operates within the limitations of a strict budget, then you may be well advised to get on the record with your bid as early as possible, otherwise you may be shut out. Other people will enter their raise requests, and while he may not automatically agree with them, he will be in the process of earmarking the raises he will probably be handing out. The more money that he earmarks for other people, the less there will be left for you. So in such a circumstance you should open the campaign well in advance of the actual time of decision.

To what extent does your boss have to get the approval of others to give you a raise? If you have good reason to feel that he talks it over with his own boss or bosses early in the game, then you should seriously consider providing him with early warning. Your beforehand disclosure will alert him, and he may be tough in the negotiation, but this can't be helped. You want him to have the maximum leeway possible when you confront him, and this may mean that he must alert his own boss early to the possibility of a large increase for you.

Another consideration, of course, is the strategy you are going to use. If you plan to make a painstaking case for a raise that you have every reason to think is well "within the ball park," then advance notification can't hurt.

But if you have decided on a "blitzkrieg," if you are going to name a very substantial figure and bluff it out, then don't drop any advance hints of your approach. Furthermore, if you are going all-out for a whopping raise, and you want and need to take the upper hand in the negotiation, delay the negotiation session until close to the time when the boss must make up his mind. Wait until he is in the throes of preparing his budget. Don't give him too much time for a comeback.

Now let's consider another variation of the situation. Your boss is likely to be talking with others about your request after he gets it. You are confident that you can convince him that you deserve all or most of what you are asking; but you also know that your boss will need help in selling your raise to others. You will present your request to him in terms that he can use in backing you up. You will want, as nearly as possible, to put the actual words in his mouth and the proof material in his hand — as recommended elsewhere in this book. If this is the situation you face, don't let the boss know how much you're asking before you cover your demand in detail. If he gets your figure too early he may start talking about it to others — without having the advantage of the selling ammunition you plan to give him. So do everything possible to avoid tipping your hand. Keep away from the subject until you are able to put your request in the context of the case you are prepared to make, and that you want him to make for you in turn.

In considering when to mention your asking figure, observe what others around you are doing. If everybody is pestering the boss about a raise far in advance of the time when he will actually decide — and if you don't have to worry about his making so many commitments that he will have little left over for you — there may be an advantage in "playing against it." The boss may welcome your restraint in not irritating him about money before the appropriate time. You can capitalize on this when you actually meet with him by saying, "I wondered whether I should begin talking to you about this earlier, but I decided that you had a lot of other things to worry about, so I thought I'd wait until we could wrap the whole thing up today," etc. It can get the negotiation rolling on a pleasant note.

Any decision to disclose your request in advance should be subject to your judgment about the penetration and rapidity of the company grapevine. If you give early notice of a big raise demand, and the news leaks, your boss will be under pressure from a lot of other people who think they deserve as much as you. When this happens your hopes — justified though they may be — are likely to be doomed. The boss will feel obligated to cut you down.

In general, think about revealing how much you want in advance when enough of the following conditions prevail:

- You have a strong case, and one that is apt to be strengthened by developments between the time you tip your hand and the actual negotiation.
- Your boss needs time to get used to the idea, but is not likely to use the time to figure out ways to combat you.
- Your boss must make preliminary judgments about how much of a gross figure he must set aside for raises.

You should probably hold off on revealing your figure in circumstances like the following:

- Little or nothing is going to happen in the interim to make you look more deserving.

- The boss is a congenital bargainer, who will begin to carve away at your request as soon as he knows what it is.
- The boss has the leeway to make the decision, and is apt to make it fast.
- You are thinking of taking a strong stand, boldly striking for a very large amount.
- Your boss has to sell your raise to others and needs the supporting arguments you can provide.
- News of your request is likely to get around and stimulate others to jack up their own demands.

Take all the factors into account and make a reasoned decision on whether to name your price ahead of time or wait until you are in the arena. Too often people do it one way or the other without giving any thought at all to the appropriateness of the move given the circumstances.

Your Visible Posture During the Raise-Getting Period

When the boss knows, or suspects, that you are asking for a healthy increase, he will look at you somewhat differently than he did before. You are doing your day-in-day-out job. But there are ways and ways of doing a job. Since you are under scrutiny, you will do well to give thought to how you look during this critical period.

There are certain things you should not do. One of these things is "making waves." For some time you may have wanted to raise some hell within or outside your operation. Perhaps somebody in another department is not cooperating; it may be that the treasurer's office is giving your department the short end of the stick on something. This is not the time to start fights. You can *talk* about making waves with your boss, if you feel that a show of aggressiveness will help. But, even though you are justified, it's not a good idea to get involved in internecine warfare on your own. It raises eyebrows; it causes headaches; it sucks your boss into the arena; and the time for decision on your raise may come before there is any resolution of the struggle. This is not a healthy atmosphere within which to try for more money.

Don't come to the boss — if you can avoid it — with major problems or with questions that he will have difficulty in answering. It may be perfectly reasonable for you to do so, but the boss is unlikely to react happily to your information or your query. Rulers no longer behead the messengers who bear bad tidings, but the impulse is still there, buried under layers of civilization. If there is a bad situation that must be brought to your superior's attention, try to work it so that he learns through some other means. Perhaps you can put it on the grapevine so that the boss's secretary can pick it up and relay it. The person — no matter how blameless — who is prominently identified with bad news may not be a good bet for a raise.

There are exceptions. If you can bring the boss news — no matter how bad — along with some good ideas for correcting the situation, then you are in good shape. Or if you provide information that the boss needs and isn't getting from other sources, he may appreciate it. But if you are just the person who walks in and says, "Things are going to hell in the shop," the eye he casts on you is apt to be jaundiced.

Don't try to "come on strong" by acting in ways that are at great variance with the way you normally act. For example, a raise seeker who customarily lounges at his desk is suddenly to be seen striding up and down the halls, looking serious and carrying pieces of paper as if they were the formulae for the hydrogen bomb or Coca-Cola or something equally vital. This ploy is easily seen through. Belated attempts to make an impression of business or efficiency can only work against your chances of getting the raise.

Don't "go public." Avoid talking about the progress of your raise negotiations with anyone. Keep it to yourself that you have asked for a raise. There may be times when strategy dictates that you should "go public," but this is almost always after you have received a tentative turndown or you are being stalled.

Don't incur prolonged absences from the work scene if you can help it. When an employee is not around, no matter how much good he may be doing wherever he is, a boss — influenced by the possibility of having to fork over a big raise — can easily come to the unjust conclusion that his subordinate is goofing off.

This is a minor point, but it's usually a good idea not to appear overly complacent, as if you were already counting the money. Confidence is one thing; complacent assumption that the boss will have to meet your demands (or the boss's perception that this is what you assume) may harden his heart and cause him to dig in his heels.

These are the negatives. Now for the other side.

Be a problem solver. Maybe there is some small but nagging difficulty that has been around for a while. Maybe you even had a pretty good idea of what to do about it a month ago. Now is the time to get in there and clear it up. And make sure you get credit for it, not by obvious boasting, but by self-effacing references to all the help you received from others, including the boss. He may not remember what kind of help he gave you, but you can always assert that it was something he said or wrote that set you on the right track.

Big problems are different. If you could solve the big ones any time you wished, there would be little need to worry about raise-getting strategies. But there is frequently the opportunity to contribute something toward the resolution of a major problem. You may look for and report ways in which similar difficulties have been overcome in other companies. You may offer a description of the difficulty that does not necessarily contain any solutions, but appears to help at least in showing what must be done. At the very least you can indicate your determination to go all-out in overcoming the obstacle, even though you haven't an answer right at the moment.

Approach your working life with a confident air — not smug and complacent, but confident. Be positive in your utterances — about the chances of solving problems, about the likelihood of reaching next year's objectives, about the future of the department and the company. Show that you are thinking right. This connotes a healthy frame of mind. A lot of bosses tend to relate negativism to neuroticism, and while there may be times when it's good to be negative, raise time is not one of them. Julius Caesar liked to have men around him who look as if they "sleep o' nights." In that he was not too different from a lot of bosses.

You want to look good; but never at the boss's expense. Make him look good too. This does not mean agreeing enthusiastically and loudly with everything he says — the yes-man is old hat. There's a better way to do it.

Take for example this excerpt from a meeting. Luther Lemmon is planning to hit Fred Gray up for a nice increase. In the conference, Gray announces a new plan. Many of those present cry with alacrity: "That's great! . . .First-rate thinking, chief! . . .Bullseye!" and the like. But Lemmon looks pensive. "At first sight it shapes up as something with a lot of velocity, but I wonder . . .Fred, do you think you could spell out more of the long-range implications, particularly as they might affect reorders?" Now, Luther Lemmon has every reason to believe that Fred Gray has given a lot of thought to those long-range implications, and in this he is not disappointed. The boss comes through with about ten minutes of facts and figures. At the end of this Lemmon says, "Boy, that was some piece of thumbnail exposition. It clears up my reservations. I'm sold."

Lemmon's ploy is consonant with the discovery we discussed earlier. Behavioral scientists found that we are much more likely to respect the person who disagrees with us at first and then is won over by our arguments, than we respect the person who agrees right away. Lemmon established a modest position of independent thinking with his mild demurrer. Furthermore, he gave the boss a chance to look good.

Initiate promising-looking plans and programs. This is the time to launch into operations that have what appears to be a lot of potential. Undertake them with every indication of zest and confidence. In effect you are saying to the boss, "Look at the big payoff you'll have when I bring this off. And of course I will work even more wholeheartedly and devotedly at it after I get my raise. If you are well-launched on a project that may be profitable, the boss may be reluctant to disturb your concentration by haggling over money. He may still haggle, but there may be less zip to his haggling.

Be reassuring. You are around to solve problems, not create them. Your role is to make life easier for the boss, not harder. (Or at least this is a useful way to see your role when a raise may be in the offing.) Through every possible word and deed you should be conveying to your superior this message: "In whatever part of the operation that concerns me, you can rest assured that I will take care of it in a way that works and makes you look good, with a minimum of worry and effort on your part." Be particularly diligent about following through on things, even when it's not necessary. Leave no loose ends dangling. The theme of many points of contact with the boss should be, "That job is taken care of satisfactorily; you can count on it. I'm here to report as much as you want to hear about it." The employee who helps to bring peace of mind is an employee who is more likely to come away with more money. Work effortlessly. Don't appear to be laboring at your job. It is interesting to note how some actors who have achieved great reputations, get away with it. They appear on the screen, standing still and mumbling. Audiences go wild. "Discerning" critics remark, "Look at the beautiful economy of the way he works. He does hardly anything."

You can be the capable and assured individual who handles things with "no sweat." If you look like your rushing all the time, or if you complain about there not being enough hours in the day, the boss may suspect that you're in trouble — and he will wonder if a raise is really justified.

Remember that you're on display at raise time. The boss is looking at you for clues to your ability and your determination. Show him a picture of calm efficiency, supportiveness, positivism, forward-looking pursuit of profitable goals, solution of problems. Of course these may be "surface" things, but, let's face it, what appears on the surface is what is seen, and what is seen is important in creating impressions, sometimes vivid impressions. Look at all times like somebody who rates a raise.

4

special strategies

Making That One Big Score

You have watched the scene in the movies many times. It's the one about the desperado who is also a dreamer. You may see Robert Redford in the part currently, or Humphrey Bogart in an old one on the late show. Toward the beginning of the film the crook calls his associates together and dumbfounds them as he reveals his plan for the super-heist to end all heists. The camera zooms in for a close shot. The hero's eyes light up as he tells how he is going to cap his career by pulling off that One Big Score.

But there's no reason why the concept of the One Big Score should be restricted to bandits in the movies. A good honest working person can — if the circumstances are right — hit for the One Big Score that gives him a quantum jump in compensation.

The essence of this strategy is that you go along for a considerable period, never agitating for a raise, taking what you get. You wait until the time is ripe. And then you demand a huge raise; one that seems to the boss to be outlandish ("You must be kidding!"). If you have used the strategy properly, you will get that raise.

Not everyone can do it. The most important requisite is that you must have worked your way into a position in the company which makes your continued contribution *absolutely vital* to the boss at the critical moment.

One of the beauties of this campaign is that you don't have to hold down what is traditionally thought of as a "big job." In fact you may be better off if you occupy a lonely position in a little backwater of the corporate stream. Most businesses involve certain pivotal tasks that nobody ever thinks of as being important — until management is threatened with the defection of the individual who performs the task. These chores are often performed by a person who — when thought of at all — is taken completely for granted. The worker goes on day after day, doing something that nobody pays attention to. But this is also work that nobody else can do. When and if the happy moment comes that this faceless functionary turns out to be essential, the stage is set for the Big Score.

Greta Carpenter had labored for many years in the nonglamourous back office of Felder & Farrow, a large advertising agency. Greta was attached to Accounts Payable in the Financial Division. Her title — well, she didn't exactly have a title. In the places where it was necessary to give her a formal designation she was labeled "Assistant to the Group Superintendent." Most people had no idea of Greta Carpenter's responsibilities, although they knew in a vague way that she had something to do with paying fees and residuals to the talent used by F & F in its commercials.

As it must to all organizations, computerization came to F & F. The bright new consoles were installed in a special air-conditioned space and began to hum busily, spewing out payrolls, billing statements, payorders, and so forth. Everyone was very proud of the new system, except of course for those who were fired because their manual jobs were now taken over by the machines.

Greta Carpenter was not one of those fired. She had been around for so long, grown gray in boredom, that she blended in with the dingy decor of the financial floor. Every day she still seemed to busy herself with ledgers and files that she got from someplace. Since no one could describe exactly what she was doing, Greta had achieved a high degree of protective coloration. Her immediate boss was not precisely keyed in on her tasks, and was too embarrassed to admit this to his boss when the subject of Greta's continuation came up. So he maintained that Ms. Carpenter was doing something that needed doing, and not too many questions were asked. Further up the line nobody even knew she existed. So Greta survived the perilous moment of computerization and again receded into near-invisibility.

One other factor that weighed heavily in assuring Greta Carpenter's continuation was that she never made waves. Greta had never asked for a raise. She had received increases, of course, in line with department-wide adjustments, but she had never complained or requested anything more for herself.

When the computer made it necessary for management to get rid of a lot of people, there was of course great distress in the executive suites. Few people really like to wield the hatchet. So, for those who knew about Greta, she remained as a vestige of the good old days of the company, and a symbol of management humanity. After all, they hadn't just fired people *wholesale.* For the higher-ups who did not know Greta Carpenter existed, there was balm in the message from her more immediate bosses that at least one of the old crew would remain on the payroll. This gave all concerned the comfortable reassurance that F & F really did, after all, have a heart.

And then funny things began to happen to F & F. The star of a series of commercials for the agency's most-valued client failed to show up for a shooting. When reached, the star declared that she would no longer work for a chicken outfit like F & F and then slammed down the phone. Several prominent agents refused to send people to casting at F & F, and as a result some important campaigns had to be placed in a very expensive limbo. Soon after this the agency was thrown into consternation; a picket line had been thrown up outside the skyscraper inhabited by the company. The line was manned by actors and actresses whose names were emphatically not household words, but whose nondescript faces were known to millions because of their constant appearance in commercials. Advertising agencies always hire the same people for television commercials; it is a matter of professional pride. Clients are unhappy if their ads do not feature the same talent which has failed to lighten up a dozen previous campaigns.

Word filtered up to the top at F & F. The actors were picketing because they were not being paid for the work they had done for the agency. A demand thundered forth from the president's office: "Find out what's wrong and get this thing straightened out immediately!" Once the problem was identified it seemed that it would be simple enough to handle it. The agency was not broke (although, up and down Madison Avenue, people were beginning to talk). But the problem turned out to be not so simple. Paying commercial talent (unless the deal is a "buy-out," a flat fee) can be complicated. The payer has to know exactly how many times each commercial in a particular pool (one of dozens) has been run on every station in the country.

Now, it would seem that such an assignment would be duck soup for the computer. And in fact the chore had, supposedly, been programmed for the EDP equipment. But something had gone wrong. Perhaps the programmer had not talked with all the right people before translating the task into magnetic symbols on tape. Or maybe the input to the computer was inadequate. At any rate, the vaunted machine was not doing its job in this area. The episode will not be unfamiliar to anyone who has witnessed the installation of a data processing system in any organization.

Obviously it would take some time to get the machinery properly geared to the task. High-priced experts would have to be called in. Meantime it was essential that commercial talent be immediately paid what was owing. The situation was slipping beyond embarrassment; F & F clients, not wholly unstimulated by competing ad agencies, were beginning to ask if F & F was really sound financially, or if the agency had completely lost control of its operations.

The head of the financial department, gaunt and white in the lips, was handed an ultimatum: get it all cleared up by the end of the week. He summoned his minions. The answer that became immediately apparent to everybody was that the job would have to be done in the way that it was done before the onset of the computer. But who would do it? All the people who had handled the task manually had been fired; well, practically all. There was that old girl, what's-her-name, Greta Carpenter.

Greta was summoned to the boss's chambers. She faced not just her immediate boss but a whole panoply of top financial executives, most of whom had seen her around but had never connected the name with the face.

Greta's boss started to explain the situation to her, but she already understood the situation. That was promising. Then came the big question: could anything be done about it quickly? Greta nodded. Smiles broke out; for the first time in three days a little color crept back into the faces of those forming the assemblage. How could it be straightened out quickly? Greta, in her tiny but well-modulated voice, started to explain, but the explanation soon lost all the others. Never mind the explanation; *could she do it?* Greta sat and thought. They hung on her answer, anxiously watching her lips. Then Greta Carpenter spoke. Yes, given a free hand, she could do it — and by Friday.

A huge sigh of relief. Greta's immediate boss, basking in the glory thus reflected on him (he, after all, had had the foresight to retain this invaluable person) said, well, then Greta should get started right away. Anything she wanted in the way of authority or assistance would be hers immediately.

But Greta lingered. "There's just one thing. I've had some expenses recently and I'm thinking of incurring a good many more. I was wondering. . .I've never asked for a raise, and I haven't had one for three years. Would it be possible. . . ."

Yes, yes, of course there would be a nice raise for Greta, just as soon as this thing was over with. They would talk about it next week, perhaps over lunch at Jimmy's . . . . But Greta, in her gentle, firm way wanted to talk about it now: "It would clear my mind for the assignment if we had it out of the way." The others looked at each other. Then the senior official made a snap decision: "You're right, of course, Greta. Starting next week there'll be ten dollars more a week in your pay envelope. To hell with the delays and paperwork; I'll walk it through myself." He sat back, beaming magnanimously. "Does that take care of it?"

"Well, not quite." Greta looked down at her clasped hands and then glanced up shyly. "I was thinking more of $35,000 a year, with a five year contract." Smiles all around the room. Of course she was joking. But they were rather weak smiles. She *was* joking, wasn't she? She didn't look like she had ever joked about anything in her life.

"You're putting us on, Greta?" said one mogul tentatively. Greta at last made it plain that she was not putting them on. She had stated her requirements. If they were not met, well, she had a little money in the bank, she had always wanted to take a long trip, and after that, well, perhaps there was someplace she could work into, some small agency. . . .

There was a spate of remonstration. Where was her loyalty to the agency? After all, Greta had been retained on the payroll when many other heads were rolling. To this she said mildly, "It turns out that that was a good thing, wasn't it?" This line of argument petered out. Then there was talk about being realistic, a smaller raise ("something in the ballpark") and of course there could be no question of a contract. Who needed a contract? After all, from henceforth Greta would have earned the undying gratitude and eternal loyalty of the organization. Greta just sat there, smiling.

There was another argument: "Greta, you're one of our oldest employees — I mean you are a trusted and valuable veteran of the F & F scene. You know how things work. There are ranges for salaries. We could not possibly come anywhere near the kind of thing you're talking about. It would skew the whole compensation scale for the entire division. You can see that, can't you?"

Greta nodded. "Yes, I can see that," she said. They sighed in relief; but then they gasped at her next words. "That is why," Greta continued, "I have thought of a solution. Since my receiving this increase and contract — which, although reasonable, might seem to some to be a little high — would throw off the wage scale, I suggest that you place me outside the scale. My title is not terribly important; 'Special Consultant to the Financial Division' or something like that. You could make me a vice president if you like, it doesn't matter. I believe there are 146 vice presidents in the organization now. The important thing is that I would be given a special assignment as an in-house consultant, which would then very easily justify my compensation."

There was more argument; but the deadline hung ever more heavily over them, and at last Greta was in possession of a contract which she had checked out with her lawyer before the end of the day. Greta Carpenter straightened out the mess. She remained with F & F for the life of her agreement, expecting that that would be the end of it. But by that time F & F was used to her in the in-house consultant's role, and who knew? Maybe there would be another problem. The contract was extended with a raise.

The elements present in Greta Carpenter's One Big Score can be found, of course with modifications, in quite a few jobs in quite a number of organizations.

Greta Carpenter may have anticipated that something like this was likely to happen after the computers went in; or, she may have just played it by ear. Either way, she was able to bring off the One Big Score because of a combination of small advantages that added up, for one climactic moment, to a single huge advantage.

You don't have to decide now that you are going to plan for years in order to make your coup and avail yourself of a really big jump in salary. But you can begin to do certain things that will help to place you in a favorable position if the moment comes.

The first requisite is to develop some knowledge or skill that nobody else possesses. It need not be a spectacular attribute; in fact, quite the contrary. It should be something that you know or can do that goes by unnoticed now, but which may conceivably become important at a future date. It doesn't necessarily have to be a skill. Jerry Bulger was a plodding functionary in the service department of a company manufacturing industrial equipment. Jerry was no Einstein, but he was a friendly fellow and he built up comfortable relationships with a lot of people who worked for the customer concerns. These were not big people;

they were small, like Jerry. But small people can become big ones. One of the friends whom Jerry made was Arthur Gatch, an engineering assistant with a medium-sized firm named Finley Associates. Within the space of seven years two things happened at Finley Associates. The development of a new process turned the company into a relative giant in the industry; and Arthur Gatch shot upward through a combination of luck and skill to become president.

Now Finley was a very important customer for Jerry Bulger's outfit. But Finley began to express some dissatisfaction with the products manufactured by Jerry's company. Suddenly an entree was needed to the highest echelons at Finley. It turned out that the best — and almost the unlikeliest — medium for such an entree was Jerry Bulger. Jerry agreed to use his old cordiality with Gatch to smooth things over — but not before Jerry's company came through with a raise that was triple the sum of all the raises he had ever received in the past.

It sometimes can happen on the basis of someone you know. More often the One Big Score is made possible by your ability to do something that no one else ever thought it important to master. One man engineered an enormous increase for himself because he was the only person in the company who was able to talk on the telephone with the proper tone of apologetic obsequiousness. His company had not had much use for obsequiousness when things were going good; but a wide-ranging product failure suddenly made this ability a valuable commodity.

Anyone who stays around an operation and keeps his eyes open learns how certain things get done. These may seem to be small things, beneath the attention of top management; but they keep the business going. They command little attention and are not thought to be worth much money because of their simplicity. A lot of people in the firm can do these things, or so the thinking goes. There may, too, be a feeling of confidence that it would be easy to replace any of the lowly employees who handle such chores.

It may be true at the beginning that others in the company know or can do the same things you can. But, as in the case of Greta Carpenter, the number of these others may be diminished, either by attrition or in one fell swoop. The specialty may be one that management takes for granted, in which case there may be no great effort to train somebody else to do the job.

The kinds of attributes that fall into this category include the following:

- Emergency procedures that have not been used for some time.

- Liaison work that unobtrusively expedites the flow of work from one department to another.
- Special relationships with outside people who are important to the company.
- Technical knowledge of standby equipment lying idle.
- Any particular ability that is not spelled out in a job description.

Your own particular job may not offer the opportunity to develop such a potentially valuable ability or piece of knowledge. But this should not impede your search. Volunteer to learn to do things that others do not want to do or that do not fit any particular job category. When you have it, don't flaunt the knowledge. Save it for when it may be useful.

Greta Carpenter had never asked for a raise. Certainly it is not to be recommended that anyone forego raises simply because he dreams of hitting the One Big Score at some time in the future. This approach to getting raises is something of a long shot; if you are able to use the other strategies in this book, you are well-advised to employ them. The individual who does manage to chalk up such a coup need not have been a total cipher about asking for money before the big moment; but he probably will not have been a tiger about requesting raises either.

Here's the reason. The employee who battles skillfully and tenaciously for more money is not inconspicuous. He attracts attention. The boss will want to know everything he can do, and the worker will naturally exploit everything he's got. So the small unnoticed skill may continue to be small, but it hardly remains unnoticed. The boss who parts with a large raise for Jim Twombly will want to know all about what Twombly can do. Furthermore, that boss is now conditioned to place a dollar value on Twombly's knowledge and ability. He will think about what happens if Twombly is not around to do the job, and try to cover himself accordingly. So Twombly is not in a position to spring a surprise. His abilities have been noticed; the possibility of his no longer using those skills in the interests of the firm will have been anticipated. The boss may not be able to cover himself completely, but he will certainly have taken some steps in the interests of self-protection.

Let's say that you have developed a hole card that might enable you to hit the boss for a healthy raise at a time when your services are at least temporarily essential. And you see the opportunity beginning to shape up. It's important to play it cool. This is the point at which the old service injunction "Never volunteer" is well worth heeding. Be patient. Wait to be discovered as a solver of the problem. Of course you may want to plant hints and float clues that will lead the boss to you — but if at all possible don't go bursting in exclaiming that you have the solution. Managers tend to be skeptical of people who claim they have the answers to problems that have baffled the so-called experts. This often happens; the colorful Viscount Melbourne once said, "What the wise men said would happen, has not happened; what all the damn fools predicted has come to pass." But it's best to let the boss find this out.

If you proclaim yourself as the savior, and in the next breath announce that you will not pass your miracle until your palm is crossed with a multiplicity of silver, your ploy may have the opposite effect of what you intended. When a boss *knows* he's being held up — and knows that *you* know — he is apt to turn irrationally stubborn. ("I don't care if the whole place falls apart. I'll be damned if I give that pirate a cent!") He will try a lot harder to solve his problem another way — and if he tries hard enough he may come up with a solution.

What helps the One Big Score strategy to work is the fact that, in adversity, the boss will be approaching the problem with at least mild panic mingling with his paucity of specific knowledge. He will happily grasp at a straw — if he spots the straw. But if you are under the straw asking a lot of money for its use, then he may rev up a maximum effort to find support elsewhere. Greta Carpenter's bosses might have found just as good an answer elsewhere if they were inclined to look hard enough; the fact that they were the ones who approached her (not vice versa) made them less likely to do so.

One of the saddest things in all this is that a lot of people have the chance to bring off the One Big Score and never realize it. Ted Bosco has gone along for years, doing a routine job. One day he is summoned to the boss's office. That dignitary, after preliminaries that are a lot more cordial than Ted can ever remember having come his way before, coughs and asks, "Ted, what are you working on now?" Ted tells him. The boss says, "I see. The usual stuff. You know, Ted, I think a change is good for all of us now and then. How would you like to try your hand at something different — say, the Zigmoid account?"

Ted is suffused with gratitude at being given a chance to do something more significant than what he has been doing. He leaves the boss's office, his head in a whirl, thinking that he has been done a favor. The fact is that Ted is the one who is doing the favor, and it's a big one. There is something — Ted is of course ignorant of it — that makes his sudden attention to the Zigmoid account essential. Ted will pitch in, handle the crisis, and not ever become fully aware that he has rendered extremely valuable service. He will then be relegated to his mundane job and, at the end of the year, be given his usual paltry raise.

When you are asked to do something special without there seeming to be an obvious reason for it, give yourself a little time for thinking and fact-finding. They may really *need* you. You may have become, for this moment, the indispensable person, or at least a much more important one than your career and paycheck thus far would indicate. If you think this could be the case, now may be the time to try for the Big Score.

You are probably not risking a great deal. Your boss may be dismayed and annoyed that you are asking for a big raise in return for the special service you are being asked to perform. He will try to talk you out of it, but hang in there. An earnest effort to talk you out of it — rather than a scornful dismissal — is a clue that you really do have a strong hand. You may not get all you're asking for — but you will probably get something. And the boss will likely develop a grudging respect for your acumen.

The worst that can happen is that you have miscalculated; you don't hold nearly as strong a position as you thought. So you give up your dream of the One Big Score, laugh it off, and do the job you've been asked to do. The boss is more likely to be surprised and amused than permanently irritated at your effort; at least after the initial shock wears off and you show you are willing to do the job with good grace.

And at least you may have positioned yourself for a somewhat stronger effort the next time raise time rolls around.

The "PITA" Principle

Our minds are cluttered with homely aphorisms — "Haste makes waste, A stitch in time saves nine," etc. Such adages become truisms, and when this happens we scorn them. We dismiss them as having no validity.

But truisms become truisms because they are *true* — or at least because there is enough truth in them to make them descriptive of some universal condition. The old folks got to saying these things in recognition of human attributes that cannot be changed, only endured. One such truism is the hoary adage that "the squeaky wheel gets the grease."

This one, if it is ever quoted any more in a business context, is said mockingly. According to approved notions of management practice, the squeaky wheel is not supposed to get the grease. The employee who becomes a constant irritant is, by all logical interpretations of sound executive philosophy, a drawback to the organization. Not only is he not to be rewarded; his behavior should be modified or he should be gotten rid of.

No boss worth his salt will ever admit that he greases the squeaking wheel; that he provides a raise to eliminate, at least temporarily, a source of annoyance to himself. Raises are not supposed to be given out for such ignoble reasons. Increased compensation, by all the books, is recognition of past achievement and motivation for future accomplishment. If things went according to theory the underling who complains continually about not receiving enough money would not only never get a raise, he would ultimately be out on the street looking for another job.

Alas — or maybe not alas — it doesn't work that way. The employee who creates enough annoyance with the money question will often wind up with a bigger raise than the dedicated individual who goes along quietly, doing the best he can and "understanding" the problems of his boss. Of course it shouldn't be — but how often have you seen it work exactly that way?

Let's face it. Squeakiness — at the right time and in the right place — can serve you as a tool for getting more money. Like any other tool it must be used properly. Here is an analysis of the technique.

Everyone has heard of the "Peter Principle." What are we talking about here is the *PITA* Principle — PITA standing for "Pain In The Ass." Judicious application of the PITA Principle to your boss can pay off in more dollars. But of course, as is the case with most principles, the PITA approach is not universally usable in every combination of circumstances. There are basic ground rules.

Your boss must be the kind of employer who responds favorably to the PITA stimulus. PITA is not a bland technique. There is always a response. Sooner or later the boss who has been feeling the ache in a vulnerable spot will do something about it. If what he is apt to do is fire you, then this is hardly the preferred strategy.

Fortunately there are a lot of bosses who will respond the way you want them to. Human nature guarantees this, and certain currently popular philosophies of management make it even more likely.

Most people do not welcome headaches. If your boss is like the general run of mankind he tries to avoid trouble to the maximum extent he can. His ideal is for everything to run smoothly, with no complaints from higher up or lower down. Furthermore, he probably likes to be liked. He may acknowledge that no good manager can possibly be adored by everyone, but this is an intellectual concept. In the gut, most of us will do what we can to strive toward universal popularity. Unless your boss is stamped from the Vince Lombardi mold — and there are few of those — he will be affected by the squeaking of one of his wheels.

There is an additional factor. Your boss probably has his own boss or bosses. He is accountable to somebody. You will have already made a study of your superior's reporting pattern and come to some evaluation of his standing and his vulnerability within the organization. When we extend upward the proposition that no one enjoys nagging annoyance, we can see that this quality in your boss's boss can work for your raise or against it. Your boss's boss undoubtedly does not like to be asked to approve raises (if, indeed you are in a position in which your requests must be passed on by higher ups.) So it may be that, for you to get what you want, you will have to stimulate your leader to apply PITA to *his* boss to get the raise approved.

However, here is an important point to bear in mind. A squeaky wheel *can* get the grease — but only if that wheel is bearing a load, or at least appears to be bearing a load. A "fifth wheel" that issues forth strident squeals is more likely to be junked than to be greased. Likewise, a wheel on which two or three of the spokes are freshly-broken should not call for lubrication. (There is an exception to this last point which we will cover later.) So apply PITA to your boss by all means, but pick the right spot.

For example, here is Emil Karswell, an employee who is in a miserable state of mind. For one thing Karswell has just seen an important project fall apart. His department was supposed to finish a key assignment by the 15th of the month. Through a concatenation of untoward events that deadline has been rendered inoperative. It's not all Karswell's fault; in fact from his point of view none of it is his fault. Supplies did not arrive when they were supposed to, another department of the company failed to produce a key component of the job, and so on. In any event the project is a bust.

That's just one thing that is making Karswell unhappy. Another thing is that he needs more money. He is contemplating without enthusiasm stripping his paltry bank account and selling his few remaining stocks to pay a whopping tuition bill. The combination of these two problems has made Karswell less inhibited than usual about asking for money.

So he sees his boss. First they talk about the project. Karswell arrays his excuses. The boss may not buy every one of them, but there are sufficient extenuating circumstances for him to let his subordinate off the hook in terms of responsibility for the disaster. But then Karswell swerves into the money question: "On another subject, Phil, I was wondering just when I can expect the increase we talked about. Things are pretty tight, and it's been two months now. . . ."

The timing is wrong. This is not the moment for the wheel to squeak. It gives the boss a PITA all right, but along with that unpleasant feeling the boss is afflicted by an almost irresistable urge toward THOOHA — Throw Him Out On His Ass. The boss does not necessarily blame Karswell for what went wrong, but he certainly is not in a mood to consider handing out a raise. So the boss enunciates what Karswell should have been at great pains to avoid — the Definitive Negative Answer. He says, "I wasn't going to get into that now, Emil, but since you've brought it up let's dispose of it. I'm afraid there is no chance in the foreseeable future for a raise. We are going to have plenty of trouble recovering from this fiasco. I hope and trust that you'll be devoting all your time and energy to getting the department squared away so there is no repetition of this. Let's see how that works out and maybe we'll talk about money around the end of the year."

And that is that. Applying PITA at a time of maximum poor results ends in a reversal of the stimulus. The boss is activated to give you an even bigger pain in the same place.

The wheel should at least be rolling when it squeaks. Miranda Gunderson has not enjoyed any spectacular successes in her job recently but neither has she tasted the dregs of bitter defeat. She has been coping, that's all. So Miranda begins to become more vocal about what she is doing. She trudges into her boss's office and sticks on his desk a routine report of the type she has been placing there at the same time every week for the past year. She sits for the customary brief discussion, but as she does she sighs and rubs her eyes. The boss asks what's the matter.

"Oh, it's just that I'm so tired," answers Miranda. "That status report. I was busy at home on it till nearly midnight. I was tempted to give up on it, but I know it's important to have it for you on time." Now, the report is not all *that* important — in fact it is so routine as to be nearly soporific — but bosses do not tell subordinates that their work is unimportant. That would fly in the face of modern management theory. The idea is that the boss must always act as if each chore done by his workers is an assignment of consuming challenge and moment. Admitting otherwise would be to flout approved concepts of motivation.

So the boss does not say, "Miranda, it's not worth sweating over." Instead, he says, "I appreciate your efforts to finish it on time, but why the problem? You've been doing this report for so long I would think it would be second nature by now. What's the matter, is there something particularly different about this one?"

Well, there isn't, and there's no point in Miranda pretending that there is. "No, Al, but maybe that's what's making it so tough. I know it's important, but the constant repetition seems to make it more difficult every week to keep it up and continue to do a good job on it. It's hard for me to rise to the challenge and still derive a sense of fulfillment from it."

Miranda is talking the right language. Managers have been hearing and reading a lot these days about how stultifying repetitious work can become for the worker. They have all heard of the revolt of the employees at the General Motors plant in Lordstown, Ohio, where the workers embarked on a campaign of deliberately sabotaging the production of the Vegas because, motivational experts agree, they had become so terribly frustrated by the dullness of repetitive jobs.

Miranda's boss isn't going to tell her to forget about the report. Some bosses might reexamine such a routine chore and ask whether it is really necessary — but not many. The boss is stuck with his position that the chore is an important one. Miranda does not pursue it; she goes through the discussion period, showing that she is making a heavy and successful effort to be particularly bright and responsive. At the conclusion of this session she brings up money: "You know, Al, I've been meaning to bring this up for some time, and I haven't. But the stress of producing that report last night convinces me that, in all fairness to myself, I have to say something. I need more money. You don't have to give me an immediate answer, I'm not going to quit or anything like that, but I'm going to have to get $250 more per month. When do you think you'll have an answer?"

Miranda can point to no single success to justify her request; so she uses the very dullness of her job as a pretext. As we mentioned, this is not at all a bad ploy in this day of management concern about the erosive effect of repetitive and unchallenging work. She is using the principle embodied in the anecdote about the tourist who approached a weaver in a town in Mexico and placed an order for five elaborately decorated shawls. The weaver, famous for his work, said the price would be $60 apiece. The tourist agreed; and the craftsman, in his enthusiasm went on, "They will be beautiful. I will put a burro on one, an eagle on the second, an Indian mask on the next. . . ." "Oh, no," the tourist interrupted, "I want them all the same."

"In that case," responded the craftsman, "The price will be $100 each. It is so boring to repeat the same thing." The by-rote nature of your job need not be a drawback in agitating for a raise. Properly exploited, it can be a positive argument.

Miranda continues to bring up the question of a raise, working slight variations on the theme: "Sometimes it gets so tiresome that I have to make a tremendous effort to keep on doing my best. . . .This was tough but I was able to handle it for you. . . ." etc. There soon follows the query, "Have you been able to do something about my raise yet?" The boss knows it's coming, it gives him a PITA to hear it, but he does not feel in a position to issue a flat turndown. As time goes on the emphasis in Miranda's repeated question shifts from *if* to *when.* She begins to take it for granted that the increase will be forthcoming, with the only question being one of timing: "I hope I'll have that raise by the end of next month, Al. How long do you think it will take to put it through?"

In the end Al responds to this recurring pain in the end and comes through with the raise. It's not as big as Miranda had asked for, but it's more than she was willing to settle for.

Miranda Gunderson has used certain tactics in her application of PITA. As mentioned, she has squeaked while obviously carrying a load. In addition, she has presented the request so as to avoid the Definitive Negative Answer. In first bringing it up, Miranda emphasized that Al did not have to give her an "immediate answer." In the majority of cases, the boss will take the lead thus provided and forgo the chance to issue a flat turndown or to bargain hard in order to reduce the raise to a minimum. He will put the problem off till *manana.* But the employee's increasing references to the subject have a cumulative effect in increasing his PITA.

Miranda has done something else that's important in applying this principle. She has modulated her requests. Sometimes they are based on the repeated complaints about the difficulties of her job and her struggle to make ends meet. At other times, however, she will point to some little effort she has made to do the job better. This may be a miniscule effort indeed, but the boss is not about to say, "Come of it. What you're doing is nothing." No, he goes along with the propos tion that the employee has accomplished something of significanc

And Miranda has adroitly shifted over from *if* to *when,* moving into the "assumption" mode that is discussed elsewhere in this book. After a while it becomes a foregone conclusion that she will get the raise. When using this tactic it is often helpful for the employee to say something like, "You have assured me that I'll be getting the raise, Mr. Jones, and I appreciate that, but can you give me a time-line on it?" The PITA-plagued boss can come to a point where he doesn't remember whether or not he might have said something that constituted at least a basis in fact for such an assumption, and he dismisses the option of denying it.

Overall, the worker who deploys the PITA strategy must always be able to step back and view the situation from enough distance to provide an objective evaluation of progress. The boss has to be the kind of person who wants to get rid of nagging headaches. If he has come under some new stress that might impel him to emit a final, "once-and-for-all" refusal, then the pressure should be eased. And the worker should appear to be continuing to do the job well enough so that the boss is not tempted to risk the much more intense pain of seeking a replacement.

You can use PITA to obtain the raise you want. If you have applied the needle expertly, the boss will ultimately be driven to rid himself of this nagging pain by giving you what you want.

But, some may ask, is this really a nice way to go about it? Is it fair? Is it cricket? Is it undue tormenting of a person who, after all, may not be able to help the fact that he is your boss?

Considerations like this should not objectively, enter into the matter. Excessive solicitude for the employer can make you an accomplice in your own exploitation. Nevertheless, the desire to be liked and to be fair works both ways. PITA, like many of the other principles examined in this book, rests in part on the boss's desire to do the right thing by you, if he possibly can. You may, understandably, feel the same way about him.

But being fair to the boss should not entail unfairness to yourself. If there is a more painless way to get a raise, by all means employ it. But, if there is not, then PITA should not be ruled out of consideration. After all, the boss will feel good when the pain stops. And your little ploy is helping him to do the right thing.

Many workers who have eschewed the PITA approach on humanitan grounds have come to look back on their forebearance with frustrated regret. Homer Green was such a one. Homer liked his boss,

Fred La Salle. La Salle always seemed to be ready to pass along a compliment and to be a cordial comrade, even if he was a little slow about coughing up more money. One day Homer went in to ask for a raise. He undertook the first steps of the PITA method, and could see that it was working. But it was working only too well. Homer noted the agony in Fred La Salle's face when he brought up the question of more money. When Homer applied the stimulus two weeks later, La Salle appeared even more anguished. So Homer decided to cool it.

One of Homer's colleagues evinced no such compunctions. Spud Dellinger listened to Homer's remarks about not pressing La Salle too hard and scoffed at them: "Screw that. I'm gonna stick it into him until he comes through. To hell with how he feels."

Dellinger had not been in the department as long as Homer Green, and in Homer's opinion he did not do nearly as good a job. So Homer shook his head and pursed his lips as he listened to the continuing saga of Spud's PITA campaign.

To Homer, Spud was just causing unnecessary agony to a kindly superior, and he would not get the raise anyway. All Dellinger would do would turn La Salle's good will into animosity.

And so it was with some considerable astonishment that Homer Green listened one day while a jubilant Spud Dellinger rubbed his hands and exclaimed, "I got it! Two grand and a bonus! Now I can get that Riviera and wheel around this town in style!" Dellinger went on to describe how he had carried on his process of nagging until La Salle, in exasperation, erupted "All right! I'm going to put it through! Now will you shut up about it?" It was at least some consolation to Homer to reflect that, while Dellinger might have gotten his increase, he had certainly ruptured the pleasant relationship between himself and Fred La Salle. But Homer did not even enjoy this consolation for long. The following week he watched with dismayed amazement as La Salle, laughing and joking, escorted smirking Dellinger out of the office, obviously with the intention of treating him to lunch. In all the time he had been there, and notwithstanding all the pleasantries that had passed between them, Homer Green had never been treated to lunch by the boss.

What Homer had overlooked is that there is a principle of human nature that comes into play in a situation like this. This principle has been described by the psychologist Leon Festinger, who calls it *cognitive dissonance.*

Here's how it works.

Have you ever noticed how, after making a major purchase — a car, let's say — you keep on paying attention to the advertisements for the automobile you have just bought? Logic would dictate otherwise; after all, why examine the claims for the product after you've bought it? Well, you are led to do so by an unresolved conflict that has been set up in your unconscious mind. You laid out a lot of money for the car. Consciously, you are convinced you did the right thing. But beneath the surface of consciousness you still have a fear that maybe you were "had." So you continue to seize upon material that will supply evidence to support the action you have taken. One experiment that demonstrates cognitive dissonance in operation was undertaken with a group of teen-agers who were asked to rate twelve hit records in order of preference. After the ratings were made, the teen-agers were told that they would receive two of the records as gifts; typically they were records that were rated low on the list. Then the youngsters were asked to rate the same records again, and this time they gave their gifts a much higher evaluation.

Festinger's theory is that, when we are confronted with two sets of facts that create an uncomfortable psychological imbalance, our minds tend to "adjust" these facts to make them more harmonious — and thus reduce the dissonance.

Homer Green's boss may have the uncomfortable feeling that he has been pressured into giving Dellinger more of a raise than the insistent subordinate deserved. So Fred La Salle's mind makes an adjustment. He can't take back the raise, so he unconsciously elevates his opinion of Dellinger's worth to justify the raise and exorcise the imbalance. And, worse for Homer Green, the process of adjustment may extend to him. La Salle may have a guilty feeling that quiet, loyal Homer deserved just as large a raise, or one even bigger. But instead of conferring the increase on Homer, La Salle is placed in a happier frame of mind because his unconscious performs another contortion. It downgrades Homer. So La Salle winds up thinking more of the squeaky wheel who finally extorted more money from him, and less of the employee who refrained from needling because the boss was too nice a guy.

There have always been inequities in compensation. In the Bible we are told how the Lord preached the sermon of the laborers in the vineyard. Some of the men worked the full shift, through the heat of the day. Others arrived at the eleventh hour, putting in not nearly as much effort. When it came time for payment, however, the all-day crew was discomfited to see that the latecomers were getting exactly the same amount of money for not nearly as much work. They protested, but the vineyard owner pointed out that he was paying the first gang what they had contracted for, and what he paid the others was a matter of his choice. This has seemed to some to be not quite fair; but perhaps the eleventh-hour arrivals applied some version of the PITA Principle.

PITA will work when you have a boss who dislikes headaches but will not be tempted to dispel them by risking loss of your respect and liking. You should be sure that your current level of performance and standing, while not necessarily spectacular, is not bad enough to create any real danger that the boss will catalyze a "take-what-I-give-you-or-get-out" confrontation.

Apply the stimulus gradually. Call attention to the difficulties in your job and whatever accomplishments the boss is willing to permit you to cite. Pose your first request in an open-end fashion; don't demand an immediate response. This is a technique of attrition. Keep on plying the PITA-producing lever until you get your favorable answer.

And don't worry too much about making the boss your enemy. After you get what you want he may be even more strongly in your corner, if only to justify his concession. And as for the discomfort the campaign causes him, well, all bosses suffer a certain amount of discomfort, if not here, there, and if not for this reason, then for that one. True, the boss may truly suffer a PITA as a result of your efforts, but if it didn't come from you it would probably come from someone else not nearly so deserving. Once you have the raise, it is surprising how quickly his pain will be eased and your feeling of guilt dispelled.

Threatening To "Drop The Bomb"

Remember the "credibility gap?" A few years ago it was one of the "operative" terms in foreign relations. Two giants, the U.S. and the U.S.S.R., confronted with each other across the curve of the world. Each possessed enough nuclear capability to wipe the other off the map. The capacity for destruction was — as it remains today — mutual. The U.S., outnumbered in troops and outgunned in conventional weaponry, depended upon this overriding threat to maintain peace between the two powers, uneasy though it might be.

But then people began to ask questions about credibility. To keep the peace, they said, it is not enough to possess enormous capacity for destruction. If that capacity is to serve as a deterring threat, then the other party must believe that you will use it. How credible was the U.S. commitment to go to nuclear war under certain contingencies? For example, if the Russians invaded Western Europe, without directly attacking the United States, would we *really* launch the warheaded missiles from their silos to blot out Moscow, Leningrad, etc.? More important, whatever we might finally do, what were the perceptions of the Soviet leaders? Were they convinced that we would push the button?

So the question of credibility became a momentous one. Capacity for destruction did not matter. Even the intention to use that destructive force did not matter. What mattered was the believability of the threat. If the enemy did not believe we would make good, then the result would be disaster.

Often a raise negotiation is based on one big threat. . .*the threat to quit.* Sometimes the threat is explicit. More often it is implied. The effectiveness of this strategy depends heavily on its credibility.

But even before we get to credibility we must first talk about the potency of the threat to quit. Helen Ambler works in the research department at Duvall Publications. She wants a $2000 raise. She has told her boss, Nancy Witkin, that she must have the increase, and that nothing under that figure will be acceptable. And the word has gotten around — Helen Ambler has helped it get around — that she is ready to resign if she is turned down.

Nancy Witkin is convinced that the subordinate is not just bluffing. Ambler is too proud to go this far out on a limb and then crawl back off of it. Some people can do that — go all out in making threats and then just laugh it off if the threats don't have their desired effect. Not Ambler; she will go through with it. So the element of credibility exists.

The only trouble is that Nancy Witkin does not give that much of a damn whether Helen Ambler quits or not. Helen is a useful, if not a sparkling, worker. But things have not been booming at Duvall Publications, and the research department is far from overworked. The hole that would be left in the department by Helen's departure could be covered, and Nancy Witkin is not averse to being able to show a decrease in her payroll costs. It would make her look good. Furthermore, if the workload increases, Nancy is ready to bring in a couple of trainees. The department has become rather static; it's time the boss figures, to introduce some fresh blood and new methods. The fresh blood will have to come about through replacement of researchers who leave voluntarily; Nancy Witkin is not ready to do anything so drastic as firing people to effect personnel change. And, the new methods can be more easily instituted through the training of new people rather than the retraining of veterans who have become set in their ways.

So Ambler's threat has no force. Nancy Witkin will offer a nominal raise. She thinks it's the fair thing to do, and she does not want to feel that she has forced Ambler out. But she is quite sure Ambler will not accept it.

If you are considering the threat to leave as a bargaining tactic, you must first be sure that the boss wants you to stay. Most bosses do not welcome resignation; replacement is troublesome and expensive. But you will want to judge just how much the employer wants you to stay. If you are a real ball of fire, superb at your job, you are usually in a strong position. Not always; the boss may be scared of you. He may welcome your removal of yourself as competition, even though he would never have the guts to fire you.

However, even if you are not supremely effective in every aspect of your job, the boss may have good reason for wanting you to stay on. You handle chores that would provide headaches for others, including your superior. You know your way around the place and can get things done by dint of experience and goodwill. You are familiar with procedures in a way that others are not. All of these factors can make your departure mighty inconvenient.

So, before going any further in considering the threat to quit as a lever to extract more money from the company, ask yourself a few questions:

- How's business? Could they get along with one less body?
- Would the boss like an opportunity to cut the payroll?
- Could I be replaced easily by others already on board?
- Do I have some special knowledge or skill that gives importance to my continuation?
- How strongly does the boss feel — for whatever combination of reasons — about keeping me on?

If the answers to these questions, and others that will be suggested to you, favor the use of the big threat, then you have a possibility at your command. But as yet it is only a possibility. There are other factors to be considered.

The winning of an increase largely through the threat to quit is a rough tactic. Even when it is successful, it can produce fall-out that may bring about lingering, unpleasant side-effects. Of course it can be said that the possibility of leaving the company is present in almost any raise negotiation conducted on an individual basis between worker and employer. True. It's a free country. But here we are considering the situation in which the menace of departure is used actively and deliberately as a bargaining lever.

A boss may knuckle under and come through with the raise. But he won't like it. He may feel that he has been "blackmailed." (He hasn't; real blackmail is an extreme ploy that we take up elsewhere in the book. But that doesn't stop some employers from thinking that way.)

Of course the resentment is often transitory. The boss forgets — or nearly forgets — what took place during the raise negotiation. He resumes full cordial relations with the subordinate and things proceed as they did before the raise episode. The employer is happy with the results and does not dwell on how they came about.

However, this is not always the case. Some bosses will harbor a continuing grudge. This can make the job unpleasant. It can also lead to a situation in which the boss begins to make moves to make sure that he can never get caught in such a spot again. This might mean that some responsibility would be taken away from the hard-bargaining worker, or that management will take steps to see that a relief pitcher is warming up in the bull pen just in case.

Realistically you have to be ready for such eventualities. So again it's not a bad idea to ask yourself some questions:

- Is my boss the kind of person who will hold a grudge against me?
- What actions might he take to make it tougher for me?
- Could he get up a contingency arrangement that would make me expendable?
- If any of these things happened would they be highly unwelcome to me?
- How much does the raise mean when the process of getting it may leave a bitter aftertaste?

After having considered all these questions you may be fully prepared to use the threat of quitting as a bargaining tactic. Now you will want to think about how to make your threat *credible.*

Of course the ideal position is to have a good job waiting for you. If another employer — or even multiple employers — are just waiting for the chance to snap you up, then you can bargain hard without a care in the world. And you probably don't even have to do much about establishing credibility; if you are in this happy posture the boss is probably well aware of it. But most of us are not that lucky. The availability of another job is not by any means a sure thing. Even if another job may be available, we have good reason to want to stay where we are — friendly relationships with colleagues, convenience of place of work, accommodation to working conditions, pleasant familiarity with the way things go (few of us, particularly as we grow older, really lust for violent change), vesting in a pension plan, and so forth.

So the individual who decides to use the "big bomb" approach is usually in a position something like this. He wants very much to get the raise; it is almost a necessity. He is willing to take the risk of tough bargaining to get it. But he would much rather that the raise be granted than have to make good on his threat to leave.

An important thing to be sure of is your actual chances of moving to another job; *actual,* not imagined. Many "job offers" are illusions. Over lunch, or at a conference, or during a party, or even while waiting for a train, John Smith says to Jim Jones, "Say, why do you waste your time over there? Why don't you come with us? A guy like you would be a lot better off with a live-wire outfit like ours."

If Jones is naive enough to get tough with his boss on the basis of this kind of "offer" he may be in for some unpleasant surprises. Job offers are easy to hand out if there is no serious chance that they will be accepted. People will do it simply as a way of inflating their egos and building themselves in the eyes of others. Jim Jones may go all out for his raise; fail to get it; and come back to Smith, only to hear something like, "You didn't take me seriously, did you? I was just making conversation." Or, "Gee, Jim, I did have some interest at that time, but you know how fast things change. . . ."

First of all, John Smith may not be in any position to offer anybody a job. The whole thing may be baloney. Or, even if he could hire Jones, it may not even have crossed his mind that the other would take him up on it.

You need more than casual comments on which to base the assumption that you have good prospects for moving to another job. Review the situation. Are you in a line of work where there is free and easy movement between companies? Even if this is the case it doesn't guarantee that you are all set, but it helps. How often have you been approached — with some seriousness — about going to work for somebody else? How recently have you been approached? Our minds can play tricks on us. A man may form the comfortable assumption that he is a hot number on the job market because he has received, say, six other offers; but all of these offers may have come more than five years before, with none since. Business conditions vary rapidly. And people change. He may not be the man he was five years before, at least not in the eyes of those who wanted to hire him then.

Research your job possibilities if you can do so unobtrusively. Be cautious rather than daring. Before making any contact, *assume* that word of it will get back to your boss and ask yourself what that does to your situation.

Don't tell people at work what you are doing. It may be that, when you begin preparations for the negotiation, you will want it known that you have been looking around. But premature disclosure can provoke management into counteraction that will turn your hole card from an ace to a deuce without your being aware of it.

Get the real facts about job volatility in your line from people who have current job hunting experience. A person who has been looking for work for eight months may be understandably ready to tell you that there is not a prayer, and you will have to judge how much of this is his fault. On the other hand the soul who was able to walk from one job right into another may declare that it is a cinch, and you have to ask yourself how much luck was involved in the episode and how applicable the experience is to your own setup. But you can get a feel for the job market by talking to those who are grappling with it now.

Talk to people. Employment agencies are apt to be a waste of time. They may send you on interviews, but the possibilities may be inferior to the job you already have. And, if you are at the management level, don't bother to talk to executive search agencies. If the head-hunters want you they will come to you. If, however, you have been approached by a search professional you may not be justified in feeling that you are a sure thing for another good post, but you should certainly consider this an encouraging sign.

When you find other employers who indicate interest, don't be satisfied with generalities. Look for specifics. It's not enough for another employer to say that he would welcome you in his company. Welcome you where? What would the job be? How much would it pay? When would you start? And so on. You may find that when you switch the conversation from vague nebulosities to specifics, the rosy pictures dissolves rapidly. If, however, the employer is willing to talk nuts-and-bolts, you are getting someplace.

You're not likely to come up with a sure thing. Few outside employers will be willing to say, "Whenever you make up your mind to quit, the job will be open for you" — and mean it. There are always risks. You must judge the risks and decide whether to take them or not.

One experienced raise negotiator — call him Bruce Caldwell — has developed a rule of thumb that he applies to the possibilities of moving to other positions. "If there's only one possible job in the offing I want to be at least 80% sure that I can get it. If I have looked into two possibilities, I want to feel that I have a 65% shot at each. If there are three jobs that I might be able to get, my objective judgment must be that I have a 50% chance at all three. Anything below 50% I simply do not crank in as a factor. I am tough on myself in assessing these situations. If, realistically, they are in my favor, I go right down the line in demanding a big raise. Otherwise I can't use this ploy." Bruce Caldwell has never had to move to one of his other job possibilities. He has been with his present employer for twelve years and has gotten some hefty raises by being willing to deploy the "big bomb" threat. And Bruce Caldwell, while a valuable worker, is not unique, nor is he a superman. He has always evaluated the situation carefully before setting this particular raise strategy into action.

If you feel that the move is worth making, and that you have solid possibilities for another job, then you are in good position to base a demand for more money on the threat to leave. Of course you can use the threat even if you don't have firm possibilities — but there are problems with that. Your credibility is likely to be lessened, and your resolve is not apt to be rock-hard. (Of course some people will go all out on a threat to quit without having any idea whether or not they can get another job, and not worry about it at all — but most of us would worry more than a little.)

Let's assume that all the elements look favorable enough to make the "big bomb" strategy attractive. Now you must make it *credible.* Your task is to get the boss to believe that, if you don't get the raise you ask for, you are likely to leave in the near future. Here's how one enterprising raise getter handles it.

Jerry Considine, has decided that this time he is going to make a quantum jump into a higher salary bracket. His boss, Phil Schaffer, has never been easy pickings at raise time, but Jerry is convinced that the threat of his departure would be heavily influential in tilting Schaffer toward a favorable decision.

Considine's opportunity to begin his campaign comes up during a conversation with Schaffer about an important new project scheduled to be undertaken by Considine's group after the first of the year. Schaffer has listened while Considine reviewed the responsibilities that would be assigned to each of his subordinates. Then the boss says, "You're putting a lot on Sam Orkin's plate. Do you think he'll be able to handle it?"

"No problem there," says Jerry. "Sam's been my right-hand guy for more than a year now. One of the things they tell you first is to always have your own replacement ready, and I've tried to do that with Sam. I hope you'll agree that he has come along fine. He's able to step into my shoes at any time. Maybe I'll get a chance to talk to you more about that when it's appropriate." Schaffer notes this remark without commenting on it and they move on.

Jerry Considine prepares a detailed plan for the new venture, along with alternate plans that will come into play under certain circumstances. One of these, "Plan B" is a set of revised departmental charts, showing the realignment of responsibilities suggested by Considine in case one or more key people become unavailable. Part of the package is a projection of what the department might look like *without* Jerry Considine. In going over these submissions Schaffer makes a casual observation: "I see that on this one you've dealt yourself out of the picture."

Jerry smiles. "It's a good idea to be ready for anything. You never know. Life is funny. I just thought I'd get something on paper to cover every possibility." Schaffer smiles in response and says, "Well, this is one possibility that I hope we can assume just stays on paper." Jerry nods and nothing more is said.

But Jerry continues to comment, from time to time, about the value of contingency planning and the existence of preparations to assure continuity. He does this when talking with Schaffer and he alludes to the fact in other ways. At a meeting of his department Jerry says, "The assignments are clear-cut. Everybody, including me, should know what he's supposed to do, and by this time we should all know what we need to do it. If there are any problems they should be discussed now. Furthermore, we have a flexible organization here. I'm counting on every one of you, but if somebody got sick, or for some other reason wasn't able to follow through to the end, I am assuming that we would be able to cover. Incidentally, that includes my part in the project, of course, just as it does yours."

A few days later, when Jerry is presenting the plan to the heads of other departments whose cooperation will be important, he says, "This is not a strategy that stands or falls on the availability of certain people. We've all seen bad things happen when too much responsibility was keyed to one individual because he happened to have certain capabilities. This is not that kind of plan. Even if there are personnel changes, it should continue to run smoothly, and you should have no liaison problems with the department. That goes for me as well as for the other people who'll be working on it." Phil Schaffer is not present at either meeting, but Jerry Considine has a pretty good idea that his boss is not unaware of what is being said.

Furthermore, Jerry knows something else. In continually alluding to his program as being workable even in the face of substantial changes in the management of his department, he has been painting the lily. The people who will run the campaign *are* important, and Jerry is the most important of all. Certainly he is not indispensable. Things could go on without him. But Schaffer is not likely to contemplate that possibility with any pleasure. This doesn't mean that Schaffer will automatically fork over a lot more money. Phil Schaffer knows that Jerry Considine likes his job and he has always assumed that Jerry is a fixture — but Jerry's current tactics are designed to make him wonder a little.

Year-end approaches. Schaffer and Jerry are in another conference. Schaffer says, "It looks good. You've done everything possible, and I think it will work. This program could be up to speed by next Labor Day. Now. It's never too early to look ahead. Have you given any thought to where we go from there?"

Jerry Considine becomes evasive. "Gee, no, Phil, I've been so up to my neck getting this plan on track that I haven't had time to think that far ahead." Schaffer pushes a little, evincing genial incredulity that a buttoned-up guy like Jerry hasn't given at least some thought to new plans that might be undertaken in a year's time. But Jerry insists that he has not done so.

"Well," says Phil Schaffer, "once you are running with this maybe it would be a good idea for us to talk about what comes next. I'd like to do that, say late in January. Really do it right. Maybe get out of the office, away from the phones, for a day or two and chew over the possibilities. How does that grab you?"

Jerry allows as how he's going to be pretty busy, and he asks that Schaffer be prepared for the chance that the get-together might have to be postponed. Schaffer brushes this aside; "Come on, Jerry. You've got this deal worked out so well that, hell, you won't even be missed for a couple of days." Jerry says okay. Then, as they are breaking up, Jerry makes a request: "On that future planning thing, Phil. I'd like to have Sam Orkin sit in on it if it's all right with you." It obviously is not immediately all right with Phil; he asks why. Jerry says something about Sam being second-in-command and that it's a good idea for him to establish better contact with Schaffer and be up-to-date on general planning. Schaffer says they can talk about Sam's inclusion after the first of the year.

When the time comes for Jerry Considine to ask Phil Schaffer for a raise, he puts his demand strongly and flatly. "That's what I want, Phil. You're going to say it's a lot. I'm not going to argue with you. You may feel it's too much, and maybe I can sympathize with that. But I don't want anything less."

Schaffer tries many approaches to pare Considine's asking figure. Considine will not budge. Finally the boss says, "Jerry, I just don't know if this is in the ball park. I wasn't expecting a request this high. You say nothing lower will be satisfactory. Let me ask you. Suppose I can't give you what you want?"

Jerry will not play. He blandly insists that the request is justified. He is sure that, after due consideration, Phil will see it his way. And that's the end of the meeting. The successful end of the negotiation comes two weeks later for Jerry, when Schaffer tells him his raise is approved.

Jerry Considine's campaign was successful, not just because of the things he did but also because of the things he did not do. He did not, for example, spread the word around that he would leave the company if the raise did not come through. He did not try to magnify his importance to the organization by emphasizing the weakness of his subordinates and his own key role in plans. He did not tie any of his words and actions in with his demand for a raise.

Instead, Jerry accomplished his purposes by indirection. He went out of his way to underscore the strength of his subordinates, their ability to step into his shoes, and his conviction that nobody, including himself is indispensable. Jerry's true convictions might not have squared exactly with his earnest words, but the boss did not know that.

Jerry Considine appeared utterly cool and sure of himself throughout. He gave every indication that he was a conscientious employee who was just about convinced he would be leaving and was taking every possible step to see that the transition to his successor was as smooth as possible.

And Jerry definitely withheld himself from long-term discussions, let alone commitments, strengthening his boss's growing impression that this was a man who was serious about leaving. By conveying through indirection this impression, by making every word and action consistent with the picture of an employee who was preparing to resign, and by sticking calmly to his plan, Jerry induced the boss to assume that he would be going. He never even had to mention it. And in every respect Jerry Considine has maintained his image as a fellow who is sincere about doing anything — within reason — for the good of the company.

You may not be able to get through the raise negotiation without uttering the actual threat to quit. Whether you do or not is not too important. What is vital is that — by visible but indirect means — you *plant* the idea in the boss's mind that you will leave shortly if you don't get what you want. This oblique approach is far more effective than bluster or deliberately-floated rumors.

Imagine that you will quit if you are not given a raise — and follow the scenario presented by your imagination. It's the best way to establish credibility in the "big bomb" approach.

5

interview ploys

Letting the Boss Answer His Own Objections

You go into a raise negotiation prepared with answers to the objections you anticipate that the boss will voice. Your tendency is to want to use the ammunition you have pulled together. Some of the positive points you will bring up yourself. In areas where your case is not so strong you will wait for the boss's questions and objections and then try to refute him with a compelling argument.

Here's how that works. Grady Morton has made his pitch. Now the ball is in the other court, and Morton's boss prepares for a powerful shot. The boss Warren Ottinger says, "Grady, I'm sympathetic to what you've said, but the budget won't permit it."

Morton answers, "The amount of work I have to handle has gone up this past year. I'm supervising seven people instead of five. And next year the load will increase again. I'm doing what I can to hold costs down, but as we've already discussed, we may have to hire two more. Also, we expect that Del Sharp is going to retire, so this will involve breaking in another replacement. The volume of transactions that we handle was up 25 percent, and that will continue to climb. In the light of all this I feel that the raise is justified."

"I know you're doing the best you can," replies Ottinger, "but so are others whose work loads have also increased. With the economy the way it is, we have to watch every penny. I've tried to stretch the budget as far as possible to cover salaries, but we're at the limit. I may consider a little more money for you, but I can't consider anything like what you're asking."

They go back and forth. Grady Morton keeps talking about his increased work load. The boss keeps talking about the budget. Grady may get someplace, but his chances are not great.

This employee is handling the boss's argument in the time tested "yes-but" fashion. The boss advances a reason for not giving the raise; the subordinate says, in effect, "Yes, but. . . .," and makes a counter-argument. Then the boss says, "Yes, but . . . .," and offers a reprise of his objection. Back and forth, without any positive result for the raise seeker.

This is the traditional and most obvious way to attempt to overcome managerial objections. There is a better way. The better way is to try to get the boss to answer *his own* objections. After all, when the boss argues against himself, the argument is likely to be more convincing than when you make it.

The key to this method is the *reflection strategy*. You reflect back to the boss his own position with certain changes. He responds, not to your countering arguments, but rather to the reflection.

Here's one way that it can work. Grady Morton's boss says, "Grady, I'm sympathetic to what you've said, but the budget won't permit it."

Morton replies, "The budget won't permit anything like the raise I've asked for?"

"No."

"And the budget is all set for next year?"

"Yes it is."

The subordinate's questions are restating and seemingly strengthening the boss's objection. Why is he doing that? We'll see in a moment.

"Warren, what you are saying is that this rigid budget won't allow change of any kind."

Ottinger considers this. "Well, I wouldn't say *rigid,* or that it can't be changed in any way." Ottinger can hardly say anything else; they both know that budgets have been revised in the past. Here the subordinate is still reflecting the objection, but with a little twist. He has placed a negative connotation on it, and has made it stronger than the boss is willing to acknowledge. So the boss backs off slightly. Now the subordinate moves to take advantage of this small shift: "Then there are cases in which the budget could be modified, if there were good enough reasons for it."

The boss has to agree with the obvious, but, because he feels that he may be opening up his defenses a tiny bit, he adds a qualification: "Yes, it can be changed if there's good reason to do it. We'd be foolish to put ourselves in such a box that we couldn't move bucks around at all. But that doesn't cover this situation."

Ignoring the last comment, Grady Morton pursues the strategy: "For instance, if next February we were to get a very large government order for the 900 line, I imagine there would be enough flexibility to tool up to meet the order."

Ottinger laughs. "Sure we would, if anything as welcome as that came along. You have to stay flexible." For the moment the exchange has taken a course that seems to leave the topic of Morton's raise. The boss is defending the company's planning. He is reassuring the subordinate that, yes, that organization leaves enough leeway to be able to put money where it is needed most.

"So really," says Morton, "the budget always allows for changes, when those changes are such that they require a new look at the established pattern." Here again the subordinate is simply reflecting back the manager's comments, so the manager agrees.

Now Morton says, "My example was about tooling up, but of course if we got an order like that we'd have to hire people in that area, so I guess the budget would allow for that as well." Ottinger shrugs; "Certainly. There would be no sense in getting the capacity if we didn't get the bodies."

Morton sums this up: "Then the budget can be modified to take care of changed needs regarding people as well as regarding machinery." Ottinger purses his lips, but he can hardly disagree with this way of putting it, since the statement merely rephrases what the boss has just said.

"Well," says Grady Morton, getting it all together, "that's my point. My situation has changed. That's what I want to go over with you." And he begins to spell out his reasons for requesting a raise.

The budget objection has been bypassed. Morton did not refute it. He got the boss to answer his own objection by using the reflection technique. Consider again what this subordinate did by using a few simple questions.

First he reflected back the objection in a stronger form, beefing it up to the point at which the boss had to back off a little ("Well, I wouldn't say *rigid*. . . ."). Morton did more, however, than just strengthen the objection. He gave it a negative connotation with which the boss was reluctant to identify himself.

Following up on this slight concession, Morton turned the position around and got the boss to admit that the budget could be revised if there were sufficient reason to do so. In saying this, Ottinger was simply acknowledging the other side of the coin. If the budget is not rigid, then it can be modified. And the boss was put in the position of defending his and the company's foresightedness by asserting that "you have to stay flexible."

At this point the subordinate asked, in effect, if his manager felt that the needs of people were as important as the need for equipment in considering changes in the budget. Again, the boss could hardly deny this. He can't, after all, look as if he doesn't care about people.

And, having blunted the objection, the subordinate proceeded to identify himself with the boss's position, claim that his changed circumstances fitted into the framework that the boss himself had just set up, and shift the discussion to the merits of his claim.

All of this took place in an atmosphere of calm questioning and unbelligerent agreement. The manager and the raise seeker are not arguing; they seem to concur on everything. But the employee winds up by surmounting a tough objection and giving himself a chance to sell his raise.

The first requirement for this technique is that the boss be willing to answer your questions. There's no reason why he should be unwilling. Your questions are not antagonistic. If anything they seem to indicate a sincere search for information. When the boss reaffirms his objection, your next question appears to reinforce his argument. When he backs off a position that you have made too strong, he does so of his own volition. You haven't forced anything. He is backing off, not backing down.

Your series of questions almost dictate the answers (which is what a skilled lawyer does in cross-examining a witness). Each question grows out of the boss's answer to the last one. You reflect back his answer to him with a slight twist, but without overt opposition. You are leading him along the path of least resistance, not fighting him.

You have taken control of the interview at this point. Your control will last as long as you don't make it obvious that you have taken control. Don't be misled into posing a question that is too combative, that evokes an emphatic negative answer. Maintain the atmosphere of general agreement and enlightening discussion.

The boss may see where this is leading. But even if he hesitates to go along with a question, you can point out that he has, in effect, already answered it — "This is just another way of saying what you just said a moment ago, etc."

When you have led the boss to take a position that can encompass your request, state the proposition in the same cool unbelligerent way in which you have put your questions. Then assume that the objection has been disposed of, and go on to pursue your goal.

You have really nothing to lose. The worst that can happen is that the boss stubbornly insists that, no matter what he has just said, his objection still stands. Inside, he is apt to be at least a little shaken. You can shift to a more aggressive posture with a better chance of success.

Subliminal Trade-Offs

Boss Max Kubelik leans back as he listens to Fred Miller's pitch for a raise. Miller is doing a good crisp job of ticking off his reasons, but Kubelik's mind seems to be wandering. As Miller pauses, the boss comes on the air. "You were saying a minute ago that you were able to handle the "B" component runs on just two presses, Fred. I haven't been over there in a while, but the way I remember it, I can't figure out how you do it. When I was in your job we had trouble, even when we ganged the jobs. You see, the operators. . . ."

Miller restrains his impatience as the boss launches into a reminisence. "He's trying to get me off the track," the subordinate says to himself. When he has a chance he breaks in: "Well, you've seen the production sheets, Max. What happened was that there was a field modification on those presses that came down from the factory. They run at a higher capacity now than they used to. If you want to go over the reports again. . . ." Kubelik says no, there's no reason to go over the reports. Miller does not want to dwell on the point. He can't take credit for the modifications in the equipment, and so he wants to move along to cover points that will help him get the raise. He determines that he will try to keep the discussion focused on the main topic — his raise — without wandering off into side issues.

Maybe Fred Miller is making something of a mistake. He assumes that Kubelik's chatty excursion was an attempt to divert him. But maybe it wasn't. As a matter of fact, what we have just seen here is an example of a manager, who has been promoted to a level at which he doesn't have to "get his hands dirty," yearning for a little shop talk and nostalgic rambling back to the old days. Miller assumed that it would have done him no good to gab about machines and small details of the job. But he might have been giving the boss something that the boss will never come out and ask for, but which he needs.

There are things that you may be able to give the boss that would have no weight at all when placed on the scale of objectivity, but which have subjective importance to him — and which may make him more receptive to your raise request.

One such "subliminal" selling point is the opportunity to talk shop. A boss who has come up through the ranks often thinks back nostalgically on his earlier days. Occasionally he feels the urge to get into the thick of it again, but he can't give in to that urge. The currently popular philosophy of management dictates that a high-level executive should not get involved with operating problems. He must leave those to subordinates, confining himself to "big-picture" thinking, long-range planning, and abstract decision-making.

This can get boring. The executive may yearn for the chance to at least talk about the kinds of nitty-gritty problems he used to solve. It's a form of escape. But his subordinates don't afford him that opportunity. They don't chat; they report.

If you have this kind of boss, you may do him and yourself a favor by getting into an occasional chat about the details of your operation. Don't go to him with problems. Work the shop-talk in unobtrusively: "Since you used to slave out on that plant floor yourself, you may be interested in something we found out last week. Got a second for some nonessential conversation?" The boss may welcome it. This may be just what he needs. And at no cost to yourself you can solidify your position with him.

Another thing you can give the boss — something not included in the job description — is information. This is emphatically not to suggest that you should become some kind of informer. But the higher a man climbs on the ladder, the more remote he becomes from what people on the lower levels are thinking and feeling. You should not be obvious about this, or do it too often, but every once in a while provide a few tidbits of knowledge that may have nothing to do with the official transactions that pass between you and your superior. It gives him a chance to see a different side of you. You demonstrate that you can be an observer who is sensitive to trends and implications. And it provides him with input that he may not be able to get as readily anywhere else.

And then there is loyalty. Of course you are loyal to the boss when there are no great strains placed on that loyalty. But sometimes it's not a bad idea to convey the impression that your loyalty can be stretched beyond these conventional boundaries. Remember Viscount Melbourne's remark, "I need men who will support me when I am in the wrong."

There will be times when your boss is definitely in the wrong. He may be fighting a quixotic battle with another department when all the logic is on the other department's side. Others will try to tout the boss off his crusade, and they will avoid being pulled into it. You should say what you think. If you think he is wrong, tell him so. But then, after you have spoken your piece and he insists on going ahead anyway, get in there and support him 100 percent. Now this is a selective stratagem. You certainly should not indulge in it to the endangerment of your job, not to the distinct detriment of the company. But once in a great while, when your boss is way out on a limb and the bough is cracking behind him, give him a full measure of cooperation. Once may be enough. He'll remember it.

Some bosses want and need a sounding board. Suppose you are talking to a manager. You finish with the business at hand and he says, "There's something I'd like to bounce off you." And he launches into description of a wild, far-out idea. Your first impulse may be to come back with constructive criticism. Examine that impulse carefully. The boss may not be looking for constructive criticism at this stage. His idea may be at such a nebulous phase that he wants only to talk about it, and have somebody listen, nodding his head. You may wish to indicate in some way that you don't buy it altogether — "Boy, that's something I never thought about. I'd have to really consider it before I could give you any kind of reaction, but it sure is an eye-opener." Fine. This may be what the boss needs — a ready and sympathetic ear.

The boss has troubles too. From time to time he may tell them to you. Some subordinates react unsympathetically to this. They feel that their problems are greater than the boss's, and that they will be damned if they are going to let him cry on their shoulders. This attitude shows through. The boss, a little embarrassed, will not repeat the experiment.

Listen to the boss's troubles sympathetically. You may learn something. You may be in his shoes one day. But, whether or not that is a possibility, you will be giving him a chance to get something off his chest. He may be a better and happier boss as a result, and he will also probably feel more sympathetic toward you and your needs.

Are these things toadying? They could be called that. But they could also be called friendly cooperation, human understanding, or establishment of better rapport. If being nice to the boss goes totally against your grain, don't try it. There are many other approaches you can use to get a raise; this is not a major one in any case.

But it does help to offer the boss certain subliminal trade-offs. Not that you point to them in asking for a raise. You do no more than say, "And of course I will give you the same support and loyalty that I always have." It can't hurt.

Package Deals

Harry Drago faces a dilemma. He would like to give Floyd Wick a good raise. Wick is a valuable man; he has pressed hard for more money; and Drago is afraid that Wick will leave the company within six months if he doesn't get what he wants. (Whether or not Wick is really determined to go is not the point; the point is that the subordinate has successfully convinced Drago that this is a strong possibility.)

Floyd Wick sits across the desk, waiting. Drago has considered his options. He cannot approve anything more than a modest increase in salary; the top brass has given a flat "no" to that. However, there are items under the heading of compensation that he can play with.

"Floyd," says Drago, "I am going to level with you. I can't give you much in the way of a salary boost, for the reasons that I have already indicated. But I think, on the whole I can do a lot better than that for you. Let's see what kind of a package we can put together." And, as Wick watches alertly and somewhat skeptically, Drago starts to put figures down on a piece of paper.

Harry Drago is doing what a lot of bosses do. He is "putting together a package" which will include nonsalary items that comprise benefits and some kind of bonus plan.

Wick's skepticism is justified. When the boss begins to put together a "package" in lieu of the salary raise you have demanded, it is well to scrutinize what he is doing with the same care you would use in watching the hands of the fellow at the carnival who manipulates the walnut shells and the pea — and sometimes for the same reasons. There can be a lot less to this kind of "package" than meets the eye. But not always. You should not respond automatically with cynicism. The right kind of package can be lucrative. And if a package is all you can get, well, you will want to get as much as you can out of it.

"Let's add up," says Drago, "what the company will really be paying you." When the boss says this, he is about to add up the benefits that the employer pays for. Although these benefits are still referred to as "fringes," there is nothing "fringey" about them to the boss. Benefits add up to more than 25% of the total labor cost of American business, so it is no wonder that the boss would like to get more credit for these items than he usually receives. Indeed, in more than a few companies the cost of fringes may run as high as 40 percent.

Traditionally your boss is stuck with the fringes — the health plan, the life insurance, the retirement benefits — and he knows it. The word "plan" is usually a misnomer when applied to fringe benefits. In most cases there has been little planning in their establishment. They just grew. For example, if you work in a nonunion job for a company that is partially unionized, you are likely to be getting a "free ride" by being given the same fringes that the union has bargained into its contract.

Top management is not very happy with the benefits picture. Benefits cost a lot of money. And yet management complains that it does not receive credit for all that it spends on fringes. New employees, from the highest to the lowest, usually receive neat little booklets telling them all about the fine extras for which the company foots the bill; but alas (from management's point of view) members of the working force tend to take all this for granted, never regarding it as part of compensation.

There is, perhaps, considerable justice in management's lament. However, that is not our problem. If the organization has, for whatever reason, gotten itself into the box of laying out large sums for insurance and retirement benefits, you will of course accept these things. However, when they ask you to think of them just as you would dollars in the pay envelope, it is time to say, "Thanks, but no thanks; I'd rather have the cash." They, naturally, have contractual obligations and they will have to go on giving you the fringes whether you say you asked for them or not, and in spite of your ingratitude. If you wish to shed a tear for the ownership of the firm at this point, do so. It would not be inappropriate. But our interest is in getting you more money, one way or another; so the only proper posture you can have in considering the basic fringes is, "Of course, they are nice. Now let's put them aside and talk about what you're going to *pay* me." This makes management unhappy, but in many ways they have asked for it.

The whole benefits system, besides being very expensive, has been so fouled up by industry that we may find ourselves being less sympathetic toward management's plight than we might otherwise have been. A good example is health insurance, with the employer picking up at least part of the tab. But how good is the plan? Look at Blue Cross, the most widely-known scheme. Blue Cross has gone sky-high in price. But, as Peter Drucker points out in *"Management: Tasks; Responsibilities; Practices"* (Harper & Row, 1974), "it does not provide for payment of medical and hospital bills when the worker needs it the most, that is, when he is out of work. But it pays full expenses for the minor illnesses of his family while he is employed — which is a major reason for the high premium." It might make more sense to protect the worker against disastrous charges while he is working, while assuring him of coverage while he is out of work. But this is not the way the plan is structured, and there seems no way of changing it.

Employers have been disconsolate because they receive little in the way of kudos for their retirement plans. But here again the schemes have often been rigged so that they are emphatically not in the interest of the employee.

Typically, a pension plan would require the worker to be with the company for five years before he would even begin to "vest" in the plan. Then, from the sixth to the fifteenth year, he would vest at the rate of one-tenth of the retirement plan per year. So he would have to remain on staff for fifteen years before qualifying for the full value of the pension. Spreading unhappiness with this kind of arrangement has led to the swelling impetus toward legislation that will give the employee assurance that he is amassing retirement benefits as soon as he is enrolled in a plan.

Nevertheless, as unsatisfactory as some of these fringes have been and continue to be, they constitute a massive trend in American business. Increasingly we see a picture of businesses which are in effect "owned" by the employees. The employees are not in any way direct owners, or even voluntary owners. Their ownership is exerted through trustees, via the medium of the massive benefits arrangements. But the worker sees little real benefit from all this, and it is not to be wondered at that he receives the gospel of his financial dominance with a grain of salt and often with active hostility.

Management associations may refer in glowing terms to this trend as "profit sharing." The individual worker sees very little of it. Drucker also remarks, "The real property of the employee...and the income on which he depends, is his job. Profit — even if he gets all of it — is a fringe benefit, and not a very big one. *Rational behavior for the employee is clearly to maximize wage and salary income, even at the expense of his own share in profits.*" (Italics added.) This is not the presidential candidate of the Socialist Labor Party talking; this is Peter Drucker, America's leading corporate philosopher. We would be foolish not to heed him.

When the boss talks about profit-sharing we are tempted to nod our heads and indicate unqualified approval for the proposition that we want to share in profits, even at the risk of some security or some sacrifice in fixed earnings. After all, we are beneficiaries of the free enterprise system, are we not? If we say, "I'd rather get it in the pay check," doesn't that stamp us as lacking in the gumption and enterprising spirit that have made America great?

For example, when Harry Drago says, "Would you be interested in a profit sharing arrangement?," shouldn't Floyd Wick reply with an enthusiastic affirmative?

No he shouldn't. There are always hitches. To begin with, when a boss talks about profit sharing as compensation, he is almost never offering the subordinate a larger share in the high policy-making councils of the company. He is not suggesting that you sit on board meetings, decide on investment policies, place your hand on the real levers of privilege that make the organization go. He is suggesting that your compensation be keyed, in some way, to the success of the company or a division of it.

But when you point this out he is likely to say, "Ah, but on the other hand you are not taking a risk. You will get your basic salary no matter how bad things may get. But if things go well, look at the money you'll earn." This is not profit sharing in the true sense. You are being asked to settle for the possibility of a bonus geared to performance.

That's what is happening right now between Drago and Wick. Drago has gotten through with his notations on the fine benefit package — retirement, insurance, health — that Floyd has been getting and will continue to get. Wick is not exactly out of his mind with enthusiasm. He is reminded of the way a life insurance salesman, in giving you the "total package," adds in your social security and other goodies that the insurance company has no hand whatever in providing. However, Drago has just been leading up to his big pitch.

"Floyd, you've made a case for your performance during the year, and I'm impressed with it. You point out that your continued high productivity will pay off big for the company in the coming year. I am glad to hear it. I believe it. But — do *you* believe it? Are you willing to let us put the company's money where your mouth is? I am going to offer you a deal whereby you can't lose anything — at the very worst you will make the basic salary you receive right now — but under which, if things go well, you can really get up into the big money. Now — do you have enough confidence in yourself and the organization to go for that?"

Sounds fine. Can Floyd Wick really say no to that? Well, he should say neither yes nor no until he knows more about it.

When you are offered a "profit sharing" deal, the first thing to do is determine its real nature. It is probably a bonus arrangement, contingent on certain things happening. What things? Therein lies the potential value, or lack of value, of the proposition. The first question is how much will be paid when? How will the bonus be computed? A plan which is extremely hard to understand is not likely to work in your favor. Along with this you will want to know if the performance on which the bonus is based will be reflected in figures that will be made available to you as soon as they become available. You don't want to buy a pig in a poke. If management indicates that you cannot see the raw figures – that you will just be told how you came out – then you don't want any part of it.

The bonus should be simple. At any given time you should be able to figure out accurately how you are doing.

How frequently would the bonus be paid? Is it to be one lump sum at the end of the year? That's no good. Indeed, you can point out that experts in motivation reject such schemes because they do not provide frequent enough reinforcement. If you want a bonus arrangement at all, you may want one that is paid, say quarterly, with a fresh start for the next quarter. Ah, the boss may say, that is not fair to management; suppose the company does very well the first quarter and you collect a big bonus. Then it does very poorly the following three quarters. You still receive your basic pay. At the end of the year, because of the abnormally high performance recorded in the first quarter, you come out with more than you are entitled to.

Fair or not, that is the kind of arrangement you want. Because, after all, you do not have anything like full control over the factors that go into the performance that serves as the basis of your bonus. And this leads to the next question: what are the measures by which your bonus will be figured and to what extent do they lie within your control? If you are a salesman and payment is keyed to volume, you have a reasonably strong grip on the situation. But if you are depending on company performance, or even the performance of a unit in which you play only a part, you are relying on what others do. Your bonus is not a clear function of your own efforts; it can be blown by the unlucky concatenation of outside events, the incompetence of your colleagues, or the machinations of your superiors. Therefore it is not unfair for you to receive extra money when things go well within a limited period. After all, you are taking plenty of risks.

What is the base of the bonus? If it is a small percentage that uses current performance, or last year's performance, as the starting-point of computation then it may be a lot more lucrative than one which features seductively high percentages and sums, but which comes into play only if the organization performs at an out-of-sight level.

All these are considerations that should go through the mind of Floyd Wick, and through your mind when the boss offers you a bonus. If you cannot get any more in wages, bargain on the bonus along these lines:

- Make the basis of computation simple and clear.
- Get paid as frequently as possible, and never accept a provision that requires you to give anything back.
- Try for high percentages, but, even more important, make sure that the base point at which the bonus begins to pay off is as low as you can make it.

As it stands now, a bonus plan of some kind is about the only thing of true potential value that a boss can offer you if he is not giving you a salary raise. For a while in certain industries, executives were bemused by the possibilities that they saw in owning company stock. Characteristically, a company — with great fanfare — would notify a newly-promoted manager that he would now enjoy the great privilege of possessing a "piece of the action." Everything was automatic. A loan was arranged, and the lucky employee became the owner of, say, 100 shares, with more to come as he went along. However, at the same time he signed a piece of paper requiring him to sell back the stock if he left the company. This play had, for a time, great influence on many executives of the more credulous kidney. However, stock performance in general has shed a cold light of reality on such cosmetic fringes. The granting of stock options has come to be thought of as an equally dubious boon.

But otherwise the fringe package is pretty well fixed. Everybody gets the same benefits. The life insurance premiums may vary, but they vary in accordance with salary range. So everybody is apt to be getting benefits that he does not need and coming out short on things he could use more of; and the company is picking up an enormous tab and complaining bitterly about it.

The thoroughly unsatisfactory nature of the whole fringe scene has led toward a burgeoning movement that may result in a refreshing infusion of flexibility into the salary/benefits mix. Dr. Mortimer R. Feinberg, president of BFS Psychological Associates in New York, refers to the coming "compensation cafeteria." This is of interest to you, because you may be able to work out, at least to some degree, a "mix" that is more in your favor than the standard package would be.

Stuart Corning, Vice President, State Street Bank of Boston, describes the "compensation cafeteria" as a means by which "the total mix of a man's salary and compensation can be adjusted depending on his age and needs."

Here are three examples provided by Dr. Feinberg of how it might work.

Tom Smith is 45, married, with three children — the oldest a freshman in college. He is satisfied with his present salary — but is concerned that, if anything should happen to him now, the children would not be able to get through their schooling.

Here is the present "mix" for Tom Smith — and how it might be changed to more closely meet his needs.

	Current	*Proposed*
Salary	$25,000	$25,000
Pension	2,265	1,765
Profit Sharing	3,000	3,000
Life Insurance	712	1,212
Major Medical	302	302
	$31,279	$31,279

Tom gets the same salary, a little less in pension, but more insurance — his principal current concern.

Here's another case. Jeff Jones is 26 and single. Salary is important to him. He wants to have fun and maintain a life-style; and his contemporaries judge accomplishment by salary, not fringes. Here is Jeff's current package, and the one proposed for him.

	Current	*Proposed*
Salary	$15,000	$18,000
Pension	1,360	460
Profit Sharing	1,800	0
Life Insurance	403	103
Major Medical	77	77
	$18,640	$18,640

Jeff is getting more of it up front, where it counts to him.

A third example. Alec Brown is 54. His children are married. His needs are simple. He is interested primarily in his estate. Here's how it might be mixed for him.

	Current	*Proposed*
Salary	$45,000	$40,000
Pension	4,077	9,717
Profit Sharing	5,400	4,760
Life Insurance	878	878
Major Medical	302	302
	$55,657	$55,657

The individual figures in each of these examples are unimportant. The principle is important, to the extent that it spreads through industry. It may be that, frustrated in your desire for a raise in salary, you may serve as a pioneer of the compensation cafeteria in your company by getting management to at least work out a "mix" that is more favorable to you.

We've already gone over the questions you will want to ask about any profit sharing plan. Look with equal care at other elements of the mix. The health care plan, for example; can it be stretched to cover your kids beyond their majority, even though they are not students? (More and more kids choose not to go to college right away, or to drop out for at least a year.) Does it cover psychiatric care? Can you obtain a plan that is *really* "major" in that it offers this important benefit? (If you do get a plan that provides psychiatric care, you may do well to arrange for reassurance that the company will in no way be privy to your availing yourself of the privilege. Many employees are afraid to get needed psychiatric help under a company plan because they fear it will endanger their jobs. This seems to be particularly true of middle managers. In one company that adopted such a plan, it was found after a couple of years that members of top management and rank and file workers were making ample use of it. Middle managers and supervisors, however, used it hardly at all.)

Your questions about a retirement pension are simple and clear-cut. How quickly do you vest in it fully? If possible, you should become fully vested immediately. And, along with this, is the plan portable? At what point may you leave your job, for whatever reason, and take the plan with you? If there are substantial strings on a retirement plan you may properly scorn it as a meaningless gimmick used by management to force you to stay around.

Let's go back to Harry Drago and Floyd Wick. Drago outlines a plan involving a certain limited sweetening of the fringes and a bonus arrangement that looks, at first glance, very promising. Wick asks a few questions, enough to elicit the information we have suggested he needs in order to evaluate such a proposition.

Then Floyd Wick says, "This is something I wasn't prepared for, Harry. I still feel that I deserve the raise I asked for, and I'm disappointed that you can't see your way clear to give it to me. However, I will consider this, but as you must understand I need some time. Can we get together again Monday or Tuesday?" Drago has little choice but to say yes.

On the following Monday Wick comes in prepared for a fresh negotiation. He has a new set of proposals, all aimed at improving the package that Drago has presented. "The percentage on the bonus plan is okay, Harry," he says, "but the method of computation is a little complicated. I don't see how I can follow it. Let's base it on straight volume before taxes. And as you describe it now it doesn't start low enough. We would have to have the best year in our history for me to get anything. I expect to do fine with my end, but I'm depending on a lot of other people as well. So we'll have to change that."

Wick bargains hard, using the original package as a base and working up from there. Drago fights, but Wick wins on more points than he loses. And he winds up with a pretty fair mix.

When the boss suggests nonsalary supplements instead of the raise you request, he has opened a door. That door may lead into a dead end if you go through it too quickly. Your strategy should be to keep the door open while you shine a light into the maze into which it leads and take your time in planning your next moves. It's usually best to find out as much as you can — then break off the interview so that you can come back with some counterproposals designed to sweeten the package. You are apt to be able to improve them to some extent. After all, the boss has indicated his agreement with the principle by broaching the possibility, so you are entitled to work for as favorable a deal as possible in exchange for giving up your well-deserved salary requests.

Don't go for a package deal until you are sure you have gotten as much as you can in salary. Don't buy the assertion that you should begin to look on all of the compulsory fringes as compensation. Make sure that the package you are offered is likely to pay off. Then work hard to sweeten each aspect of it.

Playing One Against the Other

The offer of another job can be a powerful lever in prying loose a raise. *Can* be; it's not always. Certain conditions must be present. The outside offer should be of some substance. It doesn't have to be a hard and fast open-end offer ("You can start here any time you want.") but the possibilities should be pretty good. Bluffing about moving to another job when you've got only a deuce in the hole is a special and extreme technique. Furthermore, for the threat to have weight, your boss should be convinced that you really have the option to move out. Furthermore he should be concerned to keep you on his payroll. If he doesn't give much of a damn one way or the other you are not able to exert much leverage.

The employee who hesitates to use the "other job" tactic because it is too rough and risky can sometimes achieve similar effects through deployment of a more circumspect stratagem. This is the "other department" ploy. It involves playing another manager off against your boss. This approach can be tricky, but on the whole it presents fewer perils than the threat to leave for another job.

Here's one way it works. Kris Nordstrom works for Tom Bean. Bean is a square shooter, but a fairly demanding boss. He runs a taut ship. He is not open handed with raises. Kris Nordstrom is not too happy with some aspects of her job, but on the whole she thinks she is pretty well situated. She knows the ropes, likes the work, and would like to keep on doing the work. But she would like to get considerably more money.

How to get it? Kris does a good job, but Bean takes superior work for granted. He is proud of his department, and expects all his subordinates to take the same pride in the humming efficiency he has managed to engender. Kris gets pleasure out of being associated with a first-rate operation, but the satisfaction does not soothe her itch for a raise. She is good. She could probably get another job, but she does not want to leave the company. She knows Tom Bean well enough to realize that his reaction to an ultimatum is not likely to be positive. Bean's feelings would be hurt if Kris let it be known that she had been looking for another job. While he values her contribution he might just say, "Fine, go ahead and take the other job."

During Tom Bean's vacation Kris Nordstrom has a lot of time on her hands. She is asked to help out in another department and, for a number of reasons, she is glad to oblige. The manager of this other department is Otis Cumberland. Cumberland is quite a different proposition from Tom Bean. He takes a relaxed attitude toward the running of his department, socializes with the troops a lot more, enjoys heart-to-heart chats and, sometimes, personal service.

Kris is not much impressed with Cumberland's way of doing things. She prefers Tom Bean's cooler, more efficient approach. But her temporary association with the other department presents an opportunity.

At the end of the first day that Kris Nordstrom is assigned to him, Otis Cumberland calls her in to talk. He expresses beaming appreciation for the quickness with which she has caught on, and the effective help she has already been able to contribute. Among other things Kris has been genially cooperative about going for coffee, and she did a little personal shopping for Cumberland during her lunch hour. Ordinarily Kris is by no means a "go-for," and Tom Bean doesn't expect her to be one, but this is all part of her plan.

During the few days she spends with Cumberland, Kris Nordstrom goes out of her way to impress. She does things that she simply would not do as part of her usual job. Cumberland is pleased, and Kris takes the opportunity to say, "This has been a real pleasure. Quite a change of pace. I've enjoyed working here. If you feel I've done all right, I'd appreciate it if you could let Tom Bean know about it." Cumberland hints at the possibility that the chance for a transfer would not be out of the question at some point; and Kris does not act as if the idea is an anathema to her.

Word gets to Tom Bean. He mentions it to Kris with an air of studied amusement: "Otis Cumberland thought you were a big help, Kris. Quite impressed. Wouldn't surprise me if he had some thoughts about luring you over there to work for him permanently. Not that that would be in any way in the cards, of course."

With a different boss and in different circumstances Kris would answer this question (and it really is a question, although not phrased as one) differently. But to Tom Bean she says, "I did my best of course, and I think Mr. Cumberland appreciated it. They don't have anything like the organization we have here, of course. It was fun. Easy, really, once you are used to handling what I handle in this job. Mostly I enjoyed the chance to give them an idea of how much we're on the ball." Bean seems satisfied, and they get back to business.

But Kris Nordstrom has made a little ripple. Two or three times subsequently she manages to "help out" briefly in Cumberland's department, on her lunch hour, and in between regular assignments. Once she stays late to "help Mr. Cumberland organize his reporting system a little better." Tom Bean may not be overjoyed at this but he makes no comment.

The time comes for Kris to make her pitch for a raise. Bean is cool when he learns the figure; "That's high, Kris. You're doing a good job but that kind of increase would not be warranted." Kris's response is wistful; "I wish you could say yes. I like working for you. But you know, really, in the past year I've gotten a better idea of my value to the company and how much I can do. In a way you spoil us, Mr. Bean. Your standards are so high you make other jobs seem easy. I want to continue here, but I do need this raise, and I think I've earned it and can continue to earn it."

Kris has issued no ultimata. She has expressed her desire to stay in her present assignment. Her manner conveys that she thinks a move to another assignment would be less satisfying professionally. But at the same time she projects the image of someone who may unhappily be driven to consider such a move because of her need for money.

Tom Bean's pride in his department starts to work on Kris Nordstrom's side. Bean likes Otis Cumberland all right, but he is amusedly contemptuous of the slack way in which Cumberland runs things. He thinks it would be a shame if somebody as good as Kris went to work for Cumberland; a shame and a waste of talent. Furthermore it would be a waste of Tom Bean's efforts, because he takes a lot of credit for shaping Kris Nordstrom into the efficient worker that she is today. Beyond that, it would be a blow to Bean's pride for one of his key people to indicate a preference for working elsewhere in the company. Bean is confident that his people respect him, tough as he may be sometimes, and that they want to work for him. For Kris Nordstrom to even evidence the desire for a transfer would not feel good to Bean and it would not look good to Bean's bosses. He is not the kind of man who welcomes being put at a disadvantage, particularly by the likes of Otis Cumberland.

Bean tries to talk Kris into agreeing to a lower figure, but she is — regretfully — adamant. Kris Nordstrom gets her raise.

Any interest you can arouse in another department or another boss is potentially useful. At the very least it can shed a favorable light on your efforts. Used with a little more purpose, as in this case, it can be a way of exerting indirect pressure on the boss. You get yourself liked by another manager. You let your own boss know about it. You emphasize your desire to stay where you are, but you hint wistfully at how nice it is to be appreciated and how you feel you might get a better financial deal with the other boss, no matter how inferior the spot might be in all other respects. By using this approach you're in an off-the-hook position. You have not sought out the favor of the counterpart managers.

There are variations on this technique. Here's an example of one. Stan Fessler's job has, for some time, involved him in considerable contact with the customer service department. Stan has gotten to know Wade Seminick, head of customer service pretty well. Fessler has asked questions about the service department and shown a flattering interest in what they do. Culling the fruits of his homework he has even been able to make a few suggestions to Seminick, one or two of which are not bad.

Seminick says, with a simle, "Hey, Stan, ever think about coming over on this side of the fence? You might not be too bad at it." Fessler displays pleasure at the suggestion. A few days later he says to Seminick, "I've been thinking about what you said, about me maybe having a better future here. I don't know. Can you tell me more about it?"

The customer service manager may or may not have been entirely serious when he made the initial comment to Stan Fessler. At any rate he now talks about the possibility with at least superficial seriousness, although he adds that there is no opening at the moment. Perhaps Seminick is just being obliging to someone who has been cooperative; perhaps he is really interested. It doesn't matter. Fessler strings out these conversations with Seminick until the period approaching raise time. Then he talks with his own boss: "By the way, I've been trying to keep good liaison with customer service, as you suggested. So I've been talking to Wade Seminick quite a bit, and I think we have a nice relationship built up, which means things run smoother between us and them. I've even been able to suggest some things to him. Wade went so far as to make me a tentative offer, if I ever wanted to switch over to that department. I just forgot about it at first, but it came up again the other day. Then I thought, well, maybe I'd better talk it over with you. I'm happy here, even though I don't feel I've moved along fast enough in some respects, but if it were for everybody's good all around I'd certainly consider moving to service. What do you think?"

The worst thing that can happen is that Fessler's boss asks Seminick about and Seminick disavows any serious interest. This would mean only that Fessler misunderstood. But Fessler's boss might not take Seminick's comments at face value. He may still harbor some suspicion that the other department head would like to take one of his men away from him. This, in turn, might mean that Seminick has seen possibilities in Fessler which Stan's boss has not seen, and can bring them out. That is not a prospect to enchant Fessler's manager.

Or, Seminick might say, yes, Stan has some possibilities. We might be interested in him, but of course that would depend upon your own plans for him and his importance to you. Fessler might just come out of this with a transfer to a job for which he has specifically been requested; not an unfavorable situation. Or his boss might say, no, we want to keep Stan around. This would enhance Stan's bargaining power at raise time.

In the variation just described, the idea is to evoke some interest, however mild, from another manager and treat it seriously. You really can't be blamed for wanting to seek new pastures, and if you have unwittingly magnified the solidity of the other boss's interest, you can't be blamed much for that either. You can't lose in the by-play, and you may well come out of it with a bigger raise than you might otherwise have gotten.

There is another interesting twist on this tactic. In principle it resembles the ploy used by a marginal British business promoter (call him Featherston) a few years ago. Featherston was waiting — in a London restaurant he could ill-afford — to meet two money men whom he desperately needed to impress. A few tables away he recognized a solitary luncher. It was Aristotle Onassis. After some thought Featherston got up and diffidently approached the magnate: "Excuse me, Mr. Onassis." Onassis looked at him coldly, but Featherston hurried on with his plaintive story. He so needed to impress the men who would be joining him in a few minutes. Onassis could be of so much help. "All you have to do, Mr. Onassis, is, when you go past my table — perhaps on your way to the men's room — please say hello to me. That's all I ask." Onassis at first tries to brush it off, but finally — perhaps touched by Mr. Featherston's earnestness — he agreed.

The money men arrive. Featherston is giving them his pitch. A man appears alongside their table. They look up to see that it is Aristotle Onassis. Onassis smiles at Featherston and says, "Hello, Mr. Featherston." And Featherston replies, "Buzz off, Onassis. Can't you see I'm busy?"

The adaption of this bit to raise getting goes as follows. You cultivate another manager in the company, get him talking about possibilities in his department. He doesn't have to be serious about it, or even hold out any hope. You take what he says as a serious offer, however — *and then turn it down.* You can now say to your own boss, "Jim Callaway wanted me to come over there with him but I turned him down cold." And then you ask for more money.

It's always good to make yourself a cooperative and valuable worker, outside your operation as well as inside. It can be additionally useful to see that your boss gets the idea that you are well thought of and even coveted by other bosses — however much substance there may be to it. This enables you to work a species of the "other job" routine without going to the trouble of trying to line up an outside job, and without incurring the risks and possible unpleasantness that the outside-job threat entails.

Naturally there is always the possibility, remote though it may be, that you will actually wind up being transferred; so it's just as well to make sure the other department is one in which you would not mind working.

6

weakness into strength

Strategy for Covering Your Weak Points

Russ Murray has been Director of Mail Order Sales for Upshur & Company for two years. In a week he will be talking to his boss, Andy Garra, Marketing Vice President. The subject will be more money for Russ. He hopes he can manage to get a substantial raise.

On the whole Russ Murray can look with some satisfaction on the job he has been doing. When he took over the operation he did a lot of things right. He had several heart-to-heart talks with Garra. Murray knows the requirements of his job that seem most important to his boss. He was able to work out with Garra an informal set of job standards, and since then Murray has managed to produce a good record against each of these criteria — with one exception. But the exception is a major one, and it looms as the biggest stumbling block to the raise that Russ desires.

One of the things that Garra emphasized was the necessity for coming up with a way of selling Upshur's "Majestic Line," the company's most expensive service, by mail. It had never been done successfully in the past.

Murray worked hard on methods of moving the Majestic Line. He experimented with various lists. He tested letters with widely-differing appeals. He tried premiums and money-back guarantees. But progress was practically nil.

Andy Garra is a tough bargainer at raise time. Murray knows his boss well enough to know that the failure to achieve a breakthrough on

Majestic will be thrust at him as a reason for denying anything but the most nominal raise. So Russ Murray will have to come up with a means of countering this ploy.

For the past few months Russ has really been going all-out on Majestic. While most of the tests have not shown enough promise to be expanded, one particular appeal — applied to a new list which Murray just found out about — looks as if it might have some possibilities. It's too early to come to any definite conclusions, there will have to be a lot more testing, but there are enough clues in the initial test to justify a certain amount of optimism. Of course there have been other efforts that showed initial promise, only to peter out when tried more fully.

Russ Murray looks over the preliminary findings on this test, called Project 35. His first inclination is to write it up as quickly as possible and submit it to Garra in advance of the discussion about money. But then Murray gives this idea a little more thought. He broadens his thinking to take in the whole strategy that he will use in trying to get the raise. And then he decides not to inform Garra in advance (there is no administrative procedure that compels him to do so). Instead Murray goes back into the files of past efforts and begins to do some paperwork.

The time of the confrontation arrives. Russ Murray tells Andy Garra what he wants in the way of a raise. He reviews the reasons for his request, hitting the high points of his performance. And then Garra, as Murray knew he would, brings up the big question. "Before we go any farther, Russ, I'll agree that you've done some nice things with the department. But much as I'd like to concentrate only on the successes, I have to point to the Majestic thing. Let's face it, you haven't gotten anyplace with that part of the job, and it's a damned important thing. Really, before I could consider that kind of raise I would have to see much better results in the Majestic area. So far you haven't come up with anything."

Murray nods. "Andy, I know that of the objectives we talked about when I took this job over, Majestic has been by far the roughest. I could expand on some of the things that I think you'll agree I've handled quite well, but let's stay on the Majestic issue. I took on an assignment there that had never been done in this company before, isn't that right?"

"Sure, but that's part of your job, Russ. The assumption was that you could get someplace with it. You *did* take it on."

"And I said I would do my level best with it. Of course I've been busy with a lot of other things. For one thing there was the campaign on "Happy Days" — and the big mailing on "Canopus." Maybe I'm being immodest, but I think you'd have to agree that those efforts went pretty well."

Garra says, "Yes, I have no complaint with your work on those campaigns, Russ. In fact I'd say you showed me that you really have something on the ball. But I keep coming back to the failure to do anything on Majestic."

"Well, you agree that I have done all right in most aspects of my assignment?" Garra nods. Murray continues, "But Majestic is the big problem. You will go along with me, won't you, Andy, when I say that Majestic presents one hell of a problem?"

"Sure it does, but I figured when I gave you the job you would be able to at least open up some cracks on it. So far we haven't seen a damn thing. It's this total absence of results in that area that gives me trouble about being able to justify a raise anything near the size that you're asking for."

"So it boils down to Majestic. Obviously we haven't had any big success with it. . . ."

Garra interrupts. "It's not a matter of no big success, Russ. It's a matter of no accomplishment at all. If there were even a hint of progress I might feel differently, but. . . ." Garra shrugs and spreads his hands.

Murray leans forward earnestly. "Well, I feel somewhat the same way you do, Andy. In fact, faced with the string of bum results on Majestic, I was on the verge of withdrawing my request to you, or at least cutting it way down, since I did not have anything even remotely promising to show you. And if I understand you, Andy, you're looking for something that gives us at least some indication that we are going to crack the problem, right?"

"Yes. But we haven't had it."

Now Russ Murray produces some papers and shoves them toward Garra. "Uh-huh. I came to just about the same conclusion when I was working these up. Nothing new to you there. Those charts show our results on various Majestic tests pretty nearly up to the present time. They're not encouraging."

Garra glances at the charts, then looks across the desk at Murray. "Yeah. That's what I mean, Russ, and that's why I say that, if we didn't have this Majestic problem, we might talk some numbers, but as it is, I don't see how I can respond to you."

I can understand your position, Andy, and that's why I had just about given up hope. Until something happened. Project 35. Take a a look at these." He hands another sheaf of papers to Garra. The vice president looks at them, reads them more closely, and then looks up. "I haven't seen these results before."

"Just came in. We were working them up until late last night. I think you'll agree that it looks as if we might have the breakthrough on Majestic."

"This is just a small test, Russ. No way to tell until we see more results."

"Of course not Andy. But it's the most solid results we've had. I'm going to move full steam ahead to expand on this, I'm hot on it. I bring it up now because you were saying a moment ago that the only problem you have about my raise is the lack of even a hint of progress on Majestic. You indicated that everything else was satisfactory. Well, there's what I would call more than a hint of progress. I want to capitalize on this, Andy. I think it can mean a lot to the division and to the company. And I want to do it with a clear mind, so I'd like to get this financial thing straightened out. That's why I put it to you very sincerely that the raise I want is reasonable and will enable me to work with absolute concentration on this project."

Garra says, "Well, now, Russ, I have to admit that these results are promising, but they are just preliminary. Why don't we wait to see how it pans out?"

Murray is ready for this one. "Andy, when we first talked about this job we agreed that it involved risks. You have to keep testing things, and some of them obviously don't work out the way we had hoped. Furthermore, we can't rush things. When you come up with a good test, you have to give yourself the time to exploit it with the greatest of care. Now, on the objective level I will of course give this an all-out effort, no matter how we come out here. But I'd hate to think that, subconsciously, I was forcing the thing in order to get results to qualify for a raise that I really need and that I think I have qualified for now. And I don't think you would want to impose that kind of pressure on me, would you, Andy? I mean, considering what's at stake here."

"No, I wouldn't want to do anything like that. But this test on Majestic, this Project 35, this is not really solid yet."

"Andy, I know something else about you. You're not the kind of boss who changes the rules in the middle of the game to suit himself. A moment ago you were talking about the need to come up with even the suggestion of a breakthrough on Majestic. Well, we certainly have that here. And let's look at the whole picture. You agree that I've done a good job on 'Happy Days' and 'Canopus.' In addition to that I could point out the results on 'Saratoga' — high-volume at the lowest cost per order we've ever had, when you weigh the figures. My operation has run smoothly; you haven't had to put out any fires there. Now, putting all these things together, and adding the development of Project 35, which you admit to be promising, don't we have a picture that justifies the increase I am asking?"

There is more discussion. Garra comes back again and again to Majestic. At one point he observes, "Following through on those results is going to be tricky. You can have problems in analysis that could skew the whole thing."

Murray responds, "Yes, and that's why I want to be able to get this raise thing settled and devote my whole heart and soul to the job. And, incidentally, Andy, I'm going to be calling on you for your reactions and your know-how on this, if you have no objections. I'll need all the help you can give me. Let's face it; Majestic is the one area where we haven't accomplished what we thought we should have, and I feel that strongly. I want to handle this absolutely right."

Andy Garra offers considerable resistance; but in the end he agrees to give Murray the full raise requested.

Bosses will often fight against your pitch for more money by zeroing in on one particular area in which you have not shown much accomplishment. When you anticipate that this will be the case, you can handle it according to a number of principles.

Find some evidence of progress in the weak area, no matter how tentative it may be. If you can't find any, try your best to develop something that could be called hopeful.

Hold this material for the raise interview. Don't fire it off to your boss in advance. If he has a week to think about it, he will tend to discount it more and more as the days pass, and you will not be able to exploit it fully when the crunch comes.

Highlight your accomplishments in asking for the raise, even as you anticipate that he is going to bring up the weak spot. When he does, don't try to deny the failing. Admit that it has been a problem.

Encourage the boss to concentrate on this problem. Get him to describe it as the largest (and, if possible, the only) obstacle to your raise. If the boss thinks that you do not have any answer, he is likely to be led to expand on this point to the exclusion of others.

Get him to voice his approval of your other achievements. He will feel fairly relaxed about doing this if he is convinced that the raise stands or falls on your utter lack of results in the questionable area.

Pin him down on the point that he would look favorably on the increase if you were able to show something of promise in the weak area. Encourage him to talk about the total absence of results and the weight that this absence has in influencing his attitude.

Produce your evidence of improvement or promise — some tentative results, a plan, some documentation that points toward at least a glimmer of light at the end of the tunnel.

When he comments on the slightness of your evidence, remind him that he resisted your request because there was nothing at all to show that you were making progress on the weak point. Appeal to his sense of fairness.

Add up both sides of the ledger. Put your pluses on one side. Put the minus on the other side. Emphasize that your evidence shows this minus will start looking more like a plus.

Spell out your intentions of moving ahead and capitalizing on the improvement you have shown. Refer to the fact that you can do this best when your mind has been set at ease by getting the salary question resolved.

Reduce his argument to absurdity. Ask if, in effect, he requires perfect performance in every area before giving out raises. Remind him of the motivational effect that a raise is supposed to have.

Put things in context. Refer back to the job standards that you and he have agreed on. Point out again how well you have met the majority of them.

Ask for his help in continuing to make an improvement where you are deficient. Emphasize your dependence on him as leader and guide.

Patiently stick to your guns, referring to his desire for a hint of progress and to your respectable performance in the other areas.

And chances are you will wind up with the raise you want, or something pretty close to it.

When the boss is led to put all his eggs in one basket — to base his refusal on your shortcomings in just one area — you have a chance to overcome his resistance by encouraging him to exaggerate his focus on that one weakness, and then by producing some evidence of accomplishment on the questionable point.

When You've Goofed

For the raise seeker, a serious blot on the record is certainly an unwelcome event. But such a setback need not altogether destroy chances of getting a raise.

Harold Greenwood had a good record at Arcturus Inc. He was looking forward to salary review time, when he fully expected to go up against his boss Cal Freund for a large increase. Greenwood was preparing to document his case and play his strong hand with the utmost vigor.

And then came a most dismaying surprise. Greenwood was responsible for relations between Arcturus and one of its long-standing customers, Peterman & Sons. Things had gone smoothly on this front for a long time. Greenwood did not, frankly, pay much attention to Peterman. He left the routine work up to others. But something came unstuck. Peterman & Sons received a delivery of the wrong materials from Arcturus, and the error was not discovered before the customer had to curtail production to a serious extent. Greenwood's belated efforts to patch things up fell short, and the Peterman company withdrew its favor, and much of its business from Arcturus.

A bad scene. Harold Greenwood was very upset. Of course part of his discomfiture stemmed from his having let Arcturus and Cal Freund down, but Greenwood would have been less than human if he did not consider the effect that this episode would have upon his chances for a raise. Several possible means of handling the problem ran through his mind.

One possibility was to say as little as possible about the foul-up and hope that Freund would forget about it. Greenwood discarded this alternative, reasoning correctly that while a boss may cease talking about a mistake of this magnitude, he will certainly not forget about it, particularly at raise time. Another course might have been to blame the whole thing on others in the organization and the customer company. Harold Greenwood certainly did not bear all of the responsibility. But he concluded, again rightly, that this alternative was not only sneaky but self-defeating.

Here's the way Greenwood handled it. Just after the dust had settled he had a talk with Cal Freund. Greenwood minced no words: "Cal, I really blew that Peterman thing. I can't tell you how hard it's hit me. Nothing like this ever happened before." He went on to indicate that he took total responsibility for the calamity, that he regarded it with the utmost seriousness, and that he was even wondering if his usefulness to the company was at an end.

Freund was somewhat taken aback. At first he appreciated the fact that Harold Greenwood was not trying to weasel out of the responsibility. But then the boss became alarmed. He did not want to lose Greenwood, or to permit his subordinate to fall so far into the dumps that he would be ineffective.

So Cal Freund endeavored to show Greenwood the brighter side. "These things happen to everybody, Hal," he said. "It's not as bad as all that. Listen, I remember once. . . ." Freund proceeded to tell Greenwood about a couple of horrendous goofs that he had perpetrated in his younger days. Harold Greenwood permitted himself to be cheered up a little. "After all," the boss went on, "you've done some terrific things here, Hal. Your record is excellent. Why, the way you handled the Argo negotiation is something that a lot of people around here sat up and took notice of, don't think they didn't."

Now the position was changed. Greenwood sat and listened as his boss told him about the good things he had done. Finally Greenwood left, evidently cheered up, but not before he had said, "Well, I appreciate all you've said, Cal, but I'm not going to forget this thing. However, I guess the best approach is to see what I can learn from it." In parting, Cal Freund slapped Harold on the back and reassured him, "Right. We can always learn something from these things. And I'm sure a resourceful guy like you can really turn a setback like this to his advantage."

Three weeks later Greenwood, having scored a minor triumph, sent a memo reporting this fact to Freund. At the bottom he noted, "What I learned from the Peterman experience helped me in handling this deal. I appreciate your helping me to see it in perspective."

Now it's raise-negotiation time. Harold Greenwood is making an all-out pitch. His previous actions have, to a considerable extent, already spiked Freund's guns with relation to the Peterman fiasco. After all, it is Freund who said that the mistake was not all that bad, and Freund who admitted that he had done worse things himself, and Freund who extolled Greenwood's triumphs as far offsetting this one setback. The boss is scarcely in a good position to cite the Peterman problem as a major reason for withholding the raise.

But Greenwood doesn't leave it at that. He himself brings up the Peterman episode. He says, "I think I qualify for this raise, Cal, and I'd like to remind you of some of the reasons why. But I would not be on the level if I didn't mention the events that led to our trouble with Peterman & Sons. You were great at that time, if you remember; you reassured me that it was not the end of the world. But I've thought about what happened then, and I think I learned a lot from it. The record will bear me out, I believe. But it would not be fair if I didn't bring up that situation and ask you — do you feel that the Peterman deal disqualifies me for a raise?"

It would be pretty tough for any boss to say yes to this. Freund can do no more than shrug and remark, "It sure wasn't good, but those things do happen." Satisfied that he has done everything possible to neutralize the negative effects of his failure with the Peterman company, Harold Greenwood now proceeds to make a strong pitch for a substantial increase. It would have been better if it had not happened, but Greenwood has cut his losses most effectively.

When you blow one, and you fear the effect of the goof on your raise negotiations, you will be subjected to certain temptations. One is to try to cover it up. In the long run and even usually in the short run, this is disastrous. When the word does get to the boss — and it will — your chances of getting someplace, financially or any other way, will be seriously and perhaps permanently compromised.

It is also a poor policy to just let the thing drift along. If it hasn't been thrashed out previously, you can be sure that your shortcoming will be used against you with full force during the salary negotiation, and you will be very hard-pressed to handle it.

There may be excuses and extenuating circumstances, but if you try to advance them they will just sound like weak alibis. It's best to have somebody else, ideally the boss, make your excuses for you. Have a full-scale discussion of the problem with the boss as soon as you are sure of the entire extent of the problem. You don't want other shoes to keep dropping; this is not conducive to effective salary negotiation. Do it fast; the farther in advance of raise time the better.

Make full disclosure of the facts. If possible it is often not a bad idea to be able to tell the boss even one more bit of information that underscored the magnitude of the trouble. The boss will be more likely to feel that you are leveling with him.

Take it big. Don't try to minimize the thing. On the contrary, you may do well to exaggerate your dismay and concern. Let the boss reassure *you* that it's not too bad. Let him be the one who cites your triumphs as a way of putting it all in perspective and making you feel better about it. Permit yourself to be consoled, but emphasize that you intend to learn a lesson.

In the weeks that follow don't try to over-compensate for your error. A spasm of effort may produce some temporary results, but it carries with it the danger of making another mistake, which would be truly disastrous. Also, even if you work wonders, you will inevitably tail off and your performance will not be on the upsurge when you go in to ask for a raise. Instead, wait until you are able to call the boss's attention to some legitimate, even if modest, accomplishment, and remark that you have been able to turn your bad experience into something useful.

Be candid about referring to your goof when you lay out the evidence in support of your raise request. This gives strength to your recital of positive accomplishments by reminding the boss that you are willing to admit failure. You may want to obliquely remind the boss that he has said that the error was not so bad, and then give him the chance to turn around and say that it *was* bad, so bad that you can't get an increase. This is an opportunity that few bosses will take. Then go all-out for your raise.

Let's not kid ourselves; a serious mistake or failure is not an asset in seeking a raise. But if you keep your head and handle the situation with care, it doesn't have to be a crippling deficiency either. If the boss has taken the lead in minimizing the setback you don't have to be defensive about it. And, while it may not be altogether logical, many bosses are more sympathetic toward giving raises to the person who honorably admits a mistake than to the man who presents himself as a paragon of infallibility.

Making Something Out of Nothing

You toil away in a quiet backwater of the organization. You have done nothing noteworthy from one end of the year to the other. Your boss knows that you're alive, but that is about all. The impact that you seem to have on events, large and small, is minuscule.

Must you resign yourself to never getting anything bigger than the barest raise? Not necessarily. It would be easier of course if you had been at the pulsating center of events and had accomplished great things. But your very invisibility may offer some hope — if you play it right.

Grover Catlan has occupied a niche in the sales department for eleven years. Day-in, day-out he does his job, which involves correspondence with the salesmen — forwarding leads, providing extra copies of merchandising brochures, checking price lists, etc. Catlan has received raises — modest ones. He has not gone altogether unnoticed. If there is any money left over after the salesmen and the merchandisers and the advertising department and the service specialists have gotten theirs — then Grover Catlan gets a little too.

Now Catlan has decided that this is not good enough. Traditionally his vacations have consisted of package tours to Ausable Chasm; and for many years such leisure fare served its purpose. But Grover Catlan has been reading *National Geographic,* and reading the ads which blazon forth, in coruscating color, the wonders of trips to such places as the Galapagos, the Antipodes, and the Mountains of the Moon. Catlan has decided to change his life style to include such jaunts. This will take a lot more money. So he is on his way to ask his boss, the sales manager, for a larger raise.

Sales manager Gary Blankenship has been in his job for about two years. He stepped directly into the post, being hired away from a competitor through the good offices of a "head-hunter." Blankenship is of the new school of marketing executive — well-educated, unflamboyant, scientific in his approach, anxious to maintain good rapport throughout the ranks.

"Yes, Grover?" asks Gary Blankenship. The sales manager of course knows this subordinate by name, knows he has been around the company for years, and has some vague idea of what he does. But the chores performed by Grover Catlan are not the type to really turn a man like Gary Blankenship on. (In fact, there are extremely few who would really thrill to a recitation of Grover's day.) But of course Catlan is a member of the team, so he is to be treated with the utmost cordiality.

Catlan says, "Well, I'd like to talk to you about money, Gary. But first I thought it would be a good idea for us to review progress in decretal communications during the last twelve-month period. As you know, one of my responsibilities is to coordinate the engineering of epistolary access between headquarters and field operations. You'll be interested to hear that we have been able to successfully expedite a 15 percent increase in contactual transactions. . . ."

Blankenship looks hard at Catlan, but there is not the trace of a smile on the subordinates face. All Catlan is saying, of course, is that he answers letters from the salesmen and there have been more of them. It is the way Catlan is saying it that is interesting. Blankenship listens as Grover goes on in the same, nearly-incomprehensible vein. Finally Grover says, "That fills you in on activities at this end of the shop and plans for the coming period. Now, let's get to Big Casino. Money.

Gary, I was thinking about what would be adequate compensation for a continuation of this same level of activity and quality of contribution. In previous years I haven't had to think too much about it. But as you know, inflation makes all of us concerned with money. Furthermore, I find something to be increasingly true with regard to authority within the organization. To a much bigger extent than formerly, the new breed of marketing people tend to respond to you on the basis of what you make. So I believe it's time for the inequity to be made up. It will be best for the organization, because it will strengthen my hand. A raise of five thousand would meet my present needs."

Gary Blankenship hasn't been getting all of this, but he gets the part about "five thousand." Swallowing his astonishment he answers, as gently as possible, that of course such a raise is out of the question, but he will certainly see that Grover Catlan receives something commensurate with his ability and importance. (This is just what Grover does not want.) Unperturbed, he responds that he has stated that figure because it is justified, and furthermore he would hate to think that the rumors are true. What rumors, asks Blankenship. Well, the rumors that the sales manager tends to give the largest raises to certain of the star salesmen because they are able to build themselves up as being essential and unique performers. "Modern management theory," says Catlan with a smile, "doesn't recognize the star system. We all know that many of the behind-the-scenes functions are much more vital to continued good operation than the more ballyhooed activities. I've always assumed that you recognize this and operate on that basis."

The discussion continues. Catlan offers more of his jargonized version of the importance of the job he does. He insists upon the figure he has named, professing indifference toward anything less. He issues hints at the calamitous things that might happen if he were to leave or in some way ease off in his activities. He appeals to the sales manager's scientific knowledge by assuming that "of course" Blankenship is aware of the vital role played by corresponding operations in the maintenance of a satisfactory field effort.

Let's stop and examine what Grover Catlan is doing. To begin with, he is being audacious. Audacity is not as popular in our era of muted interpersonal relationships as it was in a more flamboyant era. Thus many bosses are less ready to cope with it. Sometimes sheer audacity can carry an argument without much more than a shred of support. In the Victorian age, for example, the exploits of the depraved poet Algernon Charles Swinburne became too much for the staid Arts Club, and the members undertook to expel him. Appearing in Swinburne's behalf was the eccentric painter James McNeill Whistler, who bluntly told the committee, "You accuse him of drunkenness — well, that's his defense." The sweeping effrontery of Whistler's advocacy outshone its blatant illogicality — "You ought to be proud that there is in London a club where the greatest poet of your time *can* get drunk if he wants to, otherwise he might lie in the gutter." (*Whistler,* by Stanley Weintraub, Weybright and Talley, 1974). Swinburne was not expelled.

An audacious demand may throw a boss off balance and make him think there must be *something* behind it. Since no manager likes to think of himself as being blind to all the angles and subtleties of a situation, the boss may examine a sweeping request with great care, on the basis that such a large demand is likely to have a foundation of some kind.

Then, Catlan has described his relatively simple job in language that magnifies its complexity to nebulous proportions. Some bosses of the old school would merely say, "Bull! That's just fancy talk for writing letters." But Catlan knows his man. The more modern the executive, the more earnestly he believes in jargon as a reflection of the importance of a function. We live in an age of inflated language and values. People tend to take other people at their own evaluation. The most pompous and self-inflated ignoramus may achieve scope and clout by presenting himself haughtily as an expert in something that no one else even understands. The self-inflater may have little if anything on the ball, but that means nothing. Before you know it he is on the "Today" show lecturing us on our inadequacies.

Inflate your own job. Wherever a function seems simple, make it more complicated. Find multi-syllabic words to describe it. Imply that there are enormous depths of insight, research and technology underlying every seemingly-straightforward move you make. You may not make much sense, but there are a lot of bosses who will be impressed merely because the subordinate is so impressed with his own importance.

Play on the boss's insecurity. The very fact that your function is obscure can be an asset. The boss does not know much about what you do. But if he's been around at all he knows how many current business projects are houses of cards that can collapse instantly. The collapse is often caused by the overlooking of some simple, mundane element. *You* may be such a booby-trap. True, you may also be practically expendable, and anybody may be able to handle your job. But often the boss doesn't know that. He can take a risk — but the stakes are high.

He would rather that you continue doing whatever it is you do, so that he doesn't have to find out about it or worry about it.

You can appeal to the boss's sense of fairness. Should the big raises go to the most obviously spectacular performers? The boss has probably always thought so, but if you question him as to *why* he may not have a ready answer. After all, you have given years of loyalty and service to the organization. You do your best; is that not worthy of reward? This argument has no connection with your value as a worker, which is why it can be so effective. (Viscount Melbourne once said that of all the honors he had received, he valued the Order of the Garter most, "because there is no damned merit in it.") Why should merit invariably be regarded highest? This concept received startling and touching articulation a few years ago when President Richard Nixon announced that he was appointing an undistinguished judge, G. Harrold Carswell, to the Supreme Court. The adjective most employed with relation to Carswell was "mediocre." Senator Roman H. Hruska of Nebraska rose to Carswell's defense. Maybe the appointee *is* mediocre, Senator Hruska declaimed, but what of that? Why should all Supreme Court justices be outstanding? Isn't it time that mediocrity received its fair share of representation?

In much the same way you can issue an audacious challenge to meritocracy. And you have a chance to get someplace with it, because the boss probably has not got a ready answer and because bosses nowadays are urged never to dismiss even the most seemingly idiotic argument out of hand.

And then you can hint that you might just leave because you don't think that much of the job. Managers are sometimes piqued by an underling's show of indifference. Some bosses tend to feel that, if a subordinate appears not to give a damn about keeping a job, he must either be in demand or not need a job. Either way this can enhance the attractiveness of the worker. Of course in show business this is an old story. Robert Morley says it is more important for an actor to learn to bluff than to learn to act. Morley recalls how he first went to Hollywood. His career had been a disaster. Nevertheless, MGM thought he might be useful in a part so they asked Morley's agent, "How much?" "Five hundred a week," replied the agent. The film moguls collapsed in laughter. "He's never done anything. He never lasted 24 hours. So how is he worth $500 a week?"

"He's not," agreed the agent, "but he doesn't want to go to America and he has a large personal fortune." The bluff lasted until Morley signed the contract, but then he had to ask for a cash advance to pay his passage (*TV Guide,* May 25, 1974).

If you seem indifferent to whether the boss keeps you around or not, he may wonder what it is you are not telling him. And, since fear of the unknown is such a powerful factor in human affairs, he may choose not to find out. He can stave off the unknown by giving you a raise.

There is something else going for you. No matter how routine your job may be, you can always argue that you do it without making waves. You cause the boss no headaches, no trouble. You keep problems away from him. Since he does not know what problems might come his way if you were not around — and he does not want to find out — he may feel that a raise is the lesser of two evils. Indeed, the very fact that you don't do very much that looks important in your job may work on your side. "I feel that I've been penalized because I do my job effortlessly," you can say. Again, this has a parallel in show business. A "great" actor stands stock-still before the camera and mumbles. "Look at the sheer economy with which he does it," exclaims the knowing critic. "No wasted effort."

So there is no need whatever to despair of getting a good raise just because your work is obscure. The very obscurity of the job may work in your favor, if the boss does not know much about what you do but just takes it for granted. You can inflate the importance of the function and hint darkly at the horrendous things that might happen if you were not around. Since one of the great practical rules of management is that one should never take on one single headache more than necessary, the boss will at least consider giving you what you want to get you to stay.

As for Grover Catlan — he did not get the $5000 — but he got half of it, a mighty fine raise.

Making A Negative Into A Positive

There are times when the boss has you cold. He points out a shortcoming that can't be overlooked. You can't deny that it's part of your job. He has talked to you about it before, so you can't say you didn't know about it. Although he did not specifically say — at the time he talked with you about the problem — that if things did not improve he would be unable to give you a raise (few bosses tie criticism, constructive or otherwise, to forthcoming raises; they are schooled not to do this) he is on strong ground in saying "no."

Are you dead? You are certainly not in good shape, but there may be a chance to salvage a raise. Here's an example of how one individual handles it.

Bryan Spelvin has put in for more money. After a few preliminaries his boss, Zane Garth, smiles and shakes his head. "I think it's only fair, Bryan, for me to say something right at this point. One of the key things in your job is to pull a higher percentage of responses on our general institutional mailings. We went over this about ten months ago, and again back in July. But I'm looking at the latest returns and I'm sorry to say it's no better. Still hanging at about 2 percent. This is important. You know it, I know it. Obviously the problem is not solved. I know you're working hard at it, and one of these days you may come up with the right approach, but right now more money is out of the question."

Garth expects one of two things, or a combination. He anticipates that Spelvin will offer alibis that shift the onus of his lack of results to other shoulders, or that the subordinate will try to make his results look better than they actually are.

Spelvin does neither. "I was going to bring up the matter of returns on those mailings. Actually, I have to tell you that last month they even slipped a little, about a tenth of a percent. I know damn well that this is not satisfactory."

Garth, a bit surprised, says, "No, it's not. So you can see why. . . ."

"But it is important," Spelvin breaks in, "So maybe it's worthwhile if we spend a few minutes on it. I have my own ideas, but first I'd like to hear from you. What do you think is wrong?"

Garth says, "Well, I believe in letting people handle their own jobs and judging by results. But I wonder if you aren't stuck with some out-dated lists. I realize the budget for new lists was curtailed, but maybe if you eliminated some of the older ones and just concentrated on the best performers, it would go better."

"I wish I could get myself off the hook that easily," says Spelvin. "I think the old lists have something to do with it. But I'm beginning to suspect that there's more to it than that. I suspect that the appeals I've been trying are dead wrong. Maybe I need a new strategy. Now I know strategy is my responsibility, but I'd like your help. Tell me. When you get this kind of mailing from other companies, what's your reaction?"

Garth is drawn into a discussion of his reactions. He is happy enough to diverge from the sensitive subject of the raise that he thinks he has just turned down. Furthermore, Spelvin's attitude is different and interesting. Twice within the space of a few sentences the subordinate has not only passed up the opportunity to try to make himself look better, but has even gone in the other direction, making himself look a little worse.

After some conversation Spelvin says, "I wonder if I could bounce a couple of ideas off you. He proceeds to cover three or four possibilities. Frankly, Garth does not know that much about it. "You're the expert," he says. "But if you want to know my gut feeling, that second one sounds like it might have promise. But I expect you to be the guy who sees these things through."

"Sure," replies Spelvin, "but it's important to me to get fresh, intelligent reactions. I'll have to refine and test these concepts. Maybe none of them is any good. But someplace I've got to come up with an approach that will jack up the returns. But maybe we can set up a goal to shoot at. What would you see as a satisfactory rate for us to pull in by the end of the first quarter?"

Garth considers this. "Well, what we would like to have is a basic 6 percent. But, by the end of March? Six percent doesn't seem to be in the cards. We would hope to see some definite improvement, however. Say, three and a half."

"Three and a half. By the end of March." Garth watches as Spelvin earnestly jots this down. "Okay," Spelvin goes on, "that gives me something to shoot at. Within that time I have to cull the lists, settle on two or perhaps three approaches, run tests of just enough magnitude to give us an orientation, and then roll on the right approach. I think I can show you some preliminary results by the end of January." With Spelvin doing most of the talking, a timetable is worked out.

"Okay," says Spelvin, putting the last flourish on his notes, "we have a plan. I'll be checking with you at points along the way. You'll be keyed in on my progress, or lack of it. I won't take up more than a bare minimum of your time, but can I count on you for some comments now and then, and for a little support with some of the other departments? To pull this off I will need plenty of cooperation."

Garth assents. Spelvin then says, "Even so, this is a rough timetable. I will have to put in a lot of overtime on it. When I'm working on concepts I like to be able to pick up the phone and bounce a thought or two off some of my buddies in the business, so is it all right with you if I arrange to have an outside phone line switched to my office automatically every night at the close of business? As it stands now you have to make arrangements during the day if you want a line. Since I'll be late most nights, and there isn't that much call for night lines, it will be a lot more convenient if I get it automatically."

Garth nods, much in the manner of a man who could not care less about such things as arrangements for night lines. However, he knows that arranging for such things can be troublesome, and he has gotten the point that Spelvin will be working hard.

Spelvin swiftly sums up the task he has undertaken, the goals he expects to hit, and the yardsticks against which his progress can be measured. Then he looks at his boss. "Is there another area that we should cover in the same way? Can you point out some other aspect of my job that needs this same kind of crash program for improvement?"

Garth may have one or two small complaints, but he decides to let them go. "No, as far as the rest of the job is concerned I think you're doing fine, Bryan. And if you get this thing straightened out. . . ."

"Okay," says Spelvin. He leans forward. "I have admitted where I am falling short. We have set up a plan and I have committed myself to go all out for improvement — while keeping the other parts of my performance up to standard. I'm going to give you my best, and I think it will pay off. Do you still feel that this kind of approach is unworthy of a raise?"

The boss is not about to say that he demands that everyone be perfect before getting more money. He still doesn't want to grant the increase; but the field is reopened, and Bryan Spelvin has a very good chance of persuading Garth that he merits a raise.

What Bryan Spelvin did, when confronted by the roadblock of a salient deficiency in his performance, was to move around it by shifting the session from a raise interview to a performance review conference.

Performance review is something that the manager, not the subordinate should initiate. Most bosses don't conduct anything like an adequate merit-appraisal system. They criticize or pat-on-the-back; but they don't sit down with an employee for a serious discussion of a problem, leading to exchange of ideas on what would constitute satisfactory performance; how those standards may be achieved; and a timetable within which the goals may be attained.

Bosses avoid performance review sessions for several reasons. They are difficult. It takes time to gather the facts on which to conduct a truly fruitful critique of the subordinate's work. It's much easier just to praise him when he does something good or knock him when he goofs. Bosses are often afraid that appraisal interviews may disintegrate into gripe sessions, alibi exercises, or even shouting matches. Then too, there is the fear that if a subordinate is able to show that he has been performing well, his expectations will be honed and he will ask for more money.

It has been suggested elsewhere that you should prepare early for a raise by establishing criteria for performance that your boss agrees with and that you feel you can handle. This does not mean you have to push the boss to talk with you about performance unless it's a raise session. However, if you have distinctly fallen short someplace — whether or not you were instrumental in setting up the standards — it may be to your advantage to have a frank talk about it right in the middle of the session at which you are trying for a raise.

You can throw the boss off balance and tend to disarm him somewhat by *going farther than he does in admitting your own responsibility.* There is an undeniable risk; the boss can come back later and say, "You yourself admitted such and such." But the risk is not as great as it may appear. The boss has probably gone a little easy in spelling out where you went wrong. He doesn't want a fight, he just wants you to settle for no raise. When you admit to being even more culpable, you may surprise him with your frankness, but you are not likely to be putting a new idea in his mind.

Get his comments on how the job might be done better, no matter how vague they may be. Get him to agree on what would constitute good performance. You can probably suggest standards yourself. Don't give yourself a setup. He won't buy that. You're in a risk situation anyway, so you may as well talk about criteria that will not be easy to attain, but that you have a fighting chance to make. You can surprise the boss favorably a second time by being tougher on yourself in terms of goals than he expected you to be.

Lay out a plan. Include checkpoints at which you will be reporting back to him with results. Establish a timetable for accomplishment. And show that you are going to knock yourself out to make it. Ask him if he has other problems about your performance. Having been tough in this one instance, he may not be too tough in others.

And then go back at him for a raise — then and there. Your argument is that, while you have admittedly fallen short on this one thing, you have the humility and the intelligence to see this and to recognize what must be done. You will be making a maximum effort to improve — and who could ask for more than that?

You may get the raise. Or the boss may say, "Let's wait and see what happens." All right. You've established some definite checkpoints. Leave it with the boss that you hope you can show him some results. Work like hell to look good at the first checkpoint. Then, when you review it with the boss, bring up the raise again, from the stance that you assumed a good showing at this juncture warranted more money.

It may work. It often has.

7

problem situations

When The Boss Says "Things Are Tough"

Businessmen tend to look on the bright side. They magnify triumphs, minimize setbacks. But not always. There are exceptions. Exceptions come when the boss is talking to the tax man, to a creditor, or to an employee who wants a raise.

When the boss pleads poverty as a reason for not giving you the raise you've asked for, you need not be thrown for a loss. "Things are tough" is a common countermeasure, and you should be ready for it. The first thing to remember is that this tactic presents you with an opening.

Here's an example of the opening and how it can be exploited. Barbara Hunsicker has just asked her boss Vincent O'Reilly for a raise. O'Reilly assumes a regretful expression: "Barbara, I just wish I could say yes, but you know how things have been going. This has been a tough year. We have to watch every penny. There's nothing personal about it, we're all in the same boat. I wish I could take home more money, but it's just not in the cards."

Barbara says, "I'm surprised to hear that, Mr. O'Reilly. And upset. I wish you'd tell me what it is about my work that hasn't been up to your requirements. I've been doing my best, and I thought I was doing pretty well." Seeing that Barbara has missed the point, O'Reilly expands on his theme. "No, no, it's got nothing to do with you, Barbara. Your work has been just fine. We just haven't done as well as we hoped to, not only in this department but across the board. So I'm afraid raises are in short supply."

"Well, at least I'm happy to hear that it's not a matter of my not performing well. When you asked me to reorganize the inventory procedures I had hoped I could do the job well enough to justify your confidence in me."

"And you did. You did a great job, Barbara. In fact you've been a bright spot in the department. I have no complaints about what you've been doing, none at all." And the boss continues, telling Barbara Hunsicker how well she has done.

Vincent O'Reilly has been led into a simple trap. Relieved at Barbara's failure to respond vehemently to his plea of general poverty, he has succumbed to the temptation to lay it on thick about her performance. After all, compliments cost nothing. (At least O'Reilly thinks they cost nothing; Barbara's strategy will be to make them cost him something.) So the boss goes a little overboard in reassuring the subordinate that her individual effectiveness is quite satisfactory.

Barbara Hunsicker, of course, missed the point deliberately. When the boss raised the general objection of lack of money, she immediately began to apply the tactic which experienced salesmen call "qualifying." Qualifying a customer means getting him to say, in effect, "The objection I have just raised is the only bar to the sale. If it were not for that we would have a deal." Once the salesman has gotten the prospect to say this, he can zero in on that one objection. Similarly, Barbara has induced her boss to give up his chance to present anti-raise arguments based on deficiencies in her performance.

Whenever the boss opens his defense by claiming an overall money problem as a bar to giving you a raise, you have a chance to cut down his maneuverability. Without acknowledging the validity of his claim, try to lead him on to speak highly of what *you* have been doing. Chances are he will — particularly if he thinks he has spiked your guns. Let him tell you how happy he is with your work. Try to establish a position in which he says, "If it weren't that times are tough I'd give you what you want. It's got nothing to do with you."

Once you have worked around to this position it will be hard for the boss to try to reverse his field later and cite your deficiencies as a reason for holding back the raise.

But what do you do about the boss's "no money" argument? Well, here we can learn something from modern tactics of land warfare, notably those executed by the German army during the blitzkrieg attacks of World War II. The essence of the lightning strike was to move fast. When the attack came up against an enemy strong point there was no effort to besiege and demolish it then and there. The strategy was to move around the strong point and carry the battle onto more favorable ground, leaving the enemy's defenses relatively intact, but impotent.

You can't demolish the argument that "things are tough." Or rather, in certain cases you can, but it's better not to. Let's say the boss, though not actually lying, is exaggerating when he raises this obstacle. Even if you have facts to refute his contention, it's unproductive to get into a hassle about actual company and/or departmental performance for the past year. No matter how many facts you have, the employer is always able to refer gloomily to "other factors." To try to get him to admit that things are really going well is to fight on the wrong ground. Whatever counter-ammunition you possess can be used better in another way.

Here's Barbara Hunsicker again. She has permitted Vincent O'Reilly to go on at some length about how she, personally, has been doing a good job; it's just that overall conditions militate against her raise. Barbara listens and then goes into action.

"Gee, Mr. O'Reilly, I never realized that things were *that* bad. The company is really in desperate shape, isn't it? I guess we'd all better start thinking about what we do next. I appreciate your telling me this, because we all have to do a lot of thinking now."

The last thing O'Reilly wants is for Barbara to go running back to her co-workers proclaiming that the sky is falling. He would be inundated with questions and, perhaps, begin to lose people. Panic is not part of his plan. So Vincent O'Reilly sees that he will have to cool it somewhat.

"Well, no, Barbara, I don't think things are as bad as all that. In fact I know they're not. It's just, well, you understand how an organization can get into a temporary bind. . . ."

Barbara looks a little reassured. "Oh. You mean this is a temporary thing. But even so, sometimes temporary things turn out to last a long time. Wouldn't it be a good idea if we had a meeting and talked over the situation, I mean how bad it is right at the moment? I'm sure everyone would understand, but it would only be fair. . . ."

"No, no. No need for that. Actually, I would expect that we will be out of the woods quite soon. In fact, things are looking up already." O'Reilly is modifying his position to such a degree that you might even say he is abandoning it. "There really isn't any case to get upset, or for people to worry. Everything is going to be fine. Prospects are quite good."

"Well," says Barbara, "I'm glad to hear that. You had me scared there for a minute, Mr. O'Reilly. But I guess you have to be conservative and always look on the dark side of things. I mean that's your responsibility, not to get too optimistic. I'm always very optimistic, and I guess that's because I have such complete faith in the company and in you."

O'Reilly acknowledges this statement of faith. He cannot do otherwise. He tries to turn it to his advantage: "I'm glad of that, Barbara, because I always try to be on the level and fair at all times. So I can assure you your confidence is not misplaced. This little difficulty will clear up and everything will be rolling along well again."

"I *know* it will," says Barbara earnestly. "I know that things are going well, basically. I remember reading that little article you had in the house organ about our big plans for next year, and I thought, boy, this is a great company to be with. And then there was that memo you sent around a couple of months ago, reporting on performance. That certainly looked as if things were going well. . . ."

O'Reilly has a momentary twinge of regret that he has permitted himself to go on record so effusively about how good things were and how much better they were going to be. After all, those statements were made for a different purpose entirely, namely to make some points with O'Reilly's bosses. Vincent O'Reilly thinks, wistfully and illogically, how nice it would be if his own employees did not read material published for them but not really meant for them. Barbara is going on: "Then I guess really that I had no reason to get so scared when you said that. We're still going to be in business, and be able to pay the bills, and all like that, aren't we? I mean, even with prices going up the way they are, there's no reason to worry about us not being able to keep going, is there?"

O'Reilly assures Barbara that this is correct. "Well," she says, "Mr. O'Reilly, I want you to know that I will be doing everything I can to help. Naturally, when I get my raise I'll be even more eager to do everything I can, but that's only human, isn't it? Everybody looks out. . . ."

O'Reilly has been staring at her. Now he interrupts. "Barbara, I thought you saw the picture. Everything is going to be fine, is basically fine now, but at the moment we're just not able to consider raising you. It's just one of those things. I thought you understood that."

"Why, I'm afraid I don't understand. I mean, paying people what they deserve is important, isn't it? I know you feel that way, Mr. O'Reilly. You've always had such good rapport, everybody says so. One of the things that's great here is the way you understand and look out for the people under you. So I don't see why you say you can't give me the raise, especially if things are all right and going to be better next year. It's next year that I'm asking about."

The boss tries to explain again. Somehow Barbara doesn't get it. She keeps referring back to his own statements, and to the undoubted fact that compensation is a cost of doing business. Occasionally she expresses renewed alarm: "How bad is it, really? Is it something that we all ought to worry about?" She emphasizes her willingness to do her best to assure the bright future, including talking it up with her colleagues. And she keeps referring to various statements, by O'Reilly and others, about how things are in excellent shape.

In the end O'Reilly has to abandon the argument that money for raises is in short supply. He tries to bridge back into a discussion of Barbara's shortcomings, which have suddenly become magnified in his mind. But he has just gotten finished telling her that he has no complaint with her work. Barbara Hunsicker gets her raise.

You can bypass the "no-money" argument by preparing yourself in a number of ways. Collect factual material that supports a claim that the operation has been functioning efficiently and at a profit. Even more important, collect the roseate statements of your employers. They are around. If the company issues an annual report you have a rich source of ammunition.

Qualify the boss's objection by leading him into a position of saying, "If it weren't for this I'd give it to you." Begin to make him back off by taking alarm, by magnifying the gloomy picture he has been painting. He, in turn, is apt to get a little edgy and will consequently modify his dire description. Keep asking "why?" If things are basically sound, then what is the problem? His explanations are not likely to be compelling. Don't let them be.

Tie your raise request to the cost of doing business. Advert to the fact that the company is prepared to honor its obligations in the coming year. And — with some luck — you will be able to bypass the "no-money" objection, isolate it, and get your raise.

Coping With a Hostile Boss

When asked for a raise, some bosses turn into Mr. Hyde. The manager who is easygoing and affable all year round turns hostile when confronted with a request for more money. This can be disconcerting. Worse, if you let it throw you, you will miss out on the raise.

Sometimes the boss's violent reaction is genuine. Sometimes it is a calculated ploy to head off the request. Often it is a mixture. Certain managers consider themselves watchdogs of the treasury, even when they are not the owners of the company. They will fight tooth and nail to keep costs down, no matter how well justified the appeal may be. With this kind of manager the raise seeker is usually prepared. He knows that it's going to be a battle when he walks in.

Then there is the manager who looks upon a demand for more money as a personal affront. Hasn't he been a fair boss? Hasn't he communicated, established rapport, offered friendly advice, been a pal as well as a superior? Isn't the subordinate grateful for everything that's been done for him? This kind of manager is hurt because the appeal for a raise strikes him as a slap in the face. Of course he's not being realistic, but nevertheless it happens.

Another problem is posed by the boss who "came up the hard way" and thinks that everybody else should do the same. He wasn't handed raises on a silver platter. He had to fight for every dollar, and often there were not many dollars. He derives satisfaction from seeing others going through the same struggles as he did.

Some bosses react angrily out of guilt. They know that they should be giving raises — but circumstances have combined to make it difficult. The manager is angry at the company, at his own bosses, at the politicians who louse up the economy, at his competitors, and at the world in general. Frequently he is most angry at himself. He takes it out on the employee who comes in and asks for a raise.

When the boss gets mad — or acts mad — in a raise interview, the first thing to do is let him get it off his chest. But while he is expressing himself you will want to listen for clues as to what to do next. Your end of the conversation should be, at first, passive. Don't be drawn into a dispute. Keep your cool. Ask questions designed to get at the root of the problem.

Here's an example. Wally Meyers has just disclosed his raise demand to Mel Roche. Roche sits there, getting red in the face, and then he explodes. "Fifteen hundred! You've got to be kidding! That's way out of line! We have a policy of paying people fairly, I think, but this is ridiculous. It just drives me up the wall when people walk in and ask for the moon. Where's the dough coming from? Did you ask yourself that?" And on for a few more choice minutes. Meyers listens, and when he gets a chance, asks a question: "What is it about my work that bothers you, Mel?"

"Nothing to do with you," Roche replies. "You've been doing okay. But I don't think you're using your head when you come in here and ask for this much money. Use a little sense. You seem to have plenty of it."

Further conversation indicates to Meyers that it's not *his* particular request that has set off the pyrotechnics: the boss would have reacted, on this day, to an appeal for an increase from anybody. Meyers continues to question and develop the information he needs. When Roche calms down a little he reveals that top management is putting the pressure on, and that Roche is going to have to go to the mat to get approval of any raises.

As they go on talking Mel Roche regains control of himself. The boss is a little ashamed of his outburst. Meyers takes it in stride; and he manages to turn the discussion in his favor. Roche is looking for help in justifying raise requests, and Meyers is ready to give it to him. Finally the subordinate works himself into the favorable position (covered fully elsewhere) of "you and me, boss against *them.*"

If you listen to the boss's tirade, and draw him out, you can determine pretty accurately whether the blast is directed at you personally or at the idea of giving raises in general. In this case, of course, Wally Meyers was faced with the latter problem.

Here's a different situation. Sid Blank asks his boss, Pat Dressler, for a raise. Here's the reaction: "You got to be out of your everlovin' mind, Sidney. Not a chance. You're lucky to keep the job. Why don't we just forget about it?"

"What's the trouble?" asks Sid. "The trouble is that you're not delivering the way you should, Sid. You must have production problems down there that I haven't heard about. The record is just not good enough to warrant a raise at this time."

Sid says, "Production is up 6 percent in my department. I have the latest figures right here. . . ." But the boss interrupts. "Yeah, but it should be up more than that. You're spending more dough, you put on two more people, you had an overhaul on several pieces of equipment. Now, maybe this is not all your fault, Sid, but you're the guy who is responsible, and I'm not going to consider any raise right now."

All right. Sid Blank has at least determined that he has run into a stone wall because the boss does not think he's doing a good enough job. Sid is prepared to document and support his request, but before getting into that he wants to set the stage. "Let me get this straight, Pat — I think in all fairness I rate an explanation — you're saying no to a raise because you don't think production has gone up enough to justify it?"

"That's the story."

"Is that the only problem, Pat? I mean, you're not saying this because there's no money for raises anyway, are you? You've always been on the level with me. . . ."

Pat Dressler asserts that he is laying it on the line; that Sid Blank's performance is the obstacle to the raise. Sid sticks with this point a little while longer: "So if production were up, say, 10 percent, you'd think differently about it?" Dressler answers, "Sure I'd think about it, but facts are facts, and we have to consider the situation the way it stands now."

Now Sid Blank knows what he's up against. He has "qualified" the boss; gotten him to say that if it were not for this one problem, the raise request would receive much more favorable consideration. So Sid can proceed to try to make his case that he has, indeed, gotten the highest production possible under the circumstances. Depending on the strength of his case and the skill with which he presents it, he may come out with a raise after all. Even if he doesn't, Sid Blank is in good position to lay the groundwork for a future raise if he jacks up performance.

Again, the key is to let the boss speak his piece, prodding him along with questions to get the information you need. You will want to find out if the beef is a general one or if it is aimed at you. If he is upset with your work, you can find out if it is one particular aspect of your performance or with several. You have a chance to "qualify" him, to win agreement that there are only one or two barriers to the raise. Having found out the problem, you can then select your tactics. You may even be helped by the boss's sheepishness when the storm subsides.

It's not always easy to retain a cool head when you are confronted with a tirade, particularly when it is not justified, or doesn't seem to be. But it's worth the effort. The less you deserve the bawling-out, the better chance you may have of coming off well in the end. Remember, giving out raises can be the hardest thing in the world for some bosses. They find it painful. So you must expect some kicking and screaming at the moment of extraction. It needn't be an insurmountable obstacle.

The "Lightning Rod" Technique

When you are facing the necessity of asking for a raise from the kind of boss who tries to browbeat you into submission, planning is important.

The experience can be analogous to that of trying to extract a fang from a puff adder, but even that can be done with a little forethought and preparation.

Think over previous experience with the browbeating boss. Fill in your intelligence gathering with observations from others who have worked with him. Then mount a strategy. One approach that has worked for some clever raise seekers is what we might call the "lightning rod" ploy. In this method, you divert the boss's fire into an area that afterward turns out to be ineffectual for him and harmless for you.

Linda Koppell works for Dean Anderson. She is asking for a raise. Anderson does not blow his top, but he shakes his head vigorously. "Sorry, Linda, I just cannot put one through for you at this time. You've done an all right job in a number of respects, but you still don't seem to be able to cover every aspect of your responsibility. I am willing to compensate good performance, but when you talk with an employee who agrees that certain things will be done, and then those things are not done — well, wouldn't you agree that this is not what you'd call first-class performance?"

"Yes, I might agree, Dean, but I'm not sure I know what you're talking about. Is there something that I was supposed to do. . . ?"

Anderson smiles mirthlessly. "You remember back in August when I talked to you about the scheduling problem with EDP? Sometimes work piles up, and sometimes the machines are busy on Mickey Mouse stuff. There are bottlenecks in keypunch. I didn't expect you to solve all the problems, but what we did agree on was that you would work out some way for us to get earlier information on EDP availability as far as this department is concerned. I was hoping. . . ." Dean Anderson continues to spell out his complaint about Linda Koppell's failure. Linda just sits there. But at last her turn comes.

She says, "Why, Dean, I did work that out with Don Kennedy. We've had a reporting system in effect for a month now. Of course you haven't seen the thing operating because in the ordinary course of events you shouldn't be bothered with these matters — that's what you said." She rummages in a file she has brought in. "Here — I just happen to have some of the paperwork on it. Seems to be working out fine so far."

Anderson is nonplussed. "Why didn't you tell me this was in effect?"

Linda looks surprised. "You told me to handle it, Dean. I said I would. You said you just wanted it handled without any more involvement on your part. So of course I went ahead and did it. I figured you would assume it had been handled."

Now Linda assumed nothing of the kind. She suspected that Anderson might take for granted that nothing had been done if he did not hear about it. But technically there was no reason to inform him ("I don't want to be that kind of person who comes bursting into the boss's office yelling 'Look what I did!'"). Anderson can hardly insist that he should have been kept informed of every detail, after he said he wanted it done without any more involvement on his part. And he will not find it easy to turn to criticism of some other facet of Linda's work. Linda Koppell has moved a big step toward getting her raise.

What Linda did, in effect, was to erect a "lightning rod" to draw off the boss's anticipated complaint harmlessly. Putting it baldly, she set him up. Her stratagem resembles the poker move (deplored in friendly games) called "checking a man into a cinch." You know that you have an opponent beaten in a stud game; but you check instead of betting, hoping that he will make a hefty bet and give you the chance to raise him, thus entrapping him in a losing situation.

When you know the boss is likely to try to zero in on some deficiency of yours to head off the raise, think about giving him a spurious target. If you can hold back something legitimately, hold it back. Let him jump on it; and then disclose that you have, in fact, handled that chore.

When the Boss Says "Trust Me"

Tony Fiore thinks he has really got it made. To begin with, he deserves the raise. He has presented his case compellingly. His boss, Grant Burgeon, has not raised too many objections, and he has seemed satisfied with Tony's arguments. Furthermore, Burgeon has been pleasant and cordial in acknowledging the good things Tony has done. Everything seems to be rolling along smoothly. And then comes the zinger. Burgeon leans back and says, "Tony, you don't have to convince me. I know what you've done. You're good, kid, and I'd be a damn fool to try to tell you you're not. Sure you have put together a record this year that deserves a raise."

Please, Tony tells himself, "Here it comes." And it comes — but it's not what Tony expected. It's a zinger. Burgeon says, "Now I'd like you to listen carefully to what I'm going to tell you, because it will be the limit of what I *can* tell you. Tony, you rate the raise right now. But I'm going to ask you to wait a while. I know this is tough, but I can't give you the details as to why. But I can say this. *Don't worry.*

You can count on me. I've always shot straight with you, haven't I? Well, okay. I'm asking you to go along with me on this."

Rough. The boss has put it on what is practically a personal basis. If Tony insists on battling for the raise he seems to be shredding the fabric of friendship, loyalty, and mutual trust between the two. But he still wants his raise. What can he do about it?

First, without dwelling on the matter we might say that you should try to avoid such a situation. This is not to say you shouldn't become friendly with the boss. But if you do establish a close relationship, think ahead. Might there be a possibility that the friendship would intrude on the raise negotiation? Using some discretion, ask others if something like this has ever happened.

Forewarn the friendly boss. After all, when there is a good relationship the parties should be able to speak frankly to each other. Drop a small hint into a warm conversation. Say "I appreciate the way you level with me, Grant. It's a good way to work. Of course that doesn't mean that when I come in to you to ask for a raise I won't give it everything I've got, and I expect you to be on the level with me then as always."

But you can't always foresee this kind of plea, or avoid it. What happens when the boss asks you to trust him by foregoing your request for the time being without learning of the reasons? Well, one response to this ploy (and, no matter how sincere it may be, a ploy is what you should consider it) is to become equally — almost embarrassingly — friendly in return. "I do trust you, Grant. That's why I'm going to tell you something I was going to skip over, because I didn't think it was the businesslike thing to do. But I really need this raise. I can't go into all the reasons right now — you can understand that, I hope — but, believe me, I need it." So now you have matched a counterplea against his. Tit for tat. The boss has asked you to make a sacrifice because of friendship rather than logic. You have every right to assume that you can ask him to do the same thing; and to act as if you will be terribly hurt if he does not understand and help.

Another technique is instant assumption of the worst. "Oh, boy," you say. The boss wants to reassure you; "It's nothing serious. Just go along with me for a while." But you will not permit yourself to be consoled; "It sounds like you're in trouble, Grant. And if you're in trouble, then we're all in trouble. You don't have to tell me how bad it is if you can't. I've got the idea. It's got to be pretty bad." And so on. Greet his request as a pushing of the panic button. Be effusively friendly and greatly worried in equal parts. You may even hint that you'll talk to your colleagues to try to rally them behind his cause. Since this is apt to be the last thing the boss wants, he may find a way to back off.

Or, set a time limit. Be gracious in agreeing to "trust" the boss, but indicate at the same time that your trust has limits: "Sure, Grant, I know little hitches come up from time to time. You can't give me a positive answer right now. I understand perfectly. I'll just forget about it for now, and I will rely on you. I won't start to sweat for, oh, three weeks. You're sure to have it cleared up by the end of the month, aren't you?" This is more or less the opposite of the "panic button" response. You make light of his implied problem, taking it in stride as something you're sure he will straighten out. Then set a short deadline. He is probably hoping that you would defer your request for something on the order of a year; but he will be somewhat embarrassed now in spelling that out without giving you some kind of explanation. If the boss says "Well, it will be somewhat longer than that, I'm afraid. . . ." you can come back with a blunt "Oh. I think in that case, Grant, I have a right to know what the problem is."

Enter into an alliance with the boss. Say, "Since the hang-up, whatever it is, concerns my raise, I must be able to help out with it. I'm sure you have enough confidence in me to let me cooperate. I'll keep it entirely confidential, of course, particularly since it involves me. What's the trouble?" This technique — like the others — probes the weakness in the boss's position. If he is asking you to be trusting, why can't he trust you in return? You, after all, are being requested to sacrifice a deserved raise for some unspecified time. You can take the position that you should be shown enough counterloyalty and trust to warrant the assumption that you can be told what's going on.

Your counterstrategy will not destroy a beautiful friendship. Friendships that cost you money are not so beautiful.

The Sham Battle

"Harvey, you're out of your mind!"

"How, out of my mind?"

"You know how! Where the hell do you get off coming in here and saying you want another two thou? God almighty, we're barely treading water the way it is, and that's because we got ham heads like you loading up the payroll! And you have the crust to ask for a raise. Guts at least I'll give you credit for. And because I admire guts, even when they have nothing else to go with them, maybe — just maybe — I'll try to let you hang onto your job. But a raise? Forget about it!"

"Two thousand, Lou."

"Listen, Harvey. So far my good nature is holding me in from saying what I really ought to say. If you leave now I'll try to forget about this crap. But don't push me too far."

"If you're finished with the fireworks, Lou, maybe we can talk like two sane human beings for once. There's my request. Two thousand. Do you want to okay it right now, or do I have to remind you why I have to get it?"

Sounds as if the raise seeker has taken leave of his senses. Is this a case of a subordinate foolishly demanding more money at the cost of imminent firing. As a matter of fact, it is not. Horrendous as the dialogue seems, it is not unprecedented. In this particular company it is not even unusual. Lou Burke and Harvey Amboy are at it again. They've gone through it before. And practically everyone who wants to get a raise from Lou Burke has to go through it. The exchange sounds like the prelude to instant termination, if not mayhem. But that appearance is deceptive. With Lou Burke, this is the way you conduct a raise negotiation.

Some bosses lose most of their inhibitions when they are asked for a raise. They consider this an occasion at which almost anything goes. They bluster. They threaten. They haggle like rug traders in a Damascus bazaar. They wheedle, double talk, evade, dissemble. And they do all this, not because they are evil people, or because they are desperate beyond belief to avoid paying out more money, but because to them, this is the way the raise game is played. And they expect the employee to see the bargaining session as a game, to play it to the hilt, and to hold no grudges afterwards.

Lou Burke is this kind of boss. He enjoys yelling and browbeating in the raise session. He is really letting himself go at the moment because he has dealt with Harvey Amboy before. Harvey knows Lou; and he is not likely to be thrown off stride by the verbal assaults of his superior. Harvey Amboy will stick to his guns and they will finally settle down to a gruelling, mutually-insulting bargaining session that will probably end in a grin, a handshake, and a thousand-dollar raise for Harvey.

For the newcomer, or for the person whose psyche is woven of such fine texture that uproarious shenanigans like this are extremely distasteful, the blustering boss is tough to face in a negotiation over more money. Such people are intimidated into taking less money than they might have gotten. They try to get other jobs where these things are handled with more dignity and sedateness.

But, when jobs are not easy to get, and when the work situation is otherwise satisfactory, it's best to try to accommodate yourself to the blustering boss. You can tell quickly enough if you've got one. Normally he is pleasant enough. It is only when you ask him for a raise that he begins to go through his bag of disconcerting tricks.

The first thing to realize about this kind of manager is that he blusters because he enjoys doing it. True, his tactics may serve as a shrewd means of cowing some employees into settling for less; but they also give the boss a chance to talk tough in a way that he enjoys. The tough-talking boss is out of fashion today. The emphasis is on establishing rapport, speaking softly, treating workers like human beings, and so on. On the whole this works well, and most bosses recognize that. Still, some occasionally hark wistfully back to the days when a boss was less like a modern manager and more like the first mate on a tramp steamer. They like to once in a while shed the trappings of civilized business intercourse and engage in a knock-down-and-drag-out verbal brawl.

So, when you ask the blusterer for a raise, you are giving him a chance to let himself go. It's a game to him. If he wins the game by getting you to modify your legitimate demands, so much the better; but he gets kicks out of just playing the game. And he enjoys meeting an opponent who puts up worthy opposition. No true game-player likes to be matched against a pushover.

Be prepared to play the game in a way that lets both you and the boss come out winners. You want to come out with a raise. The boss wants to enjoy a stimulating workout and to be able to tell himself (even if he does not fully believe it) that he has come out well in the battle of wits by getting you to back off your original demand.

Set a figure considerably higher than you are willing to settle for. This is by no means a tactic to be used in every case; there are bosses with whom it is best to state a figure and never budge from it. But the blusterer will see your initial demand as a target and rip into it, so set the target at sufficient range for him to feel it's worthwhile.

For the more fastidious, there is a temptation to set a high figure, let the boss go into his act, and then sit there, not even half-listening, waiting for the real bargaining to begin. This is not playing the game. The blusterer will recognize what his opponent is doing, and this will take the fun out of the affair for him. He will be goaded to greater efforts in order to get a rise out of the phlegmatic subordinate, and he may work himself into a position from which he will not retreat. The employee will wind up with a real fight, not just a mock battle, on his hands.

No. Name your price and then go in there and battle. You don't have to match insults with the boss, or respond to every outrageous attack on your record or spurious cry of poverty. If this is not your style, stay out of the infighting. But don't act bored or indulgent. Keep your cool and counterpunch when you get an opening. You don't have to think up rejoinders as wild as the manager's sallies. Just keep repeating that this is what you want, not a penny less, and that you will document your case.

After the first hurricane of opposition blows itself out, the negotiation will shift into the haggling phase: "It's highway robbery, but I might just, out of the goodness of my heart, be able to throw you a few bucks. I'll tell you what. I'm in a good mood, and I'd hate to see you out on the street, so let's say another ten-spot per week." The blusterer would be surprised and perhaps more than a little disappointed if you caved in at this point. For him it would be like rushing up a staircase and finding one less step than he expected.

Hang in there. Stick with your demand for a while. Then, finally permit yourself to be whittled down, just a little. "You haven't said one single thing that is a real answer to my proposition, but if we can't talk like reasonable people I guess I'll have to be crazy too. So let's settle at $1800. But that's it. You know damn well you can't buy good work for peanuts. The days of slavery are gone."

You'll come to an agreement. The boss will have some fun. And you'll get your raise.

8

the way to win

Closing The Sale

You are selling the boss on giving you a raise. At some points you are
using modifications of established sales techniques to win the negotiation. As the transaction nears its climax you will want to select the
tactics you need to close the sale.

But, before getting to closing tactics, it's important to consider a
point that many raise seekers overlook to their sorrow. You must
know what you are closing on; and the boss must agree about what is
being closed on.

Here's an example. Frank Erickson feels that his campaign for a
raise has gone well. He has laid the groundwork, documented his
request, skillfully refuted his boss's counterarguments. Now it looks as
if the boss, Will Paradise, is on the brink of a favorable decision. Erickson presses his case, saying, "I think we've gone over all the factors
now Mr. Paradise, and I believe I've shown very clearly why I deserve
this raise. So why don't we get it settled. Don't you agree?"

Paradise doesn't answer right away. He seems to be deep in thought.
Then he smiles. "Yes, Frank, I agree." Erickson feels as if a great
weight has been lifted from his mind. Success! He has achieved the objective. But wait — Paradise is saying something else. "I agree, Frank.
You've made a very good case and I have no more questions to ask.
I find it most persuasive. I'm sure that Lennie will react to it the same
way."

Erickson's eyebrows escalate. Paradise says, "Well, of course I'll have to talk this whole thing over with Lennie. He is really the guy who has the final word on anything like this." And, as Erickson tries to think of something to say, Paradise adds, "You've presented your arguments very well, Frank. I'll be getting back to you in about a week or so."

It's a let-down. But it's worse than that. Frank Erickson may or may not get his raise. But something went seriously wrong with his plan. He arrayed his arguments and deployed them expertly, only to find that he could not close the sale. He was talking to the wrong man; or at least to someone who claims he is the wrong man.

Long before you get to the close, it is vital that you find out what a successful close can accomplish. Will you be closing on the boss's iron-clad agreement to your raise; or on his conditional agreement; or on his recommendation; or merely on the possibility of his relaying your arguments to someone else?

You don't want to be trapped into making your pitch to the wrong party. If at all possible, you want the raise negotiation to contain the potential for a definite decision then and there. If your assessment of the situation discloses that this is impossible, then at least you want to be able to close on a firm recommendation in favor of your request — a recommendation that will be acted on favorably as a matter of routine. Anything short of this is unfavorable. When you undergo the effort and emotional stress of a raise interview you need to be sure that the chance of success is there.

From experience you may know that your boss has the power to say yes or no to your demand. You may be so certain of that fact that it is unnecessary to check it out. But, if there is any question, make sure. Early in the proceedings, get it established that you are asking for more money and that the person you are asking has the capability of granting your request. Usually there's no need to be gingery or oblique about this. Say it right out... "I'm going to ask for a raise, and I'm prepared to answer any questions you have about my qualification for it. Can I be sure that you can give me a decision, yes or no?"

You want a commitment, obviously not to agreement in advance, but to the power to give you a decision. If the boss indicates that the matter will have to be discussed with others, or bucked up the line, find out as much as you can about the process. Who is involved? How long will it take? How much weight will a favorable recommendation from your immediate boss carry in the discussion stage? You can, in a way, challenge your boss on this last point, by saying something like, "Well, I guess your recommendation is apt to be accepted, isn't it? Or is this a situation where that would not make all that much difference?" Many bosses would like to pass the buck on raise requests. But they are less likely to do so if they have to admit that they are not very important in the scheme of things.

If it appears that others will be influential in the decision, you may want to ask if you can talk with them. As a practical matter, that may not be possible. However, there are other ways to affect those who will have some say over your request; they are covered elsewhere. The important thing is to determine, long before you get to the closing phase, just what you are closing on.

And, as the apex of the negotiation approaches and you get ready to "ask for the order," restate the nature of what you are requesting. "This is a request for a $2500 increase in salary, starting January 1. I'd like your approval so I can make some personal financial decisions." or, "What I'm going to ask, Leo, is that you make the strongest recommendation you can in favor of this request. I know that if you do that I have every reasonable chance of getting it." When both parties are clear on the nature of the decision to be reached, then the negotiation can move on to the closing stage.

No matter how overwhelming the case, or unanswerable the logic, closing is a tricky operation. Experienced salesmen know this. The boss's instinct is to say "no." He may like you. He may acknowledge that you have done a superb job, deserving of reward. He may be fearful of your leaving if you don't receive what you have asked. And yet he will resist. It's human nature. If he owns the firm, he sees it as *his* money that he is paying out. If he is also an employee, he is spending the company's money; and his bosses expect him to make and save money, not spend it.

Such feelings are not logical; of course not. They are instinctive. And because of that they may be harder to grapple with than the logical objections that you have been answering as you have made your pitch. "Yes" comes hard when the boss is asked to okay a substantial raise. So your approach to closing must deal with some of the problems, logical or not, that linger in his mind.

Risk. If he approves a raise the boss is taking a chance. Suppose your work goes downhill? He will have blown the additional money he is paying you. Worse, his judgment may be put into question. As you try to move him those last few inches toward agreement, remember that he will be thinking about the chance he may be taking. Your job is to reassure him that there is no risk — or that, at most, it is very small.

Hope. Even though you have been rock-like in sticking to your asking figure, the boss will retain to the last his hope that you will settle for less. To counter this you must get across the point that the possible consequences of his continued resistance far outweigh any small advantage he may gain by haggling.

Face-saving. No one enjoys being beaten in a negotiation. Some bosses will, of necessity, admit that there is every reason to give a subordinate the full raise demanded. Nevertheless, something deep inside will not permit that one syllable of assent to come out. The negotiation is a struggle, and assent is acknowledgment of defeat. You will have to work things so that the boss does not view his agreement as surrender. You are out to get a raise, not pin his shoulders to the mat.

One closing effort may not be enough to overcome all this. But unfortunately many raise seekers — who handle everything else well — fall down when it comes to the close. They do little more than make one half-hearted effort to get a decision. Here, for example, is how it goes with such a person. Tim Orchard felt very sure of himself when he was detailing the ways in which he had mastered his job challenges during the past year. He was not too shaken up when the boss asked tough questions. He stuck with his asking figure, remaining calm in the face of managerial opposition. But now, when perhaps all he has to do is pin down the boss on the raise, Tim is getting gun-shy. He says, "I hope I've covered all the reasons why I ought to get this raise."

The boss nods; "I believe you have."

"Are there," Tim asks, "any other questions that we should talk about?"

The boss indicates that he doesn't think so. Tim says, "Well then, I hope I've gotten across to you with my point. This raise is important to me and I feel that I've earned it. You won't be sorry that you've given it to me." The boss looks at Tim, with neither hostility nor approbation. There is a pause. Tim begins to fidget and then says abruptly, "Well, since we've covered everything, I'm wondering. . .I mean. . . ."

"I'll think about it, Tim, and let you know."

Grateful for the dismissal that signals the end of the interview, Tim Orchard quickly leaves the boss's office. You would think that he had made a botch of his negotiation. He hasn't. But he has neglected to close the sale. He has let the boss get off the hook. Why?

There are a number of factors that cause us to be squeamish about actually "closing the sale" and boldly asking that the raise be granted. For one thing there is the fear of rejection. No matter how strong your case, you can never be sure of success. And there is something inside all of us that causes us to hang back from certainty on the slim chance that certainty may be bad news. We occasionally pass up the chance of hearing an almost sure "yes" on the small chance that we might hear an unwelcome "no."

And then there is something so cold-blooded, so blunt, about saying flat out, give me a raise. It's one thing when you're talking about the job, your accomplishments, your plans, etc. But when it comes to the close you know you are asking the boss to do something that he would rather not do. Will he resent it? Will you be storing up trouble for yourself later? Is there some way to avoid awkwardness?

Sometimes, too, we hesitate to pull the trigger because we think there may be a chance of creeping a little closer. We wonder if we have advanced every possible argument, if the boss has gotten every conceivable favorable point. We're not sure; so we branch back into a rehash of arguments that have been advanced already, and go over old ground that has already been won until we run out of time.

When you go in looking for a raise, think it out beforehand. Don't kid yourself that, after you have engaged in some pleasantly objective conversation, your manager is going to spring up, crying jovially "Enough! You don't have to say any more! You can have the raise right now!" Those things don't happen. You will have to accommodate yourself to the reality of, at the proper point, bringing the negotiation to a successful conclusion by applying the finishing touch.

Don't rest all your hopes on just one effort at closing. Be ready for delay and resistance. Be prepared to overcome the resistance by applying a *series* of closing devices, each leading into the next. If one doesn't work, it prepares the ground for the next effort.

Consider the example of a football team which works its way down to within the opponent's twenty-yard line to try for the game-winning touchdown. The coach and his quarterback do not put all their chips on one play. The plays are mapped out according to a sequence. First may come a short pass. If it works, fine. If not, the enemy secondary may have been drawn in just a fraction so that they are set up for a long pass. If the long pass fails, the opposing linemen may have been conditioned to anticipate a third pass — and be vulnerable to a running play. And so on. The working strategy lies in the sequence, not in the single bold stroke. In the same fashion a really outstanding boxer finishes off his opponent not with one blow but with a series of punches in combination.

Here is how a determined raise seeker might apply a sequence of closing devices to gain what he wants.

Alan Fournier has decided that he has answered all of his boss's questions and has presented his case well enough to merit a try at closing the deal. The boss, Dale McBride, has been tough; but Fournier feels that his points have registered. So the closing sequence begins.

Fournier repeats two or three of his major arguments: "So from July on down to the present I've had the responsibility for quality control as well as for assembly. We have been able to meet every deadline, and when we consider the pattern of overall company costs, our performance in this area has been superior. I believe I have shown the ability to handle these increased responsibilities, and I expect to continue to handle even tougher assignments next year. I think these were the big questions you had about my work. Since I've covered it all, I guess we would both welcome the chance to wrap this up and get on about our business. Will I see that three thousand dollar raise reflected in the first paycheck I get right after the first of the year, or is it more likely to start with the second one, two weeks later?"

Fournier is *assuming* that the raise has been granted, and is asking the boss a procedural question about how it will be implemented. This is a technique that slides over the necessity for the boss to come right out and say, "I will give you the raise." When you are dealing with a boss to whom face-saving is particularly important, it avoids the awkwardness implicit in his having to acknowledge orally, at the moment, that you have won. He can enter into a little conversation with you over the minor point of whether or not you start to get the raise in the first or second pay of the coming year. The response asked for is an easy one, because it involves nothing more than an unimportant fact. Even if the boss does not know the answer, he can say, "Well, I'm not sure. That depends on how they handle it in accounting." When he says this you can reply, "It really doesn't matter much. The important thing is getting it. Thank you. This raise means a great deal to me and you can be sure I'll go all out to continue to earn it."

Sometimes you need go no farther than this assumptive conclusion. But in this case Fournier's boss is not quite ready to say "yes."

"Well," replies Dale McBride, "That would be easy enough to find out, if and when we get to that stage. But we haven't gotten there. There are things about this that I would have to think over."

Fournier is not perturbed. He didn't really expect to wrap it up on his first try. And he has made measurable gains. Implicit in McBride's answer is the message that a lot of Fournier's points have gotten across. So he moves on to the next step.

"Okay," says Alan Fournier. "I agree that something like this has to be looked at carefully; certainly I would consider it carefully if I were in your shoes, Dale. So let's go over some of the points again." Fournier reaches for a blank piece of paper, begins to jot brief notes on it. "As you've said, the things you value the highest are ability to handle the rank-and-file. . .adaptability to new situations. . .cost-consciousness. . . ." Fournier lists a number of points. Then he goes back to review his own qualifications: "At the risk of seeming to blow my own horn, I think I have shown that I can handle even some of the toughest characters down in that department. For example, you know yourself that Jake Gebhardt has sharpened up considerably in the past few months — gets in on time, doesn't bitch when he's given special runs to perform, he's even helping out with some of the new guys. As for adaptability, you will remember that day when we had to turn the whole line upside down because that rush order came down from Albany. . . ." Fournier goes through his summation. Then: "Would you agree that these are the main points of performance in that job, and that I've been able to measure up to them pretty well?"

"Yes, on the whole you've been doing okay, Alan."

"Then, can we say that I have qualified for the raise?"

Fournier is making his second try for the close. He has recapped his strong points and gotten the boss to agree once again that, in general, they have been proven. He has ignored the implication contained in the comment about "thinking it over," going right on with the interview on the assumption that the decision will be made then and there. And he has directly asked for the raise.

"Alan, your record is good. But that's a lot of money you're asking for. I just don't think we're ready to give you that much."

"Because there's something about my record that we haven't talked about? I'd like to hear what your objection is. . . . ?"

"Well, it's not any single thing, Alan. It's just a matter of experience. You haven't been handling that kind of responsibility for as long as some of the other boys, and, well, I just think you need more experience."

Fournier looks at the boss. "Dale, is that your reason for saying that you have problems about the raise? Lack of experience? I mean, if there's something more specific than that, I think I'm entitled to hear about it, no matter what it is."

"No, it's the experience factor that makes me think that you are just asking for too much."

"Uh-huh." Fournier is quiet for a moment. Then he says, "Would you tell me this. Do you feel that experience is just a matter of being around for a certain number of years? Or are there other factors?"

"Well, of course it's not just being around. Some guys can be around forever and they never pick up much of anything. It's what you do with what you see and hear in the time you have."

"And, if you don't mind my asking another question, where does experience come into play? I mean, what's the most valuable thing about it?"

McBride — although he is well aware that he is being sold — has no decent choice but to consider this. "Experience gives a man a kind of bank to draw on. When he runs into a problem he is able to go back into his experience and come up with possible solutions. There's no substitute for it."

"I agree that there is no substitute for being able to come up with possible solutions for a problem. I've always tried to work that way," says Fournier. "And I think I've been successful at it. Not only tapping my own experience, but the experience of others as well. For instance when we had to figure out a way around that breakdown on four and six that time, there wasn't anybody in the place who remembered anything like that happening before. It wouldn't have done me much good to have even fifty years of experience. The thing to do, I decided, was to put together the useful experiences at hand — I came to you first, Dale — and come up with some answers. So, wouldn't you say that experience is very worthwhile, and even more worthwhile when you're able to call upon the savvy of a whole range of people, not just yourself?"

They discuss the point at some more length, McBride has to concur that experience in itself is not the big thing, it's how you call experience into action when it is needed. And he has no reason to fault Fournier's ability to do this. At last Alan Fournier makes his next closing move: "You said, Dale, that this business of experience was your reason for hesitating about giving me the money. Frankly, I think I've shown that I have what it takes under that heading. So — back to the reason for the meeting. Can we wrap it up? Will you okay that raise?"

McBride shakes his head. "Alan, you're a very persuasive guy, but I'm going to have to think it over."

What Fournier did during this phase was to "qualify" the boss; to smoke out his principal objection (or what he claimed was his principal objection) to granting the increase. Then Fournier addressed himself to this obstacle as if it were not just the principal, but the only, obstacle. He focused on the objection and discussed it until the boss agreed that it did not stand up. At that point, with the "only" stumbling block out of the way, Fournier was ready to make a strong pitch to close the negotiation successfully. It might well have worked. It didn't quite work; McBride is a stubborn adversary. But the boss is in no position to raise new objections. About all he can say is that he wants to think it over.

Fournier considers this answer. Then he says, "I appreciate that, Dale. But I'm counting on the fact that you have always been a decisive guy. We all know that when we ask you for an answer we get one, yes or no. And it means a lot to us. Now, for a lot of reasons I would like to get this settled. It's really important to me that it get settled. I've done my best to answer every point you've brought up. Do you really mean you don't know what answer to give me?"

As McBride looks at him, Fournier goes on: "I'm counting on your answer now, Dale, I really am, whether it's yes or no. I think it ought to be yes, damn right I do, but if it's no, then that's the way the chips fall. If I didn't know that you are the kind of guy who will lay it on the line I wouldn't be counting on an answer as I am right now. You know, a time comes when any answer is better than no answer. Of course the money I'm asking for is a pretty good sum, but in light of everything I think it's justified. And you can be damn sure that I will not let you down when I get it. There are things coming up next year that will call for the maximum in the way of productivity from all of us, and when you okay this, you can be certain that I'll deliver."

Fournier is doing several things here. He is appealing to the boss's self-image as a decision-maker. Nobody likes to be cast in the role of a ducker of issues or a procrastinator. When the subordinate puts the boss on the spot by asking him to show that he can make spot decisions, the boss may be hard pressed to wriggle out of it.

Another thing that this employee is doing is hinting at the unfortunate potential results that may lie in delay or in a negative answer. He does no more than hint — but he can be reasonably sure that, since the boss has come this far in the discussion, he does not want to lose Fournier, or risk his disaffection.

Then too, Fournier is reassuring the boss that he will not regret a favorable decision. He indicates that he will be grateful and that he will do everything in his power to deliver personally. This two-pronged thrust, threat and reassurance, is designed to move the boss across that last difficult threshold.

But still the boss has a problem. "I'm willing to consider a raise, Alan, and even agree that you deserve one. But three thousand? It's too high. Never mind getting into a discussion of whether you're worth it. I don't want to argue that again, one way or the other. But there are other circumstances that affect my decision. I don't want to go into them, but I'm sure you know what I mean. Your figure is too high. I want to do the best I can for you, but this is why I have to say I need to think it over."

There is a pause. Then Fournier says, "I understand what you're saying, Dale. And I guess you can see my problem, that it's god damn hard to accept not getting what you think you've earned because there are other considerations that you have no control over. But it's still important to me that I get a decision. . . ."

They look at each other. Fournier shrugs. "Well. . .I guess there's nothing I can do about these other factors, and we have to deal with the realities. You've been fair in leveling with me. I think three thousand dollars is the right figure for what I've accomplished and what I am going to continue to accomplish. But I'm willing to compromise. I will take twenty-five hundred and give you everything I've got — on the provision that you take this into consideration next time we talk about money."

Fournier stops talking. They sit there. The pause gets longer. But Fournier just waits.

Alan Fournier has gone to his next step. He has stepped down his demand to a lower figure, after refusing to consider anything lower throughout the interview. This concession is most helpful in permitting the boss to "save face." He can feel that he came out of the negotiation with something; he was able to get the subordinate to back off his original demand. Fournier would have liked to get the three thousand; but he was prepared to take the twenty-five hundred. McBride may suspect that, but he doesn't know it for sure, and so he can assume that it is his hard bargaining that has reduced the price.

And, as boss and subordinate sit looking at each other, Fournier is making one more powerful tool work for him — *silence.* You have to know when to keep your mouth shut. When you have made your rock-bottom concession, in return for an immediate answer, don't say any more. Sit there and let the boss do the talking. In this case McBride might respond by trying to haggle over the amount, by coming back with an offer of, say, two thousand. But Fournier is prepared to stick with twenty-five hundred as his final concession. He has refused to consider coming down earlier in the interview; and at this psychological moment he has the boss in a position where he does not feel like haggling any more.

At last McBride says, "All right. Twenty-five hundred dollars. The first of the year. I hope I have made the right move, Alan." Alan Fournier assures his boss that he has, indeed, made the right move; and leaves. Back at his desk, Fournier does one more thing. He writes a brief memo to the boss, summing up the agreement and repeating his thanks.

This example shows one way that a sequence of moves can be used to bring a raise negotiation to a close. The plan, in brief:

- Assume that all the questions are answered and that the raise will be granted.
- Summarize the main arguments for the raise and ask for it.
- Smoke out an objection, focus down on it as the main obstacle to the raise, answer the objection, and again ask for the raise.
- Imply the negative results that may result from delay or from a "no," and reassure the boss that he will be making the right move by saying "yes."
- If necessary, make one concession and then wait for the boss's answer.

When you get the raise, thank the boss, reassure him again — and, where indicated, formalize it by putting it in writing. You may or may not want to send a copy of your wrap-up document somewhere else in the firm, like the financial department. The big thing is to pin it down so that there can be no change of heart.

The combination illustrated here consisted of five distinct closing devices. The combination that you prepare to use may be shorter, or longer. It's best usually to be ready for more resistance than you think logical. What happens if you run through your repertoire of closing mechanisms? Well, there's no reason not to repeat them. In this example, McBride might still have hesitated and insisted that he was not ready to come through. At that point the subordinate — as long as he had not been actually thrown out of the boss's office — could have gone back to an earlier ploy and launched once again into a recap of his strong points, saying, "Well, if I can go over my main reasons once again, maybe you can see my point." Sure it's an uncomfortable situation; but it's uncomfortable for the boss as well as for you. Be ready to stand a little temporary discomfort so that you can make the boss uncomfortable enough to resolve the matter by giving you what you want.

And always think out carefully how you will close. Otherwise you may waste a magnificent effort.

Going Public

On the whole the raise negotiation is a matter that should be kept between you and the boss. Usually disclosure of your strategy of your progress is detrimental to your cause. Word gets back to the boss, and he doesn't like it. Others swarm in with their requests. The boss is put on the spot. None of this can work to your advantage.

However, there is a stage at which you might consider "going public" in a selective way; bringing others into the act. Such a move should not usually be considered unless you find that you are in a losing position. The boss has stalled long past the time when he should have responded. He has given you an extremely negative prognosis. You learn, on reliable authority, that the decision is about to go against you.

At this point you may want to look around for reinforcements. When the boss is stalling, or pleading poverty, you can enlist the pressure of numbers. Talk to your colleagues. Float the possibility that the outfit may be in trouble. Get people to talking uneasily about the possibility of unwelcome changes, like severe cutbacks, relocation, or even going out of business.

No boss enjoys talk like this. When he learns about it — and he will — he may suspect that you have something to do with the speculation. But he will not know that for a fact. And his suspicion is apt to be overshadowed by his anxiety that there be no outbreak of mass pessimism in the ranks. If the only way he can find to bolster the positive attitude is by giving raises, then he may come to the conclusion that they are not such a high price to pay after all. When you feel that your chances are gloomy enough to justify strong measures, the nudging along of some gossip can be helpful. It doesn't take much nudging;

people are quite ready to believe the worst about the company and its management.

Another source of assistance may be your boss's counterpart in another department. This is not a route to be taken without careful thought. If you enlist another manager in your cause, this outside party must meet certain criteria. He must be someone your boss respects (or perhaps fears a little) and with whom the boss has maintained reasonably cordial relationships. When you go to someone whom your boss hates, you are applying the blade of the razor to your own throat.

The approach should be indirect. Let us say that you have, in the course of your work, a fair amount of contact with the other party. You have tried to look good in his eyes. You are always cooperative, you never let him down in your role as liaison. Sit down with him for a frank and confidential chat. This is a risk, and you ought to be pretty sure that he will not immediately pick up the phone and disclose the whole thing to your own superior. Bosses, no matter how remote they may appear from each other, have a tendency to form into a tight circle when threatened with unwelcome things like raise requests. This is another reason why this form of "going public" is a delicate matter, not to be taken on lightly.

Go over your problem. Don't knock your boss. Don't say, "He doesn't appreciate me." Say, rather, "He's on the ball, and a fair guy, but he's so busy that he can't see everything. Sometimes I think he tends to take my performance for granted, and that's okay with me. I don't need pats on the back. But I do need more money, and I wondered if a word from you might be helpful. You've had a chance to observe me a little. Of course you wouldn't be mentioning our conversation, but you might just say what you think about me from your point of view."

Your hope is that the other manager — whom you will have gauged carefully — will utter a few casual words in your behalf, and that this might help to swing the balance.

There is another party, at a different level, who you may think of trying when the situation looks really tough and the raise is important. This is your boss's boss, or somebody higher up who draws a lot of water. The dangers here are obvious. Going over the boss's head is not a popular ploy. Upper-level managers do not welcome complaints about their subordinates from their subordinates' subordinates. They have enough headaches of their own.

But an oblique approach might work without involving you in too much risk. Try to make opportunities to come in contact with the higher-up. Sometimes a casual exchange in the john can be extended into a conversation in which you can get a chance to air some of your ideas. Never at any time will you even hint that your own boss doesn't listen, or that he is in any way at fault. You are a dedicated member of the team, and you just happen to be talking over team matters with one of the top players. It helps if you can demonstrate a detailed appreciation of his role and his importance in the scheme of things. Say something about some coup he pulled off, or some honor that was bestowed on him. Do your best, without tugging at his coat, to impress him.

It's probably not a good idea to even hint that you'd like him to put in a good word for you. You may even get farther by playing it in reverse, saying something like, "You know, in talking with you I've kind of gotten carried away with my own enthusiasm. I hope, if you happen to be chatting with Dan Clancy, you won't give him any reason to think I was going over his head. Not that Dan is the kind of guy who would think that, but I am scrupulous about such things." You hope he will reassure you, and then manage to drop a casual word into a talk with your boss that will indicate his favorable impression.

Going public is tricky. Resort to it only when you are pretty sure that you are in a stern chase, and that urgent measures must be taken. And, except in extraordinary circumstances, confine your outside help to people within the company. Don't, for example, have your spouse buttonhole the boss or his wife at a social gathering and talk up your raise. That's a pretty sure way of making matters worse.

Getting The Boss To Quit Stalling

"I just can't give you an answer now."
"I'll have to think it over."
"You'll be hearing an answer on this before long."
"I'll have to talk this over and get back to you."
You have presented your case for a raise, and used all of the closing techniques you are able to muster. The boss doesn't seem to have any more questions or objections. But still you can't get an answer.

Some delays are to be expected. When you know that your boss must put through a request and get an okay before he can tell you the increase is yours, you're prepared for some dead time. But the quicker you get an answer the better, for several reasons.

If the boss is just stalling you so that he can "think it over," time is not likely to work on your side. Others will press in on him with their requests. New factors may arise that will make him tighten his grip on the purse strings. (Of course something may happen that will make more money available for raises, but somehow that doesn't happen nearly as much as its opposite.) And meanwhile your arguments are becoming dimmer in the boss's mind.

For your own planning you want to know as soon as possible if you're going to get a raise, and how much. Maybe there are other job possibilities that you'd like to explore. You may have to make family plans that are contingent upon income. You must do as much as you can to resolve the uncertainty fast.

And there is yet another reason to press the boss to give you a reply. If you seem willing to endure an indefinite delay he may conclude that you are not all that determined about your raise, and begin to foster the hope that he can get away with giving you a lot less, or nothing at all. So you will want to keep the pressure on.

When the boss says that he can't give you a yes or no right now, your first response may be to ignore his ploy. Just kind of nod your head and go right into a reprise of your strongest arguments for the raise. Ask him once again if there is any problem about your work that he has not yet brought up. Then tell him how important it is to you to know right away how much you'll be making. Ask for the raise. Perhaps this next time around he will give you an answer.

But let's say he repeats the stall. Find out as much as you can about why he is putting it off. The best way to find out is to ask. Don't be bashfull about it: "Mr. Burns, would you tell me why you can't give me an answer now?"

He may say that he has to talk it over with others. Try to find out who the others are. You needn't press too hard. You can find out a lot by suggesting a name or two ("I guess any raise like this has to be cleared with Mr. Meeker.") and watching his reaction. Form an estimate of the purpose of the other conversations. Is your boss looking for approval, or merely advice? If he has to go upward for approval, make sure you have given him (in writing if necessary) the ammunition he will need to make his – and your – case. If he is talking it over with others for guidance, there may be some indirect ways in which you can influence the others with whom he'll be speaking.

Or maybe he just wants to "think it over." Ask him what in particular there is to think over. . . "Is there something about the job I've been doing that you're not quite sure of?". . ."Did you want to check out the figures for the last quarter?". . ."Is there something coming up that

I don't know about?" If the boss tells you what he's going to be thinking about, give him a fresh pitch on the question right away. You
might possibly resolve his doubts. At least you will be reinforcing your
arguments in his mind.

Appeal to his self-image as a decision-maker. With a look of disappointment and disillusion, a subordinate says, "I just assumed that you
had the authority to approve this raise." Some bosses, stung a little,
may come back to make it very clear that they do indeed have the
authority. The posture at that point is to wonder why, if the manager
has the power to make the decision, he does not make the decision then
and there? It does no harm to try this tactic. It may provoke the boss
into proving to you that he really does draw a lot of water in the organization by approving your request.

Try to get the boss to indicate the way he is leaning. You might say,
"Well, since we have gone over the picture pretty thoroughly, I guess I
can assume that if nothing negative turns up, I can count on getting the
raise." He's apt to caution you that you can never count on anything;
at which point you can get into a discussion of your chances of obtaining more money. "It's awfully tough," you can say, "to be left slowly
twisting, twisting in the wind." If he says chances are poor, then he
must have a reason for saying that. Make it clear that you feel entitled
to hear the reason, and reply to it.

If he says chances are pretty good, then your best approach is to
project optimism. Show him that you are counting on his "assurance."
Act as if you have translated his mildly rosy observation into something
pretty close to a sure thing. He may try to dampen you, but don't let
him dampen you too much — at least not so he can see.

Work for a time limit. If there is going to be a delay in learning
whether you've gotten the increase, ask how long it will be. Suggest a
time frame; "I imagine you'll be able to tell me by the end of next
week." He may want to know why you are so anxious about finding
out fast. You have a ready-made general answer: this is very important to you, there are things to think about, you want to pitch into
your work with a clear mind, and so on. Try to get something approaching a definite deadline, at least an implied one; and see that it is
not too far in the future.

Try to leave it as a "no news is good news" proposition. One raise
seeker does it this way: "Since I know you realize how important this
is to me, I'm sure you would get back to me right away if there were
any problem. So I won't let the delay bother me; I'll assume it's going

through all right as soon as the details are cleared away." Few managers are going to say that they *won't* get back to you right away if there's a problem. By doing this you are putting on a little more pressure. If he just delays unduly you can assume that the raise is okayed.

During the waiting period, remind him that you are waiting. If the boss avoids you, send it to him in writing. Cast your reminders in a positive light: "You would have let me know by now if the answer were no, so I'm not worried about that. If there is any more information I can provide to expedite the process, I'm of course anxious to do so." By tendering the boss these continuing (and not necessarily welcome) reminders you are using a variation of the PITA (Pain-In-The-Ass) principle that is elaborated at another point in this book.

Come back at him with a new selling point. If you are reasonably certain that there is going to be any stalling about your raise, you may even want to hold back on some ammunition so that you can use it to try to dissolve the log jam. Here's how one employee does it. Catching the boss at a not-too-pressured moment, he says, "I didn't bring it up when we were talking last week, because it doesn't fall strictly within the area of my job, but I know you're interested in simplifying communications between departments, so I thought I'd mention it now. I was able to work out a plan with shipping that gives us instant feedback. . . ." The employee goes on to give a brief summary of his contribution. He ends by adding, "I thought this might help to crystallize your thinking, and be of use when you're putting through the reasons for my raise." Just one more plus may be all it takes to smoke out a favorable answer.

If the delay continues, begin to talk it up around the shop. You know that others have put in for raises. Ask them if they have gotten an answer. If they, like you, are still waiting, one response might be a worried frown and a conjecture. . . "I wonder if there's something they're not telling us. Is the outfit in trouble? You'd think by now they'd be able to say one way or another." If your grapevine operates the way most do, the boss will soon be aware that people are beginning to talk. He will not be eager for the talk to continue. Give him a chance to still the gossip by asking him once again about your raise. You may even refer to the talk: "I realize that these things take time, Chet, but you ought to know that some of the guys out there are beginning to get a little uneasy. It would be good all around if you could manage to give us some answers soon."

If you are on kidding terms with the boss, introduce the light touch. "You're keeping something from me, Bob; my raise. Don't you think an old-time loyal toiler like me has a right to know about these things? Or are you just building up the suspense so that you can come on like Santa Claus?" If the boss is one who likes to kid around with the help, he may not like the point of your persiflage, but he can hardly blow up at you. It is another way to remind him that you're waiting for an answer and that you are expecting it to be favorable.

Act worried. You're usually a calm and affable operator on the job. But now when the boss talks to you, you are preoccupied and unusually serious. He may notice and not say anything — but he's likely to guess that you're reacting to the uncertainty over the raise. If he does mention it, you can be apologetic while making your point: "Gee, I'm sorry, I didn't realize it showed. The fact is, while I'm counting on the raise — you didn't see any reason why I shouldn't — it is sort of on my mind until it's all wrapped up." Whether or not you touch the boss's heart, he does not like to have gloomy people around, and he does not enjoy the thought that you might be doing less than your best because your mind may be wandering.

Stalling comes naturally to some bosses when faced with a raise request. During the interview itself you will want to do your utmost to get a decision on the spot — by challenging him, by appealing to his decision-making capacity, by reiterating your arguments, by applying a variety of closing techniques. If you cannot break through at that time, leave yourself in as favorable a position as possible. Find out as much as you can about the reason for the delay and what he will be thinking and talking about. Try to put a time limit on your agony. Get as much of a commitment as you can. Leave the boss, if possible, with the thought that you have reason to become more sure of getting the increase as the days go on.

And, by a combination of means, keep the pressure on him to quit stalling and give you your answer. If, of course, he says something like, "It's 99 percent set — just some paperwork to go through," then you can take the pressure off. The whole idea of the anti-stall campaign is to keep time from working against you, and make the unanswered question a weight on the boss's mind that he will want to get rid of as soon as he can. When you run into delaying tactics, you don't have to just sit there, gritting your teeth and taking it.

You've Got Your Raise — Now What?

The battle ended a month ago. Dan McNamara got the big raise he was after. What's happening now?

Bob Feininger, McNamara's boss, is sitting in his office, squinting at a report showing the latest performance figures from McNamara's department. The figures are, by any objective standard, satisfactory. Dan McNamara has been doing a good job. But Feininger is not happy. He is vaguely dissatisfied. It would be hard to define exactly what he's looking for, but anything short of really spectacular results from McNamara leaves him feeling unfulfilled.

A couple of McNamara's colleagues are talking over a cup of coffee. They are discussing Dan's success in swinging the increase, which McNamara has described to his friends in blow-by-blow fashion. One colleague says, "I like Dan — he's a beautiful human being — but, when you lay it all out, is he worth all that much?" The other colleague nods his head; "I'm all for a guy getting all he can get. But when they pay a fellow like Dan McNamara that much, you have to ask yourself whether it isn't a little out of line. How much do they have left over for the rest of us?"

Dan McNamara leans back in his chair, hands behind his head. He's thinking about the 34-foot cruiser that he is at last able to afford. It will be delivered next week. Dan contemplates with enormous contentment the first weekend trip to a nearby island. His eye travels to the pile of papers in his in-box, which he knows he had better get going on pretty soon. But he delays a little while, savoring again the triumph that has capped his carefully-planned campaign for a raise. Dan is luxuriating in the pleasant lethargy of a feeling not unlike that of the post-coital state.

This is a dangerous situation. You can fight your way through to a large salary increase, only to louse yourself up during the weeks that follow.

One element of the problem exists within the boss's head. He has been bested in a hard bargaining situation. He has given you the raise you want, but you had to push him to get it. Now what's happening in his mind? There may be some resentment there. The boss goes back over the steps in the negotiation. With the benefit of hindsight he sees the places where he did not perform to best advantage. "I should have said such-and-such," he tells himself. He may at least be wondering if he has been conned. This is not a pleasant feeling, and the effects can be perilous when your boss feels that you may be the one who has conned him. You may have been fair, although tough, during every step of the process. If this is so the boss's doubts are apt to fade away. But he may be smoldering somewhat, whether the heat is justified or not.

Even if the boss has overcome any feelings of resentment he may be looking for "something special" from you. The psychological phenomenon mentioned earlier, "cognitive dissonance," causes our subconscious minds to continue to grope for ways to justify an important decision, even after that decision has been made. This is the case with Bob Feininger, McNamara's boss. Feininger has no reason to expect miracles from Dan McNamara. Nevertheless he would like something — he can't describe it — that will help to resolve the "dissonance" in his subconscious mind and make him feel more at ease about the raise he has okayed for his persistent subordinate.

The successful raise getter's colleagues also present a problem, and, curiously, the friendlier they are the bigger the problem that they may present. When you manage to get more money in the pay envelope, your natural reaction is to share the news of your good fortune with your friends, particularly those friends who toil in the same vineyard and who will know better than anyone else what a triumph you have scored. So you tell your compatriots about what happened, dwelling on each delicious detail. To your face your pals are appreciative. They nod and smile. But what are they really thinking and feeling? De La Rochefoucauld observed that we can all find enough fortitude to bear the misfortunes of our friends. Conversely it is not always easy for us to endure the triumphs of our friends. Dan McNamara's motives were innocent enough. He was only giving his friends the good news — at least so far as he is aware. He was not conscious of any desire to boast or to play the big shot. However, the raise winner who talks about it to colleagues on the job may be building up resentment and trouble. His friends may not be quite so frinedly. They may even, consciously or unconsciously, move in the direction of doing things that will "cut him down to size."

The individual who obtains a fat raise after a hard fight may have caused problems for himself. Some people expend so much emotional energy in the sprint down the stretch that they breast the tape, stagger to the side of the track, and lie there panting happily for an extended time. The days just after the big raise are not good ones for resting on ones laurels or on anything else. Dan McNamara's pleasant dreams could turn into nightmares if they last too long.

Self-satisfied lethargy is not the only danger. There is also the problem of guilt. *Guilt?* Yes. Some people who manage to swing a good raise have twinges afterward. They went all-out for the money, but perhaps the successful culmination of the negotiation was something of a surprise. Anyway, the man who has gotten the raise begins to ask himself, "Am I really worth it?" His feeling that he is being overpaid may well be fostered by remarks made by the boss at the conclusion of the negotiation. . ."Frankly, I don't think you really merit this kind of money, but it looks as if I'm going to have to pay it to you."

Psychologists have studied the reactions of workers who feel they are being overpaid. They have found that, in a significant number of cases, the worker who feels this way may go into a slump. He becomes fussy and super-cautious. He worries about quality so much that his overall output declines. Functions that he once handled in routine fashion now loom as difficult challenges. More money makes him less effective. He is concerned about having gone out on a limb into an exposed position. The prophecy becomes a self-fulfilling one when his work slips and he actually does place himself in jeopardy.

So there are certain things to watch for immediately after you get that good raise. Consider your own frame of mind. Avoid the tendency to coast — this is the wrong time to do that. And examine your thinking carefully. Is there any tinge of concern that you are being overpaid? Forget it. The odds are high that you are not being overpaid. You may be getting more money than they wanted to pay you, more than has been paid before for this job, but that does not constitute overpayment. Think of the money as an incentive. If you were *not* getting it you would be working hard to qualify for it. But you *are* getting it. It is still an incentive; it just works in a different way. Now you will set out, with confidence and determination, to earn that money, and to make sure that the boss knows you're earning it. Money is always an incentive. You might as well be getting the benefit of it while you are stimulated by the necessity to earn it.

Resist the impulse to tell your friends about it. Even when they press you, evade their questions. They will say they want to hear all about it — but they don't. They may have strong suspicions that you have made a big score, but if you don't confirm it the question is still open, and they can console themselves that maybe the rumors are untrue. You'll assure yourself of more lasting friendships, greater cooperation, and fewer roadblocks on the path to your next increase if you are as closemouthed as possible about your financial accomplishment.

How about the boss's frame of mind? You should do what you can to help him resolve whatever dissonant feelings he may have about giving you the money. You can't turn yourself into a prodigy overnight, but there are certain things you can do.

For one thing, don't give the boss the least cause for suspicion that you are gloating about the money. Emphasize your earnest dedication to the job and your appreciation for his favorable decision. Be visibly busy. Look as if you are taking life on the job with the utmost seriousness.

But — avoid the mistake of going all out to produce artificially high performance in the days following the bestowal of the increase. Some people go into spasms of frantic effort to show that the raise is justified. They raise hopes in the boss's mind, but they can't keep up the pace. The boss becomes disappointed. He has been led to believe that his granting of the raise has somehow created a superman, but his creation crumbles back into normality and his doubts about the merits of the raise return with greater force.

Don't knock yourself out to set a pace that you will not be able to maintain. And don't try to handle your own feelings of uneasiness by spending a lot of time with the boss, asking him questions about the job. When he comes across with a big raise, a boss may not know exactly what to expect, but the one thing he neither expects nor desires is more problems. Do your job and stay away from him.

What, then, can you give the boss to make him feel better? Give him *promises.* This is the time to outline the big plans you've got, the big problems you are going to solve, the big goals you will begin to accomplish. They don't need to be things that can be done immediately. Long-term is better.

By emphasizing the important things you are going to do, you are helping yourself in several ways. You enable the boss to live with his decision. You show that you are not coasting. *And* — you begin to position yourself for your next raise.